"This book takes crucial questions about the teaching of language and translation skills in our high-tech, GenAI context by the scruff of the neck and gives them a really good and welcome shake. It will prove to be an inspiring read for anyone teaching or learning about language and translation skills."

Sharon O'Brien, *Associate Dean for Research, Faculty of Humanities and Social Sciences, Dublin City University*

"As the pace of technological developments quickens, translation and language educators and students alike are in need of up-to-date resources to help them navigate the changing landscape. A strength of this book is the sheer variety of food for thought with regard to possible activities to suit different teaching modes and learning styles, along with ways to assess them. It also tackles the thorny problem of responding to student (and instructor) anxieties in this highly technologized field. The path forward through the murky world of generative AI may not be entirely clear, but with this book, Anthony Pym and Yu Hao deliver a compass and a powerful torch to help guide the way."

Lynne Bowker, *Canada Research Chair in Translation, Technologies, and Society, Université Laval*

"*How to Augment Language Skills* is a must-have for language educators and translators. Packed with practical teaching tips and a captivating exploration of AI, this book brings theory to life. With a fascinating dive into Artificial Intelligence (AI), it empowers readers to enhance their language skills and thrive in today's evolving linguistic landscape. An invaluable resource that makes learning accessible and engaging!"

Defeng Li, *Distinguished Professor of Translation Studies, University of Macao*

T0384801

HOW TO AUGMENT LANGUAGE SKILLS

How to Augment Language Skills outlines ways in which translators and language providers can expand their skillset and how translation technologies can be integrated into language learning and translator training.

This book explains the basics of generative AI, machine translation, and translation memory suites, placing them in a historical context and assessing their fundamental impacts on language skills. It covers what to teach in a specific context, how to teach it, how to assess the result, and how to set up lively class discussions on the many problematic aspects. The exploratory empirical approach is designed to reach across several divides: between language education and translation studies, between technology designers and users, between Western and Asian research, and between abstract ideas and hands-on practice.

Features include:

- Fifty-seven technology-related activities for the language and/or translation class.
- Recent research on the capacities of generative AI.
- Examples of how to conduct a needs analysis in the Higher Education context.
- Comparisons of the main teaching methods.
- Ways to assess the use of technologies.
- Examples in Chinese, Spanish, Catalan, French, and German.
- A full glossary explaining the key terms in clear language.

Drawing on years of classroom experience, Pym and Hao illustrate how these skills can be taught in a range of classroom and online activities, making this essential reading for teachers and researchers involved in the teaching of languages and the training of translators.

Anthony Pym is Distinguished Professor of Translation and Intercultural Studies at Universitat Rovira i Virgili in Spain. His publications include *Exploring Translation Theories* (third edition, 2023). He has been teaching translation technologies since 2000.

Yu Hao is Lecturer in Translation Studies at the University of Melbourne in Australia. Her research interests are in translation curriculum development, translation-technology teaching, and international education studies.

HOW TO AUGMENT LANGUAGE SKILLS

Generative AI and Machine Translation in Language Learning and Translator Training

Anthony Pym and Yu Hao

Routledge
Taylor & Francis Group
LONDON AND NEW YORK

Designed cover image: recep-bg

First published 2025
by Routledge
4 Park Square, Milton Park, Abingdon, Oxon OX14 4RN

and by Routledge
605 Third Avenue, New York, NY 10158

Routledge is an imprint of the Taylor & Francis Group, an informa business

© 2025 Anthony Pym and Yu Hao

British Library Cataloguing-in-Publication Data
A catalogue record for this book is available from the British Library

ISBN: 9781032614960 (hbk)
ISBN: 9781032614953 (pbk)
ISBN: 9781032648033 (ebk)

DOI: 10.4324/9781032648033

Typeset in Sabon LT
by codeMantra

Access the Support Material: www.routledgetranslationstudiesportal.com

CONTENTS

ACKNOWLEDGMENTS

We would like to thank all the students who have attended our classes, both for language learning and for translation, both face-to-face and online. Many of the ideas in this book come from our collective experiences over the years.

We are extremely thankful to the 11 translation teachers in Australia and New Zealand who took part in an online discussion of these issues, reported in Chapter 2. We assumed you knew what you were doing, and we found real consensus among what you said. Further thanks are extended to Mirella Agorni and the translation teachers at Ca' Foscari University in Venice, where Anthony Pym wrote most of his part as a Visiting Professor giving seminars on translation technologies.

Our sincere appreciation also goes to Yizhou Wang for his help with the data analysis and visualization of our survey of translation teachers (Figure 2).

Special thanks go to the great teachers and researchers from whom we have learned over the years. Our ideas for learning activities have been inspired by Lynne Bowker, Alessandro Cattelan, Andrew Chesterman, Ke Hu, Juerong Qiu, Christopher Mellinger, David Orrego-Carmona, Robin Setton, Medha Sengupta, and Pablo Romero Fresco. Adrià Martín-Mor has been particularly provocative in alerting us to the ethical dimensions of translation technologies and the possibilities of free and open software. We are very grateful for his insights.

We also extend thanks to John Benjamins Publishing for permission to reproduce Figure 2 from our "Choosing effective teaching methods for translation" in *Forum*, 21(2), to Luis Lamb for allowing us to reproduce Figure 3 from "Assessing Gender Bias in Machine Translation. A Case Study with Google Translate," *Neural Computing and Applications*, 32(1), and to the

Department of Families, Fairness and Housing of the Government of Victoria for permission to reproduce Figure 5 *How Do I Check In*.

No permissions have been sought for the examples from machine translation and generative AI systems because, let's face it, they do not ask for permission to use everyone's online data.

GLOSSARY

Additional language   A language that is in addition to one's first language (L1). The term thus covers L2, L3, etc., as well as a "foreign language."

AI (Artificial Intelligence)   The use of computer technology to perform and augment tasks that humans can perform. Technically, AI is in at work in all electronic translation technologies. The term has nevertheless come to be associated with the use of LLMs to perform language tasks based on prompts.

AI assistant   An application of an LLM designed to help the user complete a task, usually through a human-computer dialogue.

AI text generation   The use of LLMs to generate texts, including translations, based on prompts. These tasks are currently carried out by Chat-GPT, Claude, Copilot, Gemini, PaLM, M4T, LLaMA, ERNIE Bot, Qwen, Mistral AI, Bloom AI, Perplexity, and Jurassic, among others, with many secondary platforms based on these. The term is currently unstable, with "generative AI" covering all aspects of the technology, and common parlance simply referring to "AI," while technical discourse sticks to "LLMs." Here we are focusing on how LLMs produce texts.

Augmented   Here, an adjective to describe the use of automation to enhance language skills. The adjective has come to replace "computer-aided" in the expression "computer-aided translation"; it can also replace adjectives like "semi-automated," or "semi-computerized." We seek to extend the concept to all language skills.

Augmented translation   Any translation process or product that combines human translating with the use of automated language technologies, here specifically by machine translation, translation memories, or generative AI. When there is no human translation process involved (e.g., no pre-editing or post-editing), then we refer to the process as "automated translation."

Automation The whole or partial replacement of a human activity by a process carried out by machines, with varying degrees of input and intervention from humans.

Automated translation Any translation process or product that uses language technologies without augmenting a human translation process.

Back-translation A translation that goes from the target language to the start language, usually to illustrate how an earlier translation in the other direction has handled differences between the languages.

Bottom-up A way of analyzing anything by starting from the little things and working toward the big things. You might ask students what skills they want to acquire; you arrange the answers into lessons, courses, and programs. This approach is the opposite of "top-down." Elements of both approaches should be combined.

Brief The instructions the client gives to the translator: Auftrag in German, also called "commission" in English. In translation practice, the more normal terms would be "instructions" or "job description."

CALL (Computer-Assisted Language Learning): The study of the way electronic technologies, including anything from machine translation to mobile phones, can enhance language learning and teaching.

Capacity An alternative conceptualization of "competence," emphasizing the learner's ability to operate successfully in new situations.

CAT tool (Computer-Aided Translation tool): A widespread misnomer for translation memory suites. The term makes little sense because virtually everything we do with language is aided by computers these days.

Competence A set of skills, knowledges, and aptitudes activated in a particular field of practice.

Constructivism A teaching approach based on the idea that skills and knowledge are acquired by interpreting the world, especially through practical activities. The concept is simplistically opposed to "transmissionism."

Controlled authoring The writing of a text while respecting a special set of rules. The rules may be for easy-access reading, the application of standardized terminology and syntax, or the avoidance of features known to be problematic for machine translation ("pre-editing").

Course A set of lessons covering a shared field, usually lasting 12–15 weeks or so. Also called a "subject," "module," or "unit" in some institutions.

Creativity Here, the capacity to formulate low-frequency translation solutions.

Curriculum (plural: curricula): Minimally, a set of courses in a program of study.

Curriculum development The steps taken to plan or modify a curriculum that guides and fosters meaningful learning experiences. A curriculum designer works from a needs analysis to a set of learning outcomes; based on these learning outcomes the designer plans learning activities and assessments, each designed to facilitate or evaluate the attainment of the intended outcomes.

Digital literacy   The knowledge and capacity to use the Internet and computers, including their extensions in mobile devices. Digital literacy also includes knowledge of data security and the ethics of managing data.

Documentation   The finding of information that will help solve translation problems or give background information for the understanding of a text.

Empiricism   The testing of hypotheses based on data, which can be quantitative, qualitative (including experiential), or both.

Epistemology   The study of the ways knowledge is produced, in this case knowledge about the use of translation technologies.

Equivalence   The belief that two or more texts or text elements share some common value.

From-scratch translation   A translation process that is carried out by people without the aid of machine translation, translation memories, or AI text generation; also called "unaided translation" or "fully human translation."

Fully human translation   A translation process that is carried out by people without the aid of machine translation, translation memories, or AI text generation; also called "unaided translation" or "from-scratch translation." The adjective "fully human" is a misnomer because all the technologies and their databases have been created by humans.

Generative AI (GenAI)   The use of artificial intelligence to perform operations based on inputted instructions ("prompts") and a very large database. Here, we call specific applications "AI assistants" when a human-computer dialogue is involved, or "AI text generation" when we are interested in the quality of the text produced, including the quality of translations.

Glossary   A list of terms with their field-specific definitions. Translators compile and use bilingual glossaries. Glossaries technically become "term bases" when they include such things as definitions or information on usage.

Grading   The assessment of students' work, especially when numerical values are allocated. Here, we use the term as a synonym of "marking."

Grammar translation   Originally a pejorative term for the use of translation in language teaching in Europe, predominantly from the nineteenth century. There seems never to have been any one approach that called itself "grammar translation."

Immersion   A method for teaching an additional language by having the learner speak and do everything in the foreign language. The practice is associated with the "direct method."

Indirect translation   A translation of a translation, usually into a language other than the original start language.

Interactive translation prediction   A translation process in which the translator chooses between automatically generated translation solutions.

Interactivity   Here, the degree to which language automation allows humans to intervene by making choices.

L1   A person's first language, usually in the sense of first acquisition. A symmetrical bilingual will have two (or more) L1s.

L2   A language that a person speaks other than their L1. The term is loosely used to also cover any subsequent languages learned ("additional languages").

Lesson   A unit in a syllabus, usually comprising continuous interaction between teacher and students for a period of one or two hours or so.

Literacy   The basic knowledge and capacity to carry out complex functions such as reading and writing. The term has been extended into many fields, including health literacy and banking literacy, for example. We can thus talk about "translation literacy" and "translation-technology literacy."

LLMs   (Large Language Models): The use of algorithms that work on very large databases (theoretically as big as "the Internet") to carry out language tasks like those that humans perform.

Localization   In industry discourse, the process of internationalizing a product or text and then adapting it to target locales to some degree. Sometimes, the adaptation part of the process is also called "localization."

Machine translation (MT)   The automated rendition of text or speech from one human language to another.

Machine translation literacy   The basic knowledge and capacity to use machine translations efficiently.

Marked   Adjective to describe a linguistic item that is perceived as being in some way unusual or infrequent. It does not mean there is an actual mark written on the item. The opposite is "unmarked."

Marking   In some countries, a term for the assessment of students' work. Here, we use the term as a synonym of "grading."

Mediation   The use of an intermediary person who enables communication between two languages. Here, we view translators, interpreters, and language teachers as mediators.

Metalanguage   Language about language, including the use of linguistic terminology and the various nomenclatures for translation types, processes, and solutions.

Neural machine translation (NMT)   The integration of deep-learning processes into statistical machine translation, generally from 2016 or so.

Parallel text   A non-translational target-language text on the same topic and/or with the same purpose as the start text.

Polyglot   A person who speaks more than one language.

Post-editing   The correcting of machine-translation output.

Pre-editing   The editing of a text so that it passes through machine translation with a reduced number of errors; a special kind of "controlled authoring."

Program (of study)   A set of courses, usually lasting more than a semester and leading to a certificate, diploma, or degree.

Prompt   User's instruction given to a generative AI system.

Respeaking   In conference interpreting, the spoken rendition of an incoming discourse in the same language. For example, an incoming speech in Chinese can be respoken in Chinese. This is used as a training exercise for conference interpreters. It can also be used to "clean up" the incoming speech so that it can be processed by machine translation.

Retranslation   A translation that is done later than a previous translation and into the same target language, with or without reference to the previous translation.

Rich points   Situations in a communication exchange where an expression cannot be translated in a simple way because it relates to a series of concepts that are different in the cultures concerned (cf. Agar, 1994).

Risk   Here, the probability that a communication exchange does not lead to a cooperative outcome.

Role plays   Classroom activities where students pretend to have different identities, as when a student group presents itself as a translation company.

Scaffolding   The support or assistance provided to a student by a teacher or peer in the initial stages of learning. This support is gradually reduced as the learner becomes more proficient and can acquire new knowledge more independently.

Simulations   An alternative term for "role plays."

Skill   The ability to carry out processes successfully in a particular field of practice.

***Skopos* theory**   A set of propositions based on the idea that the target-side *Skopos* or purpose has top priority in the translator's decisions. This theory is only one part of purpose-based approaches to translation, alongside theories that talk about purposes as functions without giving full priority to the target side.

Skopos   The purpose or aim of the translation; the function it is supposed to carry out in the situation of end-user reception.

Source text   Traditional term for "start text."

ST   The start or source text.

Stakeholder   Here, a person or social actor who has an interest in, contributes to and stands to gain from education.

Start language   The language the translator works from.

Start text   The text the translator works from. The term is used here instead of "source text" because translators these days work from client instructions, automated translations, translation memories, and term bases, all of which are also "sources."

Statistical machine translation   Machine translation that is based on statistical analyses of previously paired examples more than on linguistic rules; regarded as a precursor to neural machine translation.

Syllabus   (plural: syllabi): Minimally, a set of learning outcomes to be achieved in a course.

Target language   The language the translator works into.

Target text   The text the translator produces; the translation.

Teaching approach   A general set of ideas about what teaching is and how it should be organized, such as "constructivism" or "Prussian humanism."

Teaching method   A way of organizing learning activities, such as the "communicative method" or the "direct method" for language teaching.

Term base   A list of terms with their field-specific definitions. Translators can compile and use bilingual term bases. When the data only include terms without further information, it can be called a "glossary."

Text   Any contiguous set of signs, in whatever medium, that are presumed to be related to each other in a syntagmatic way (one item after the other).

TMX file   A translation memory that is in the Translation Memory Exchange format. This format enables memories to be moved between translation memory suites.

Tool   Here, a piece of software that carries out an identifiable task such as navigate through a text, apply a dictionary, propose possible translations, or check grammar. A "suite" is then a collection of tools.

Top-down   A way of analyzing anything by starting from the big things and working toward the little things. You might suppose that the aim of a teaching program is to have all students employed by translation companies. You ask the companies what skills they require, and this generates the intended learning outcomes of each lesson. This approach is the opposite of "bottom-up."

Transcreation   The part of translating where decisions are made by considering a specific receivership rather than on reproducing the form of the start text. Transcreation would include interventions such as addition, omission, updating, functional adaptation, re-formatting, and change of media.

Translanguaging   A mediating practice where a speaker uses a range of language resources and skills to convey a message in another language, often mixing languages and without regard for the formal constraints of representation that are associated with translation.

Translating   A mediating practice resulting in texts or utterances that are assumed to represent texts or utterances in another language. Here, we generally include spoken mediation ("interpreting") within the range of mediation practices.

Translation   An act of translating or the result thereof.

Translation criticism   Any activity where the value of a translation is assessed and suggestions for improvement are made.

Translation literacy   Basic knowledge of what translation is, including the metalanguage for talking about it. Translation literacy can be taught to all language students as part of their general undergraduate education (Takeda & Yamada, 2019). Another kind of translation literacy can be fostered among the clients who interact with translators.

Translation memory (TM)   A database comprising matching segments in different languages. Each match may be called a "bi-text" or a "translation unit." The database allows users to store and potentially reuse their previous translations in their new translation projects.

Translation memory suite   A set of electronic tools that recycle previous translations, these days with numerous added features such as machine-translation feeds, term bases, revision tools, and quality controls. Also called "CAT tools" (computer-aided translation), although almost everything we do with texts is computer-aided.

Translator's workstation   The set of hardware and software that a translator uses when translating.

Transmissionism   A generally pejorative term for teaching approaches based on the assumption of stable knowledge that can be imparted through discourse, as in formal lectures.

Transversal skills   Skills that are acquired in one field of practice and are useful in further fields of practice.

TT   Target text; the translation produced.

Unaided translation   Here, a translation activity that does not use a translation memory, machine translation, or generative AI. Otherwise known as "from scratch" or "fully human" translation (but there is some technology in almost all translating).

PREFACE

A vibrant multilingual society needs widespread language skills. For this, there must be people who can communicate in several languages: grandparents born overseas can discuss recipes with their children and grandchildren all in the family language; Indigenous communities can maintain language as a constant enactment of identity; traders of all kinds are able to work in lingua francas of convenience; people can have fun playing with and across languages, teasing out the joys of multiple differences. All those things can come from language learning. At the same time, that ideally vibrant multilingual society also needs professionals who can mediate between languages in a wide range of high-stakes situations, from providing social services to explaining how to act in emergencies and right the way to international conferences and negotiations at the highest levels. Of course, that varied multilingual panorama is by no means a static idyl. All those uses of language are seeing their range, quality, and speed being affected by automation, which can be used for or against multilingualism. As technologies help us increase the number of communications across languages, we might hope for more social understanding and tolerance, at the same time as the technologies could reduce the motivation for language learning, with consequently negative effects on language diversity and vibrant belonging. That is why much depends on *how* the technologies are taught and used. It becomes extremely important to ensure the technologies are integrated creatively both when we teach languages and when we train translators. It also means that language teaching and translator training must both seek answers to the same vexing question: How can we best engage with new language technologies?

Since that basic question concerns both language learning and translation, here we try to address those fields together, as much as possible. We will have rather less to say about a third constituency, namely people who use translation technologies without any connection with language learning or human translation. Those would be the users addressed in Lynne Bowker and Jairo Buitrago Ciro's ground-breaking *Machine Translation and Global Research* (2019); they could be the wider market for the excellent *Machine Translation for Everyone* edited by Dorothy Kenny (2022); they are also probably users of the generative AI text technologies (more technically, Large Language Models) that present a set of new possibilities and call for updates of even the most recent studies. That sense of a very wide automation-based translation literacy is certainly of interest to us, but we make the strategically reductive supposition that an efficient and practical way to get that literacy to people is through language learning. Lynne Bowker's initial thinking sprang from the problems of international students in Canada who were using machine translation to do research; she found that some pointers in machine translation literacy could help them use that technology better. At the same time, virtually all those international students, we suppose, had had some kind of experience in the learning of additional languages, if only to prepare them for Canada. Those language classes are a place where they could have learned how to use machine translation. That is the kind of long-term solution that we are proposing here: teach translation technologies in *both* the additional-language class and the training of translators, in the hope of ensuring that literacy in translation technologies is as widespread as possible.

To address those two fields, we draw on our experience as language teachers and as trainers of translators, as well as on our even longer experience as language learners and as professional translators. Of course, any balance is hard to attain. Indeed, any claim to equilibrium on our part would rightly be questioned, not least because most of our recent research has been more on the *translation* side of business, just as most of our personal use of translation technologies has been first and foremost in the training of translators. What we are doing here is more like trying to reach across the aisle, as American politicians might put it. That is not easy to do. Relations between language education and translator training have long been strained, to the point where some still insist translation has no role to play in language learning, while others across the aisle retort that translation skills have nothing to do with bilingualism and so require their own separate institutions and modes of training. As we survey those aging battlegrounds, we seek new ways to think about language education and translation together, within the one general frame, facing the same set of problems presented by technologies.

Here is one way to kick-start that kind of thinking (please bear with us). How can understanding be achieved across different languages? There are several possible solutions. You can learn to *speak* the other person's language; you can learn just to *understand* the foreign language (the use of mutual passive competence is technically called "intercomprehension"); you can *alternate* between languages as you speak (this would be "code-switching," of which there are various kinds, or "translanguaging" when it involves mixing resources in different languages); you can help *develop new languages*, as when pidgins become creoles and then standardized languages; or you can seek help from a third person, a *mediator*, who knows the other language better than you do. All those solutions require polyglots (people who speak more than one language) to one degree or another; most of them arise and develop quite spontaneously, without any special training, in the way that grass grows in the fields; just a few of those solutions require the specialized knowledge of a paid mediator who ideally has some training. In language education, that mediator is the language teacher; in professional translation, it is the translator (here, we use the term as including spoken mediation, otherwise known as "interpreting"). This means that mediators are just one solution among many to the problem of achieving understanding across languages, and their position is at some level the same in both language education and translation. In both those cases, mediators are paid to improve understanding across languages. In both those cases, technologies can help them do that better.

Now, there are societies where virtually everyone grows up speaking several languages and so there are few special language teachers or interpreters. This could be the case of Aboriginal cultures in pre-Invasion Australia (Pym, 2023). That would be one social configuration of mediation. In other societies, only a few select people learn foreign languages and so professional mediators become special groups. That could be the case of the professional *tsūji* or interpreters who worked with foreign languages in Early Modern Japan (Saito & Sato, 2023). In both these extreme cases, translation and language learning occupy approximately the same social position: they are specialized and marginal.

In between those positions, there are certain situations where language learning has developed without translation (since language skills can be used in all the above communication solutions), but translation has not normally developed without some kind of language learning (since mediators are supposed to have learned languages). When immigrants started to pour into the United States in the second half of the nineteenth century, there were virtually no translation services available to help them find their way in a multilingual society; immigrants had to learn languages quickly, without translation. It is from that experience that we owe much of the development of immersion ideology in language learning and the radical exclusion of translation as a way of learning languages (Pym & Ayvazyan, 2018). In other societies, the mixes have been far more varied.

Consider, now, what happens when virtually everyone can access automated translations online. Suddenly, almost *everyone* can translate to some degree or another (as in pre-Invasion Australia) but *without* necessarily being bilingual or having had formal language training. The traditional configurations no longer hold. In this radically new situation, translation not only becomes an unavoidable part of all adult language learning – since it is available to almost everyone – but translation activities can no longer be just for an isolated professional group – since that group is no longer clearly defined by any exclusive capacity. At the same time, and in a similar way, virtually everyone can potentially use online technologies, including online translation, to learn languages without a formal setting. The students who are in front of us in a language class can achieve a lot of learning outside that class: they enjoy the varied activities of DuoLinguo and the like, which includes translation activities; they consume huge amounts of audiovisual material in additional languages, often with the help of subtitles; they can have a spoken a conversation in additional languages with generative AI systems; they can instantly check whatever the teacher says with a few intelligent web searches, with or without the use of online machine translation. Just as everyone can translate, to some degree, so everyone can self-learn a language, to some degree.

If you follow that line of reasoning through, you might then ask what is going to happen to the professional mediators. Will the paid translator disappear beneath the weight of machine translation? Will the qualified teacher be replaced by the AI chat session? In short, has mediation been automated across the board? That pessimistic prospect is one very good reason why language educators and translator trainers might want to approach these problems together, rather than by opposing each other. At one level, we are all in the same boat, and it could be sinking. (No panic: at the end of this chapter, we offer reasons why that pessimism might be overstated.) At another level, what we find happening in the language industry is a move toward cross-cultural content development, to the integration of marketing surveys and adaptive copywriting, which is a major direction in which translation can be augmented, often with the help of generative AI. And who can do those new jobs? Language learners should be well placed for many of the tasks, especially if they know about communication, creativity, and cultural adaptation. On that level as well, technologies are blurring the distinctions between our currently separate activities.

Are the changes really so pervasive? From the perspective of translation, there can be little doubt that the long-term impact of automation will be considerable. Much less than 1% of the words translated in the world are now done by professionals: Pym and Torres-Simón (2021), for example, calculate that the number of words translated by professionals is just 0.68% of the words rendered by Google Translate. Translation has become a widespread social activity carried out by virtually everyone who seeks knowledge from foreign languages (Bowker & Buitrago Ciro, 2019). Vieira et al. (2023) report that, in a sample of 1,200 participants in the United Kingdom, 75.9%

said they had used machine translation, most with satisfaction and almost all in situations that would not have justified the employment of a professional translator. From the perspective of language education, too, the signs of change are difficult to avoid. Students access online translations more readily than print dictionaries; as noted, they learn independently from multiple online sites; their technological skills run ahead of those of their teachers, who are forced to play catch-up on several fronts at once (cf. Niño, 2008; Zhang, 2019). Much as it can be claimed that we now have more than 30 years of experience with the use of machine translation (Jolley & Maimone, 2022), not all educators have been on that train. Whatever the case, the centrality of the teacher, already questioned by successive waves of student-centered approaches, is now increasingly difficult to defend: that particular mediator has become more like an occasional guide to the wider worlds of language learning.

Some of the older divisions nevertheless remain and are significant. Language education is a huge industry with a very large international scholarly community, whereas professional translator training involves a much smaller community and can scarcely be described as an industry at all (translation is certainly part of the language industry, but translator training remains a rather marginal activity, with perhaps 600 or so specialized institutions in the world). The two scholarly fields communicate with each other remarkably rarely. Immersion ideologies are still strong in some parts of the language-education community (or were at the time of the survey reported in Pym et al., 2013), at the same time as some translation scholars argue that they need their own translation-specific ways of teaching languages (as in Presas, 2000), while other translation scholars want to move away from languages altogether, denouncing the historical fixation on language at the expense of other semiotic systems as "glottocentrism" (Petrilli, 2014; Litwin, 2023). The impact of free online technologies now makes those aspirations look like rather quaint remnants of a bygone age. The separate translation institutions and programs (indeed faculties, at least in Germany and Spain), splendid in their hard-won isolation, only have about a third of their graduates find long-term stable employment as translators or interpreters (Hao & Pym, 2023a). The remaining graduates use their language skills in a very broad range of occupations in multilingual societies. Translation technologies have certainly not been the cause of all these changes (the "one-third rule" of graduate employment might have been there all the time, hidden by deceptive statistics), but language automation has certainly captured the headlines as the most disruptive change in language use in our era.

A good part of our mission here is to challenge some of the more facile misperceptions of the technologies. This especially concerns the various discourses that gushed forth around artificial intelligence when Large Language Models (LLMs) were made publicly accessible in the form of ChatGPT in

November 2022 – which gained the fastest growing user base in history. The capabilities of the technology were and remain undeniably impressive, not especially in translation per se but very definitely in a wider range of language tasks. A thousand instant experts started proclaiming the end of original student essays, the end of human work on language, the end of creativity, the end of copyright, right through to and including the end of humanity as we know it. Without any real experience or prolonged testing of the technology, instant experts will always proffer negative predictions in this way. If they are wrong, everyone will be happy with the technology, and no one will remember the bad prediction. And if they are right, the experts stand to win kudos. A thousand expert voices once predicted instant doom from the "millennium bug," the fabled incapacity of the world's software to handle dates at the beginning of the year 2000. A thousand expert teachers used to instruct students not to go anywhere near Wikipedia, since it would give them dubious information and kill all capacity for research. Another thousand experts told us, for many decades, that computers would never be able to translate like humans. Why have we forgotten the names attached to all those misguided experts? Not just because they were wrong but more because they reacted out of uninformed, ingrained pessimism. This is not to say that all the predictions about translation technologies will turn out to be erroneous – the calculations of environmental impact, in particular, are to be taken very seriously. Yet, any serious learning process must start by unlearning the chattered predictions of instant experts.

In times of technological change and the corresponding uncertainties, one should test all novelties as much as possible, exploring possibilities and limitations. And then, since the technologies evolve alongside our explorations, we should invite our students to engage in the same process of testing. Instead of repeating unsubstantiated and sometimes hysterical cries of danger, instead of telling everyone what we have found to be wholly good or wholly bad, we seek to have our students interact with the technologies and reflect on what they have discovered for themselves. This is the general approach we adopt throughout this book. It might be called constructivism, but to our mind it is more like honest common sense: if we are not sure of where the technologies are going, we cannot assume to have stable knowledge to convey to anyone. We can only invite our students – and our readers – to explore.

*   *

*

The first chapter of this book explains the main translation technologies by placing them in a historical context, particularly the wider history of automation and its effects on work processes and jobs. The subsequent chapters then broadly follow the steps one might take to develop or update a teaching program. We consider several kinds of needs analyses (Chapter 2), including academic models of competencies, the requirements of education institutions, and the voices of employer groups. In Chapter 3, we base another kind of needs analysis on studies of where translation graduates go and why many graduates with language degrees become translators – the two communities have huge overlaps. Chapter 4 then deals with basic issues in the teaching of technologies, including the selection of teaching methodologies and the formulation of learning outcomes (of which we present a sample list).

We then try to be as useful as possible for anyone who is looking for ways to integrate translation technologies into their teaching. In Chapter 5, we describe some 57 learning activities that can be done in class. Chapter 6 looks at the rather more vexing question of how we evaluate the work done with technologies, and how the technologies themselves can help with evaluation tasks. Chapter 7 then offers notes on how classroom discussions of translation technologies might be based on exploration rather than suppositions.

In the final chapter, we start dreaming about the kinds of language automation that would be of most use to maintaining a vibrant multilingual society. We offer several ways of rethinking the social roles of translation. More importantly, we put forward reasons for tempered optimism.

1

WHAT ARE LANGUAGE TECHNOLOGIES AND WHY SHOULD WE KNOW ABOUT THEM?

Imagine you are teaching students an additional language (here we will call it "L2," although it may be some students' third or fourth language). You give the class a writing task, and they all submit strangely similar texts. Why? Perhaps because they have fed the same prompt into an AI text generator (ChatGPT and the like) to write the text. Or they have written in their first language ("L1") and then used online machine translation to do the rest for them. Either way, they have not worked very hard in the language you are trying to teach. What do you do?

This basic problem is being faced by teachers all over the world. And it is not going to go away – the online technologies will only get better, so teachers and students will have to get better at working with them. In this book we will be discussing some of the principles, innovations, and clever tricks that teachers can use to work with generative AI and machine translation. From the outset, though, let us assume that any long-term solution will not involve simply *outlawing* the technologies or pretending they do not exist. Teachers can always make appeals to the students' altruism, sense of fair play, or long-term self-interest: if students allow technologies to do *all* the work for them, those students will probably be the first to be replaced by those same technologies. And then, when such arguments fail, we can always make students do tests and exams with pen-and-paper, invigilated, with no computers, no phones, no online technology, and very little possible cheating – as it used to be. The trouble with that solution is that virtually none of our students is going to find future employment just sitting alone and writing with pen-and-paper, which is why few of them are likely to be convinced by appeals to altruism or praise of old technologies. Virtually all our students are going to enter employment where the technologies of language automation will

DOI: 10.4324/9781032648033-1

abound, where they will be connected with others electronically, and where they will need serious skills in the use and learning of many kinds of online tools. It might help to think here about the teaching of mathematics: students now use calculators for arithmetic, so they are getting worse at mental operations; but they get jobs using calculators, there is still plenty of useful mathematics to teach, and there is no shortage (as yet) of high-paid work for advanced mathematical skills – especially of the kind that has provided major advances in language automation. At the end of the day, prohibiting language technologies is likely to be just as ineffective as any attempt to ban calculators. In fact, it could be as counterproductive as the prohibition of alcohol was in the United States in the 1920s: a well-intentioned measure can lead to negative results.

If prohibition is not an option, then the first step toward addressing our problem is to know what the technologies are. Here we are basically concerned with automated natural-language processing, which comes in several flavors. Our focus is on generative AI and neural machine translation, which have much in common. We will outline how technologies are changing the ways we communicate. We will use this to explain why everyone should know about them, especially teachers of languages and translation. You might then still decide that the technologies are your enemy more than they are your friend. Before you make that decision, you have to know what they are.

Language technologies are historical

Each generation has its preferred technologies. A century ago, writers worked with pen and paper and sent the result off for manual typesetting – it was relatively easy to test the skills they required for the task. What those writers were doing nevertheless depended on time-bound technologies: paper and the printing press had major long-term effects when their use was generalized. Is the change to electronic communication really so different? Is it so radically new that we can only throw our hands in air and confess defeat?

Technologies of all kinds are frequently called "revolutionary" at first, bringing in change across many fields. Writing systems enabled messages to travel away from the proximity of face-to-face communication, leading not just to larger social groups but also to an awareness of human history. The invention of paper in China at the end of the first century made communication cheaper, so more people could be involved. When that technology reached Europe from the twelfth century – Europe was a long way behind! – it coincided with the adoption of Arabic numerals and gave birth to accountancy and state bureaucracies: the productivity of the monasteries grew, contributing to a huge increase in classical knowledge translated from Arabic but also in the production and consumption of wine, helped by warming climate (Pym, 1998). Paper, numbers, and the sun made the twelfth century pretty happy. The printing press, dating from the fifteenth century, led to the standardization of national languages, the separation of "legitimate" language from colloquial spoken language (Bourdieu, 1982), the assumption that languages could have equal status (thus allowing for "equivalent" translations), and expansion in the paid teaching of language as a key to social mobility. On the long view, language teachers probably owe their jobs to the printing press. If there is a particular revolution that we have to come to terms with, it helps to think historically. For example, we might compare the consequences of the printing press with those of electronic communication. In many respects, the kind of low-effort updating and variation allowed by electronic texts moves us back to the pre-print manuscript tradition, just as it returns us to languages with highly asymmetric standings – which might be a deep reason why "equivalence" is now questioned as a criterion for translation (Pym, 2015).

One might also address technologies physiologically. Consider the idea that all technologies extend the human body in some way. The printing press extended the hands that write and the legs and voice that could reach limited numbers of people. Now, what part of our body does electronic communication extend? If you think about it, the main human function that is augmented is our *memory* (Pym, 2011). Electronic systems can store far more data, from a wider range of languages and experiences, than can an individual mind, and they can use algorithms to locate and retrieve those data when called on to do so. LLMs are large language models precisely because they can process far more data than any individual human memory could ever hope to recall. They basically do what our memory does, but they go beyond the limitations of our bodies. The result might be "post-human," but we leave that for the more apocalyptic cultural theorists. For us, it is all human, albeit augmented.

Two principles of language automation

The technological extension of memory allows language *automation*: pieces of language are stored and retrieved by an electronic system, outside of the human brain and independently of what we do with our bodies. The "auto" part of automation means that it appears to happen by itself. All the technologies we are looking at here are instances of automation, occurring within the wider history of automated work, which has been going on at least since the first industrial revolution. In the case of language technologies, it can help to see automation operating in terms of two general principles, neither of which is universally valid:

- The *recycling* of previous pieces of language: What was said or written in one situation can be repeated in similar situations, with similar effects. This principle is presumed to hold for any utterance, including translations: a translation that was done of one sentence to achieve one effect on one receiver can be used when translating a similar sentence for a similar purpose with a different receiver. This principle is contradicted by the idea that language effects are always contextual, which means they are specific to the people and purposes of each communicative situation, where voices and inferences might be what counts most. That is, the recycling principle contradicts pragmatics. No matter: automation is based on the idea that recycling can work. Of course, the same simple idea of repetition without consequence is also behind the compiling of dictionaries and grammars, which only make sense if language can be recycled to at least some extent.

- The *prediction* of language production: Once you accept that recycling is possible, it makes sense to construct and draw on large databases of previous language. When you have done that, you can calculate the probabilities of past co-occurrences to *predict* what piece of language is most likely to come after the bit you are looking at. This is part of the way anyone has a conversation with someone else: we constantly predict what is coming next; we may be surprised or dismayed when our expectations are defeated, but the predicting is part of the way we communicate. Electronic technologies base those predictions on statistical probabilities. The same thing happens when you start keying a word on your phone and the next words are suggested automatically. The principle also holds when you ask generative AI to answer a complex question: the text that it generates is based on the language that algorithms predict is likely to be produced in the stipulated situation. This is also the basic idea behind neural machine translation. In the decoding phase, the system predicts the most probable word one at a time in the sequence based on the encoded input; it ensures that each word fits with the others to generate a sentence in the target language that makes sense and sounds fluent.

These two principles are not particularly revolutionary in themselves. They are neither frightening nor liberating, since they have long been involved in the ways people use natural language. The difference now is that they are used with a combination of speed, accuracy, and availability – human memory can be extended to a greater *degree* than has ever been the case previously.

The two principles underlie many of the electronic tools that none of us would want to be without. Spellcheckers, grammar checkers, and online thesauri are great advances on paper-based reference works but do not alter the fundamental principles: correct spelling can be predicted and repeated, and the words that were similar in the past stand a chance of being more or less similar in the future. In the same way, the basic idea behind web browsers is that something recorded in the past will be of use in the future. The idea was also at work in the writing of books and the building of libraries: an utterance produced in the past may be useful in the future. And then, language recycling and prediction are the basic ideas behind the advances in text-to-speech technologies, which provide a great way of revising texts (the ear picks up errors that the eye does not see), as well as the speech-to-text tools that help us follow conferences in foreign languages, that should encourage us to produce more pragmatically adept translations, and that assist us in the production of texts without risking long-term damage to our bodies.

We hasten to add that there are also numerous electronic tools that are *not* narrowly based on the recycling and prediction of language. Content-management software helps keep track of multilingual documents; project-management software helps organize complex translation jobs, including the financial aspects; electronic stopwatches record how long we spend on a task and help us charge by the hour – those are all very useful tracking technologies, not specific to language. Beyond that, email and messaging systems help us communicate instantly with each other and with clients – these are all language technologies that do not assume recycling and prediction. There are countless similar digital tools and devices that help language workers complete their tasks. Here we nevertheless focus on the core technologies that do indeed extend memory by recycling and predicting language: generative AI, machine translation, and translation-memory suites, also known as computer-assisted translation (CAT) tools.

We now look at each of those technologies in turn.

Generative artificial intelligence

Imagine you have a particularly delicate text to write in your L1: a personal résumé that you want to adapt to apply for a particular job, personal condolences on a death, or perhaps resignation from a job where you want to remain on good terms. You could spend hours worrying about the most suitable phrasing – and many more hours if the text is to be in your L2 or L3. What do you do?

A now-traditional approach would be to do a web search for texts that are similar to the one you have to write. In the case of translation tasks, the most useful are "parallel texts" – original texts written in the target language that are on the same topic as the text you have to translate. Of course, the same strategy can work when the task concerns just one language – you go looking for the *kinds of words and expressions* that are expected for the purpose concerned; you pick up the terminology, the turns of phrase, and perhaps a few ideas and formulations that would not otherwise have occurred to you. All of that can be done with some reasonably intelligent web browsing.

Generative AI now does that kind of work for us, and much more. Open AI's ChatGPT, Anthropic's Claude, Microsoft Copilot, Google Gemini and PaLM, Meta's M4T and LLaMA, Baidu's ERNIE Bot, Alibaba's Qwen, the French Mistral AI, Bloom AI, Perplexity, and Jurassic (there will be others by the time you read these lines) can put together a text based on the instructions or "prompts" you give. So can the many specialized interfaces that are based on those technologies.

You might try the following instruction: "Write a 120-word resignation from job X for reasons Y and to remain on good terms." Or perhaps: "Write a 150-word abstract for the following text." The output often reads so well that one is tempted to copy it verbatim, filling in your specific details. A more intelligent use, however, is to approach it in the way that translators have long used parallel texts and the various avatars of machine translation: draw on it to compose your own text, adapting it to your own situation, giving it your individual voice. By all means, use the ideas and expressions you would not otherwise have thought of, adopt a few turns of phrase, and gain inspiration from some of the ideas. But then, remember that the text generator is based on *recycling* and on *probabilistic prediction*: it gives you language combinations that are frequently used and thus relatively normal, middle of the road, and likely to be repeated whenever similar prompts are given. If three people give the same prompts, the three texts will initially be so similar that anyone receiving them will know the sender is visibly no longer you. You will have gained some expressions and a few ideas but you will have lost a place of your own within language; you will have lost your voice.

What we are calling "generative AI" has several different names, none of which has yet become completely stable. The most common public reference is just to "AI," artificial intelligence, as the technology at work, but that is a very loose, all-embracing term. Strictly speaking, all translation memories and machine translation systems involve the use of artificial intelligence. "AI" is nevertheless being used to refer to a set of algorithms that work on very large database to carry out language tasks similar to those that humans perform. The current technical name for that is "large language models" (LLMs). Text generation is only one of the tasks that LLMs can perform, so here we will distinguish between that general technology ("generative AI" or "GenAI," in keeping with current usage) and, when appropriate, to the part of it that generates texts on demand ("AI text generation") and then to other parts that assist with various other language tasks ("AI assistant").

Generative AI can be criticized because it offers quick and easy solutions, it can invent false references, it draws excessively on English, it sounds trustworthy when it is not, it always gives an answer even when it does not have one, it does not work for languages that have scarce electronic resources, and it can produce discourse as empty as that of politicians who have middle-of-the-road replies for everything they know nothing about. The linguist Noam

Chomsky (2022, 11.20) has consequently lamented that AI cannot tell us anything new about the world and that its only point might be to "help a student fake an exam." If, however, we accept that language technologies are based on recycling and prediction, and not much more, then there should be no question of generative AI operating like science, discovering anything new in the world (see Chomsky et al., 2023) – its databases are from the past. To the extent that the recycling and predicting go beyond anyone's individual memory, the technology has enormous potential to help in language learning, translation, and indeed all language processing. But its role should be to help, not replace.

When AI technologies are asked to "translate" (without further prompts), their current default behavior is to adopt a narrow translation concept: accurate and literal. That means they may reproduce some of the text conventions of the start language, which they risk imposing on all other languages, at the same time as they privilege middling blandness in the target language. In this, they are sometimes rather close to the initial solutions that machine translation systems give us. The benefits of generative AI nevertheless lie in all the additional information and operations that can be provided when asked for: what idioms mean in context, how the tone of a text can be modified, how reading difficulty can be reduced, how creative solutions can be forced, and so on. All those additional operations might help a translator solve a problem (if we know how to use prompts creatively), but their much more productive use should lie in the language class.

Machine translation

Machine translation is the automatic rendition of text or speech from one human language to another. Although the idea can be traced back to the ninth-century philosopher and mathematician Al-Kindi, functional machine-translation systems have only been operative since the 1950s. More important, it is only since 2015–2016 that neural machine translation has become both reasonably reliable for many purposes and publicly available on virtually every kind of electronic device.

Neural machine translation was something of a gamechanger because in many language pairs it reached the tipping point at which it became relatively trustworthy. Anyone who can use a website can now produce a usable translation from a foreign language almost instantaneously – depending on the text, the languages, and the purpose involved. That means any language-learner can lean on machine translation in virtually all their activities – even when teachers try to stop them. Any client or end-user can also draw on machine translation to try to check what their translators are doing. Any scammer can present machine-translation output as if it were the result of human work and then try to get paid for it (Pym et al., 2016). More positively, the vast expanses of knowledge and information that were in foreign languages have been opened up to general users, just as huge professional challenges have arisen for language teachers and professional translators. Whether we like it or not, machine translation has become part of our daily environment.

Machine translation has had a short but fluctuating history that can be traced back to code-breaking efforts during the Second World War – the cracking of the "Enigma code" was fundamentally achieved by Polish cryptologists in the late 1930s (Rakus-Andersson, 2004). Machine translation then benefited from the rivalries of the Cold War in the 1950s, when systems were developed for intelligence purposes to replace human translation between English and Russian. The United States and the Soviet Union were spying on each other's rocket technology, and much else, which is why both sides were working on machine translation. In Russian, Revzin and Rozentsveyg (1964) presented a comprehensive attempt to rethink general translating from the perspective of machine translation. The aim at the initial stage was to identify lexical equivalents by compiling bilingual databases and then writing algorithms for syntactic transformations. That can be broadly categorized as "rule-based machine translation." In the mid-1960s, the systems were nevertheless found to be "unpromising" by the American Automatic Language Processing Advisory Committee (ALPAC, 1966). Their unjustly infamous report did not say that machine translation was in any way impossible; it simply calculated that less effort was required to learn the foreign language – translation and language learning were parts of the deal from the very beginning. Interestingly, the report included an experiment where 23 translators post-edited (corrected) raw machine translation. It was found that "fast translators will lose productivity if given postediting to do, whereas slow translators will gain" (ALPAC, 1966, p. 94; cf. García, 2010, 2011; García & Peña, 2011, where the weaker students also benefit most from using machine translation). This reference to helping weaker translators might have opened a window to translator training. That window was shut as work on machine translation then went on the backburner for several decades. The technology nevertheless remained. In fact, linguistic algorithms with fixed bilingual databases worked well enough to be used for restricted, rule-governable semantic spaces. Canadian French-English weather reports ("Météo") used rule-based machine translation from 1977.

In the early 1990s, the IBM research group adopted a new approach focusing on *statistical* or data-driven natural-language processing (Poibeau, 2017). This was drawing on what we have described as the prediction principle: it was based on statistical analyses of previously paired examples more than on linguistic rules. Simply put, once a text has been put into a statistical machine translation system, the engine searches in databases of paired texts, generates a list of probable pairs, and finally proposes the most statistically likely output. The paradigm outperformed previous rule-based approaches and was integrated into state-of-the-art machine translation systems. Many systems at the time adapted hybrid models, incorporating elements of both rule-based and statistical approaches. If a rule works, there is no reason to throw it out.

Building on the statistical approach, neural machine translation then integrated deep-learning into the multiple filtering of candidate translations (Koehn, 2020) – there appears to have been no actual neurology taken into account. Although its quality varies greatly according to the language pair, neural output has been claimed to be indistinguishable from human translation when isolated sentences are compared for meaning alone (not for form) in its best-performing language pairs such as French-English, Spanish-English (Wu et al., 2016), and Chinese-English (Hassan et al., 2018). Over the years, most neural machine translation developers have not only expanded the number of languages their systems support but have also made the technology more functional, accessible, and interactive.

Despite those changes, no one is claiming that machine translation is perfect. The experiment on Chinese-English translation (Hassan et al., 2018) only found that there was no significant difference in the way people identified machine translation, which is technically just a null-hypothesis, the trait of a negative experiment. It did not find that there were no errors; unnatural expressions were not penalized, and it was limited to isolated sentences without context (which is not how anyone usually communicates) (cf. Läubli et al., 2018). It was also done by researchers at Microsoft, who had every interest in making grand claims. When you read any research on translation technologies, pay close attention to where the researchers work.

In practice, most professional work with machine translation uses two approaches, which can be combined:

Post-editing is when the raw machine-translation output is corrected by a human, who may be a translator or a subject-area expert.

Pre-editing is when the original text is modified to remove the features that are typically problematic for machine translation (especially grammatical subordination and pronouns, for example).

When we teach students how to use machine translation, the skills that we are mostly teaching are therefore post-editing and pre-editing, plus the ability to spot where one or the other is most likely to be needed.

There are important differences between the main neural systems, and the differences can be expected to change as the technologies develop. At the time of writing, Modern MT claims to adapt solutions to specific contexts, based on an analysis of the whole text to be translated. Perhaps more interesting for teaching purposes, *interactivity* distinguishes DeepL from its competitors. When you click on a word in the DeepL translation, the system provides a drop-down menu with a number of alternative translations. The user can then choose between the options, with each selection resulting in the entire sentence being automatically adjusted. Somewhat similarly, Google Translate nowadays offers a first translation along with several alternative translations of the same sentence: while it seems to be a single rendition on the screen, clicking on it can activate several options. Below each alternative, there is a back-translation (i.e., what the rendition literally means when presented in the original language). Both DeepL and Google Translate also allow the user to change the start text and view the changes in the translation in real time, which effectively allows for live pre-editing.

The Chinese system Baidu Translate has pursued a slightly different path by focusing on in-domain machine translation. The areas worked on include biomedicine, electronic science, technology, and hydraulics. In theory, the terms specific to these fields are rendered with high levels of accuracy. Another specialized field Baidu supports is web-based "net literature." This is because numerous popular literary genres like Kong Fu novels are being produced and made available online. They appeal not only to Chinese-speaking readers but also to those who are interested in this genre but do not know Chinese. The potential world market is around 520 million people (CNNIC, 2021). The readers tend to have high tolerance for language errors, as the plots and entertainment are what matter most to them. Machine translation in this case is often post-edited either by professional translators (who are paid very little for the task) or by unpaid fan-translators. The high volumes of text production, revision, and consumption provide the system with enormous amounts of training data, which can be used to further optimize the mathematical models. If the original text is not in a specific domain like this, then "general area" can also be selected for the translation. However, in all cases where entertainment value is what counts, generative AI (offered by Baidu in its ERNIE Bot) offers results that require fairly minimal post-editing.

Most machine translation systems can also work as intelligent monolingual or bilingual online dictionaries. When an English word is entered, Google Translate shows its meaning (in English) together with sample sentences and synonyms, then in the other pane there is a range of its equivalents in the target language. For example, the word "topic" can be rendered differently in Chinese as 主题 *zhuti* (theme), 话题 *huati* (subject of a talk), or 议题 *yiti* (issue), depending on the context. These translations are automatically listed in descending order based on frequency. DeepL also provides built-in dictionary features that allow users to check the meaning of specific words in the original text without leaving the translation. Once a word or phrase in the original text is selected, its meanings are shown in a lower pane, along with its pronunciation and sample sentences.

The glossary feature developed by DeepL extends this kind of feature to domain-specificity, allowing users to pair words and phrases in the original language with their intended translations. This process is nevertheless time-consuming at present because paired texts must be entered manually one at a time. This is a function that is better handled by translation-memory suites, as we will soon see.

Neural machine translation works alongside the other technologies we are looking at here. Its algorithms fed into the development of generative AI, which offers the added capability of adapting the translation to a specific kind of receiver. And machine translation output is usually present as a feed in translation-memory systems, where the user can decide whether to work from the machine translation or from translations that have been stored in a more specific database.

Machine translation systems nevertheless seem not to translate in quite the same way as generative AI. They work from databases of previous translations in the start and target languages (sometimes with other languages in between), decoding from one language and then looking for a good match, perhaps like a sophisticated online dating service. Generative AI, on the other hand, works from vast quantities of language, finding and formulating information, reportedly without requiring a database of parallel texts. (We return to this difference in Chapters 5 and 7.)

To test this difference, we translated the first verses of Dante's *Inferno* ("Nel mezzo del cammin di nostra vita") using Google Gemini (Chat GPT-3.5 and Microsoft Copilot gave virtually the same result):

> In the middle of the journey of our life,
> I found myself in a dark wood,
> For the straight way was lost.

This is a normal, literal rendition. When we asked Gemini who the translator was, it told us that "the translation is not attributed to a specific translator." On the other hand, the neural machine translation system DeepL gave us the following:

> In the midst of the journey of our life
> I found myself in a forest dark
> For the straight way was lost.

This is more readily identifiable as the result of a database of translations: the first verse is from Fitzpatrick and the second is from Longfellow, although the third could be from anyone.

This does not mean that one of these translations is any better than the other. It simply suggests that they have been produced in different ways. In fact, the main difference might be that generative AI can be asked to reproduce Dante's *terza rima* (sometimes with truly terrible results) while machine translation systems cannot.

Translation-memory suites ("CAT tools")

A translation memory is a database of paired segments in the start and target languages – a stock of previous translations. It allows users to store and re-use their translations in future work between the same two languages. As such, it works a little like human memory: the more similar experiences you can recall, the better you can handle a new experience, in theory.

The basic technology for translation memories was developed in the 1970s and 1980s and commercialized in the 1990s, originally as a set of macros in Word. The macros were enough to locate and present previous translations and give a fuzzy-match score. The technology is not complicated and has long been overpriced. Trados was the market leader back then and it remains so today, thanks in part to it having been adopted by the European Commission, which has the world's largest ever translation bureau.

Since the 1990s, many other electronic tools have been added to the core technology. The systems now come as stand-alone software that not only brings up previous translations but also assists with quality control (checks for spelling, punctuation, and formatting), terminology management (more or less sophisticated term bases), and project management (ranging from the simple dividing up of texts for a group of translators right through to handling finances and the scheduling of translation jobs). Here we refer to these collections of tools as "translation-memory suites," although they are also commonly called "CAT tools" (computer-aided translation tools). The only problem with that common misnomer is that virtually everything we do with written language these days is mediated by computers, including everything we do with written translation. The adjective "computer-aided" technically specifies nothing.

There is a trend for software developers to provide not only desktop tools but also web-based suites that increase user accessibility, particularly because the web-based versions are friendly to both Mac and PC users and do not depend on the updated operating systems of computers. If you are teaching these tools in a class where students have both Macs and PCs, it is tempting to stick to the web-based suites. The quality of the Internet connections then becomes crucial in order to prevent accidental data loss.

At the time these suites were being developed, machine translation was generally of much poorer quality than the renditions stored in the translation memories. That meant that the translation-memory suites found market niches quite independently of the use of machine translation. However, as the quality of machine translation increased, first with the move to statistical models and then with the step to neural machine translation, the existing translation-memory suites have incorporated machine-translation feeds. This means that the user can select whether to look for the stored translation memory first and then, if there is nothing in the database or the fuzzy match is too low, call up the machine-translation suggestion and work on that. Alternatively, and increasingly, the system will bring up the machine-translation suggestions whenever there is not a 100% match in the database. In most systems, the user can control how this works, which means that the machine-translation feed can effectively be turned off. That can make the translation class a more interesting place.

As the quality of machine translation improves, the main translation-memory suites are becoming more like sets of tools for the post-editing of raw machine-translated output. In this respect, the fundamental differences between machine translation and translation memories are becoming less important, as the two technologies converge into one. This is particularly clear in cases where companies set up their own in-house machine translation system and divide it into domains for each of their product lines. The resulting technology might be seen either as a sophisticated translation memory or a machine translation system with a very clean database. Either way, few translators working on those product lines would want to be without the technology.

When you import a text into a translation-memory system, the text is divided into segments (usually sentences) and each segment is compared against the segments already in the database. Each time a match is found in the start language, the corresponding segment in the target language is displayed as a suggested translation. There are different kinds of matches:

- a context match (101%) means that not only the newly entered segment, but also the segments before and after it are the same as what is recorded in the database;
- an exact match (100%) means the newly entered segment is the same as the recorded previous translation;
- a fuzzy match (normally between 70% and 99%) means the entered segment is to some extent similar to segments in the database); and
- a no match (normally below 70%) means the previous translation is so different that it will be more efficient to translate from scratch, although some systems allow users to modify the score at which this call is made.

A higher fuzzy match indicates that a greater level of similarity has been detected between the newly entered segment and a previously stored start text. Users can then decide whether to accept the suggestions, edit them, or ignore them and translate from scratch.

Note that a higher similarity rate does not necessarily mean that the proposed translation is the best one available. Sometimes clients provide their own translation memories, indicating that the translator should use the translations that are in it, no matter what the actual quality. On other occasions, a high similarity match may be valid for one context but not for others. This merits some explanation.

The underlying principle of a translation memory is what we have described as text re-use or recycling. This supposes that if you have translated a sentence once, you might want to use that translation whenever the same sentence appears again. In theory, the way you translate that sentence does not depend on any context. That principle can hold in a domain where the terminology and syntax are relatively fixed. In a medical translation, for example, a phrase like *chronic cholecystitis with extensive inflammatory omental adhesion* might be difficult to understand (and painful to suffer) but it will always have the same translations, whatever the target language, simply because the meaning and usage of the words are highly regulated by the medical profession – and the phrase is not likely to occur in any other context.

On the other hand, some expressions are highly context-dependent and may not be well served by a translation memory. For instance, our Chinese students always find the English word *community* challenging. The most literal translation as 社区 *shequ* can be correct only if it indicates a particular place, normally in urban areas, considered in terms of the people who live there. However, if the emphasis is on a group of people, a more suitable rendition would be 群体 *qunti*; if it refers to the condition of sharing certain attitudes and interests, then it is closer to 归属感 *guishugan* (a sense of belonging); while as a term in ecology, it should be translated as 群落 *qunluo*. In this case, the principle of text re-use is of limited help, at least on the level of terms. For this reason, professional translators usually create separate translation memories and glossaries for the different genres they work on or for each individual client.

Another major limitation of the recycling principle comes when there are different translation purposes. Even when a translator is working in the one domain and re-using high-quality previous renditions, a translation suggestion could still require extensive post-editing if the client or end-user has given different instructions. For example, if a novel like *Wuthering Heights* is being translated for teenagers, previous general-readership translations of the work could help, but the younger audience is likely to need considerable amplification or explicitation, removal of the differences between varieties of English, and perhaps some simplification of the plot. In this case, a translation memory can be of some help, but a lot of editing and rewriting will still be needed to produce a fit-for-purpose translation. These are cases where one might want to add generative AI to the production process.

As mentioned, translation-memory suites have constantly added new tools to their basic functionality, becoming bigger and more expensive. They have not been slow to add generative AI options. At the simplest level, this can be a feed that gives context-specific glossary definitions (in Matecat at the time of writing) or a link that enables the user to formulate their own prompts (as in Trados Studio). Much can be done to refine the prompts by incorporating information on the purpose and target audience of the translation (Yamada, 2023), thus potentially overcoming some of the problems of recycling.

A review of recent history as increasing perceived usefulness

If we now try to place the three technologies on the one historical timeline, the most obvious point is that the trajectories all go up together (as in Figure 1.1, inspired by a hand-written chart by Chris Manning at Stanford). This is not quite a story of one technology dying off as another takes its place.

Our depiction of the development is nevertheless made precarious by the assumption that there is just one abstract criterion that can be used as a common yardstick and that the top of the graph might be misunderstood as some kind of ideal 100% quality associated with human translation. That is indeed the operative assumption behind many of the technical tests of machine translation performance: BLEU, TER, and METEOR scores all compare machine-translation output to a reference translation produced by a human. There are several problems with that (see Pym, 2020). First, for a text of any kind of real difficulty, three human translators will give three different translations, the translators will argue about where the mistakes are, and they can all be right (cf. Quine, 1969). Second, and more importantly for our purposes, there is no way that the "human translation" yardstick can be applied in the case of translation memories, where the criterion is more likely to be the degree of matching between the new sentence and the sentence that is already translated in the database (a "fuzzy match" is not with reference to any assumed *ideal* translation). If the comparison were to be made, one would have to look at the way translators work with translation-memory suites that have a reasonable machine translation feed: you track how many times they work from the translation memory, then how many times they work from the machine translation. Alternatively, one can calculate the time taken when working with one technology or another, as was done in the early days of translation-memory software (cf. Freigang, 1998; Webb, 2000), before researchers realized that the productivity gains were not really that spectacular (cf. García, 2010, 2011). In all these cases, we would be working from data on actual use. And the third problem with using human translations as a yardstick is that LLM technologies enable the user to do much more than just straight translation – they offer many *more uses* than do the older technologies. For those reasons, we are not attempting to measure any abstract, quantifiable variable here. We are merely estimating what translators have tended to turn to at different stages of the historical development. This seems broadly in keeping with Venkatesh and Bala (2008, pp. 275–277) when they see a decision to use technology as a trade-off between "perceived usefulness" and the "perceived ease of use." We would love to agree that those judgments are made in such simple terms (usefulness and ease of use), since actual use appears in both variables. At the same time, we know there are many more factors involved: translators tend to stick with the technologies they are used to, with the ones they feel emotionally good about, or with those that their clients and partners make them adopt. All these variables are part of the deal, we know. There nevertheless seems to be a general underlying sense of usefulness that can be estimated and used to estimate some simplified lines.

In very rough terms, then, machine translation prior to the 1990s was found to be useful in restricted semantic fields; through to the mid-2000s, companies considered it more useful for translators to recycle their previous work through translation memories; then machine translation improved considerably and the translation-memory suites began to incorporate machine translation feeds into translator workstations, where they have steadily become more used; and from late 2022, LLMs seemed to come out of nowhere but were built on decades of research in natural-language processing (previously not considered generally useful), especially a variety of deep-learning models and attention systems developed by Google from 2017. Although LLMs have not spectacularly improved the quality of output for a narrow concept of translation, they have certainly shown themselves to be useful for a wide range of other language tasks. Hence, our very rule-of-thumb graph (Figure 1.1), which should be seen as no more than a pedagogical tool.

Does that mean that the older approaches simply fit inside the newer ones, like Russian dolls? Not necessarily, given that there are relative advantages to each. If a client wants to control the terminology in a translation or update a previous text, then translation memories are the way to go. If a text is to be simplified for a certain reading public prior to being translated, then generative AI is what you would first want to explore. In very simplistic terms, machine translation and translation memories can help solve problems

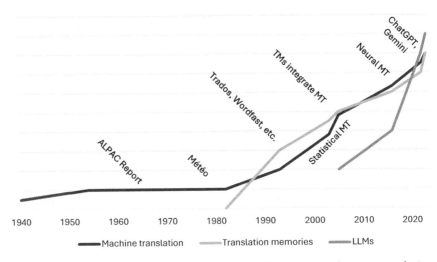

FIGURE 1.1 Estimated perceived usefulness of three approaches to translation automation

in cases where there is a right answer and a wrong answer (the "binary" problems described in Pym, 1992), while generative AI can assist with the many non-binary problems of "right, but…" or "wrong, but…" – with stylistics in a very broad sense. Such cases should make it clear that general "usefulness" is a very approximative and yet realistic yardstick with which to measure the technologies.

A simple example might illustrate what these advances can mean in terms of usefulness. Consider the following, taken from the program of a conference held in Zurich in 2018:

> Wird es in Zukunft selbstverständlich sein, Gespräche zu führen, die vom Mobiltelefon simultanübersetzt werden? Wo liegen die Potenziale und Grenzen solcher Tools? Und inwieweit wird dadurch die sprachkulturelle Verständigung in der Schweiz erleichtert oder erschwert?

If you do not know German, not to worry. You can put the text through a pre-neural machine translation system (this was the version of Systran we found on the website Babelfish in 2018) and all will become clear:

> *It is of course in the future, to talk to that be translated simultaneously from your mobile phone?* What are the potentials and limitations of such tools? And to what extent *will facilitate* the language cultural communication in the Switzerland or difficult? (Italics ours)

Well, perhaps not crystal clear. The parts in italics are more or less gibberish, although the rest is not too bad. What was the problem? If you look at the German, you find the word *selbstverständlich*, literally "self-understandable," except that it can operate as an adverb or as an adjective. Here it is an adjective, but the machine translation reads it as an adverb. Hence the gibberish in the first sentence.

In the same year, 2018, Google Translate rendered the German as follows:

> Will it be natural in the future to have conversations that are simultaneously translated by *the* mobile phone? What are the potentials and limitations of such tools? And to what extent is this facilitating or hindering *language cultural* understanding in Switzerland? (Italics ours)

This is genuinely usable, although one might quibble about the two parts we have put in italics: why the definite article for the mobile phone, and does English really need a calque of the German compound adjective *sprachkulturel*?

In 2023, DeepL offered the following as its up-front rendition:

> Will it be *a matter of course* in the future to have conversations that are
> simultaneously translated by mobile phones? What are the potentials and
> limitations of such tools? And to what extent will this facilitate or hinder
> *linguistic and cultural* understanding in Switzerland? (Italics ours)

This is entirely usable, and if there are any doubts along the way, the user
can click on the points of contention and select from a drop-down menu of
mostly viable alternatives. If you are not sure that *selbstverständlich* is really
a matter of course, click on that translation and you get the following: *given,
normal, commonplace, common thing, common occurrence*, and several
more. This kind of interactivity makes the technology a boost to creativity,
not a replacement of it.

If we move to generative AI, in 2023 Google Gemini gave the following
rendition:

> Will it be *common* in the future to have conversations that are simultane-
> ously translated by a mobile phone? Where are the potential and limi-
> tations of such tools? And to what extent will this facilitate or hinder
> *linguistic and cultural* understanding in Switzerland? (Italics ours)

The two previous quibbles are well handled here. And then, surprisingly,
Gemini spontaneously gives balanced *answers* to the three questions, even
when not asked to, basically saying: yes, it will be common; yes, it can increase understanding; but no, "these tools could also lead to a decrease in
the use of minority languages [...] This could lead to the erosion of linguistic
diversity in Switzerland." That is a good answer, albeit not necessarily useful
for anyone just looking for a translation.

In parallel, ChatGPT-3.5 gave a similarly accurate translation, with
commonplace for *selbstverständlich* and *intercultural communication*
for *sprachkulturelle Verständigung* ("language-cultural understanding"),
which are not too bad. Then we asked it to translate for a 12-year-old
reader:

> In the future, do you think it will be normal to have conversations trans-
> lated instantly by our mobile phones? What are the good things and the
> not-so-good things about these translation tools? And how will this make
> it either easier or harder for people in Switzerland to understand each
> other when they speak different languages?

The text flows well and has become more accessible, in part thanks to some
intelligent pronouns. And this, for many readerships, can be a boost to understanding and engagement, both before and after the act of translation.

The take-away here is that the technologies have become genuinely useful.

The usefulness of translation automation in language education

As translation technologies gained in usefulness for translators, there was parallel interest among language educationalists in computer-assisted-language-learning. The field developed for much the same reasons as translation automation developed: computers offered increasing capacities, in this case, with respect to the delivery of content and the organization of learning experiences over distance (Davies & Higgins, 1982).

The technologies of interest to language teaching first involved new ways of organizing learning activities and tests on computers; that was followed by the various technologies that can be used in the classroom; more recently, there is attention to the communication technologies that students can use when producing and receiving language – for example, learning on mobile phones. However, translation tasks are often thought to be incompatible with gaining fluency in a language and might thus be deemed unnecessary. Not uncommonly, recourse to machine translation is regarded as a form of cheating, raising new issues of plagiarism (Mundt & Groves, 2016), even though there is evidence (gathered from student chat rooms) that it is being used by students as a matter of course (Organ, 2023). We return to these issues in Chapter 4.

That said, a few developments in language education have opened up to translation, if not always to translation technologies. Following Guy Cook's *Translation in Language Teaching* (2010), there has been a gradual reevaluation of what translation can do in the language class, particularly with respect to the use of subtitles. In parallel, the "multilingual turn" in some parts of education theory has tried to move beyond the narrow aim of learning foreign languages, incorporating bilingual education and the use of languages across the curriculum. Meier (2017, p. 131) lines up the ideological ducks when she describes this as conceiving "languages as a resource for learning and as associated with status and power; the learners as diverse multilingual and social practitioners; and learning as a multilingual social practice based on theoretical pluralism, consistently guided by critical perspectives." That framework is much wider than the aim of producing pseudo L1 speakers. For Laviosa (2014, 2019), that was the moment when translation studies should have joined forces with language education, notably by focusing on translanguaging as a concern common to both. In 2014, the journal *The Interpreter and Translator Trainer* brought out a special issue on "Translation in the Language Classroom." In 2015, Laviosa founded the journal *Translation and Translanguaging in Multilingual Contexts*. A rapprochement was at least attempted. But it did not have very much to do with translation technologies.

Are translation technologies of any real use to language learners? Here it is instructive to go back to our sentences from German. If the learner is confused by the initial problems with *selbstverständlich* – since pre-neural machine translation was visibly confused – Google Translate not only gives a translation but also, as mentioned, offers a glossary beneath the translation, with an audio for the pronunciation. This glossary makes it very clear that the German word can be an adjective (with corresponding translations) or a verb (with some very different translations). Double-click on the same word in DeepL and you get the same information plus the verb *verständlich sein* ("be self-evident"), along with more audios for the pronunciation of each form and then whole-sentence authentic examples of how the various meanings have been translated. The learner can use this information as an excellent online dictionary.

But be careful. When we asked ChatGPT-3.5 what part of speech *selbstverständlich* is, it only gave the adverb. When we asked it a second time, it gave both the adverb and adjective. Google Gemini also said that it was an adverb only, before giving examples where it is clearly functioning as an adjective. When asked to repeat, Gemini did mention, right at the end, with apparent reluctance, that the German word can sometimes be an adjective.

Again, are these technologies useful for learners of languages? Historically, when machine translation went statistical, with a corresponding leap in quality, researchers began testing its usefulness in language classes. As mentioned, early publications explored connections between the use of machine translation and L2 writing, arguing that activities related to pre- and post-editing could help augment students' attention to form, enhance metalinguistic awareness, and improve knowledge of L2 vocabulary and grammar (Richmond, 1994; Shei, 2002; Niño, 2009). Some of the benefits have been supported by empirical evidence over the years (cf. Jolley & Maimone, 2022). Compared with a control group, learners who use online machine translation tend to generate L2 or L3 writing with greater accuracy (for instance, fewer errors in noun agreement, lexical choices, and syntax), greater lexical and syntactic complexity (Fredholm, 2014, 2015), and richer lexicons and grammar profiles (Farzi, 2016; Kol et al., 2018; Fredholm, 2019). We have noted that García and Peña (2011) found that post-editing machine translation particularly helped *beginner* students communicate more in L2, which fits in with the indications since the ALPAC report that most advantages would be gained by the weaker performers. At the same time, they also found that L2 writing tasks reduced the number of pauses and edits, suggesting less student engagement in the writing task.

O'Neill (2019) offers further evidence on the short- and long-term impacts that training in machine-translation has on the quality of L2 writing. The study involved five groups: with access to machine translation after training (Group 1) or without training (Group 2), with access to online dictionary after training (Group 3) or without training (Group 4), and finally a control group without access to either tool (Group 5). The groups' L2 development was assessed through pre-, post-, and delayed tests for fluency (total number of words written in a given time), accuracy (number of errors), and complexity (range and sophistication of lexicon and grammar items produced). The group that received training outperformed the other groups in all aspects, while it performed worst in the post-test when machine translation was removed; no significant differences were observed across the board in the "delayed" test conducted two weeks later. This suggests that the machine-translation resources are not easily internalized for *future* language production. It also shows that longitudinal studies are needed to test whether any gains are permanent.

Lee (2023) offers a useful literature review of some 87 studies carried out between 2000 and 2019 on machine translation in language learning, noting generally positive effects on language learning, particularly on writing, although teachers tend to be more skeptical than students. We nevertheless have to look closely at the dates of the studies, given that the technologies have improved in both quality of output and range of operations. Much as one might expect that their usefulness has been increasing, progress is not inevitable. Studies that examine the use of chatbots in L2 argumentative writing tasks report mixed results. While some found positive effects when using pre-generative chatbots in the preparation of writing outlines (e.g., Lin & Chang, 2020), which is a stage seen as a common challenge for L2 learners (Barrot, 2018), others observed no effects. The early systems not based on generative models reportedly could not adapt pre-set responses to provide customized feedback. Perhaps not surprisingly, a more recent study of generative AI used for student feedback on writing (Song et al., 2023) finds that not all the automatic advice is valid. For another example, the current use of the technology to generate multiple-choice quizzes is giving mixed results: some questions are great, while others miss the mark. And then, activities that were reasonably productive a few years ago, such as seeing which machine translation system makes the fewer errors (cf. Thue Vold, 2018), are perhaps now more useful to demonstrate the inherent variability of translation: the errors are becoming rarer, and generative AI usually does better on adaptive tasks anyway.

We will consider these issues in more detail in Chapters 4 and 5.

The usefulness of translation automation in translator training

In contrast to the debates and doubts that enshroud their use in language learning, the need to teach these technologies in the training of translators has become something of a no-brainer.

As translation memory technology developed in the late 1990s and early 2000s, a substantial number of translator-training institutions began incorporating it into their curricula, often with the help of academic licenses from the developer companies. Since the technology was at that stage considered an add-on to translation practices, as an advanced set of difficulties, the dedicated courses were often toward the end of the curriculum, usually in computer labs. It took a number of years for trainers to recognize that the technologies were of general use, that they affected all aspects of training, and that students had to get used to working with them over substantial period of time – which meant they should be taught near the *beginning* of the curriculum and with the students using their own laptop computers. There was also, and still is, a substantial market for continued learning: a short-term postgraduate program in offered in Tarragona, Spain, from 2000 attracted not only graduates who felt they needed to know more about the technologies, but also professional translators who were in considerable doubt about how to use translation memories when asked to do so by their employers. Those decades were not all smooth sailing, however. The downloaded software did not work for Mac computers, which were nevertheless the preference of many students, and the various updated versions had to be compatible with particular versions of Microsoft operating systems. At one stage, the program in Tarragona stopped teaching Trados (which was at that time the clear market leader) simply because of compatibility issues. Wordfast and Matecat were simple, online, and free, so we went with them. Since then, almost all the major translation-memory suites have developed online versions. Compatibility is no longer a great problem.

Shortly after the introduction of neural machine translation, Rothwell and Svoboda (2018) found that over 90% of European programs had introduced courses in technologies, with translation-memory suites and machine-translation usage being the most widely taught. The selection of tools was reported as being based on three factors: "market relevance" (whether a tool is widely used), "accessibility" (whether users can access a tool on their personal devices), and "economy" (cost of licenses). Translation teachers also predicted that their curricula would be affected by a continuous introduction of new tools. That said, fewer students were expected to choose to study translation (Rothwell & Svoboda, 2018), at least partly in response to public discourse around those same technologies. The view from Europe, though, may not be shared elsewhere (see Zhang & Vieira, 2021).

China has seen a constant expansion of translation programs. Industry reports (e.g., Translators Association of China, 2023) show that the number of Masters of Translation and Interpreting programs grew from 259 in 2019 to 316 by the end of 2022, along with 20 new undergraduate programs launched within the same three years. A 2018 survey nevertheless reported that fewer than two-thirds of the 224 surveyed Master of Translation programs had incorporated technology into their curriculum (Wang et al., 2018). The most significant barrier to offering translation technology courses was the lack of qualified instructors, accounting for 77% of the cases of non-adoption. This issue could possibly be addressed by inviting experts with fresh industry experience as guest lecturers (as suggested in Toudic, 2012;

Rothwell & Svoboda, 2018) or by providing professional development to the current teachers (Wang et al., 2018).

The development of translation technologies has been relatively slow to affect the training of interpreters, apart from the advances in microphones and headphones that enabled simultaneous interpreting in 1928 in Geneva (Baigorri-Jalón, 2014/2020, pp. 145–146) and 1929 in Moscow (Chernov, 2016) – well before the famous Nuremberg trials. Improvements in speech-to-text tools, in particular, now enable the interpreter to check for missing content, and the addition of machine translation or AI text generation offers suggestions for any transitory doubts concerning the rendition (see the survey in Fantinuoli, 2023). In situations like legal depositions or court trials, it makes sense for the interpreter to follow the written version of spoken utterances, since in most systems it is the written record that has legal validity. Other technologies of use in the booth are magic pens and tablets (all explained in Corpas Pastor & Defrancq, 2023).

Machine translation can also be used for (relatively) simultaneous interpreting. The incoming speech is fed into a speech-to-text tool; the result of that is machine translated; the result of that is then fed into a text-to-speech tool. This system has been offered by Skype Translator since 2015 and is available on systems like Meta's Seamless M4T. Google's Translatotron, on the other hand, promises direct speech-to-speech translation. These systems are eminently useful for tasks like communicating with taxi drivers, getting your clothes washed in a hotel, and communicating food allergies in a restaurant (we speak from personal experience). As yet, however, we can find no reliable surveys of how well users accept speech-to-speech systems for following an entire conference, especially since they involve listening to a robotic voice. The more viable use of machine translation for lengthy discourse would seem to be in the production of written translations that end-users can use as a set of clues and interpreters can refer to for occasional checks and inspiration in the booth.

Chen and Kruger (2022) have explored how this can work, looking at speech recognition and machine translation as supports for consecutive interpreting. In this work mode, conventional notetaking is replaced by the respeaking of the original utterance into a speech recognition system, which generates a transcript to be further translated by a machine translation system. The interpreter then speaks the final rendition with reference to the transcript in the original language and its machine translation. Based on the data collected from six student interpreters, the workflow was found to have a positive impact on the reduction of disfluencies (measured by the numbers of filled and unfilled pauses) and cognitive loads in both the L1 and L2 directions.

That said, conference interpreters and teachers of conference interpreting seem to have resisted automation for a long time (just as they have resisted the move to remote interpreting, for reasons that include the neurological effects of substandard audio feeds). The basic set of tools has been around for more than 20 years (cf. Berber-Irabien, 2010). It might be that a generation of established professionals, who reached the top of the game without any software solutions, effectively delayed general adoption of the technologies in the profession.

Although there are huge differences between the training outlooks in different parts of the world and different parts of the translation profession, there is no indication anywhere that training institutions are systemically reacting *against* the technologies, give or take a few older teachers. If the technologies are not present in some programs, it seems to be due to local reasons rather than any widespread ideological current.

Translation automation as a transformative force

A long view of translation automation enables us to address some of the more vexing concerns of our age. Here we bite the bullet: Does automation spell the end of the line for human translators? Some kind of answer can be gained from what we know about the general history of automation.

Will the number of jobs for translators decrease?

Bessen (2016) takes a list of occupations in the United States in 1950 and compares it with a corresponding list from 2010. In theory, the differences between the two lists should indicate the impact that computers had over the intervening decades. In fact, he found that only one occupation had disappeared: elevator operators (although a few survivors can be found). People have now figured out how to use the buttons in an elevator! So the effect of automation has not exactly been the destruction of occupations. What has it been? Long-term studies find some underlying trends that might help temper a few of the more hysterical reactions.

To take a classic example, when the textile industry was almost completely automated in the nineteenth century, products became cheaper, demand for them consequently rose, the production pie became bigger, and the number of jobs in the sector *increased* in some places (Bessen, 2015). This is an example of Jevons' Paradox, first formulated in 1865: increasing efficiency can lead to increased demand, which in turn leads to a net increase in resource use. The paradox can apply to increases in human resources and, more worryingly, to the use of energy in AI systems.

Within this basic logic, automation tends to reduce the number of workers whose jobs are better done by machines at the same time as it *increases the value* of the jobs that remain (Autor, 2015; Deming & Kahn, 2018). A job where a human controls, adjusts, or repairs the technology stands to increase in rewards, especially in high-stakes communications where trustworthiness is a prime value. Some people gain from automation; others do not.

The result can be a growing divergence between the upper and lower salaries in a sector, especially when "new skills are costly or difficult to acquire, so that only some workers acquire the skills" (Bessen, 2016, p. 2). Logically, divergence can be limited by re-skilling. That is, automation may not reduce the number of jobs in cases where it transforms the nature of the work and workers can gain new skills.

An optimistic view of this process contends that translator-computer interaction is a double dance of agency: there is an intimate and reciprocal interaction between human and machine actors that can lead to synergistic effects (Tsvetkova et al., 2017). Ruokonen and Koskinen (2017) describe the double dance as a dialectic process that involves initial resistance (as when software unexpectedly fails to perform and the user wants to give up) and then accommodation (as when users learn to adapt to software). This suggests that increased automation need not reduce human agency, even though no one can expect to continue to work in exactly the same way. As noted, the automation of certain processes may make the automation-resistant human skills more appreciated and more highly rewarded, which is why one might want to adapt to the technology.

That optimism, however, only holds for the winners, for those who have somehow overcome resistance and accommodated to the technology. There are whole parts of the translation industry where that is not happening. For instance, recent translation graduates in China are hired as "taggers" or "annotators" to repair the errors in monolingual or bilingual databases for the machine translation systems of tech giants such as Youdao and Sougou. The taggers receive static, low to mid-range salaries; the companies reap the big rewards. Large AI companies take the same approach but are increasingly outsourcing to workers in Kenya and Nigeria, who earn less than $2 an hour. This means human skills are being under-employed to help automation evolve, instead of automation augmenting human skills. A similar kind of gap can be gleaned from statistics on the translation industry in Europe, where the profits of the larger companies grow while many of the smaller translation companies and freelancers struggle to survive (Pym & Torres-Simón, 2021). Not gratuitously, the larger companies are the main investors in technology, while the traditional smaller operators have been left wondering where to turn. Some enroll in courses on translation technologies.

It follows that the question should no longer be whether automation will replace all human jobs. It is smarter to ask which kinds of skills will gain in value.

How can we assess exposure to automation?

A 2010 list of occupations that were likely to be "computerized" in the United States ranked translators and interpreters at place 265 out of 702, with a 0.38 probability of replacement (Frey & Osborne, 2017, p. 272). Translators were just below "packers and packagers" and just above "home health aides." That middling score is not as important as the approach. Language work in general was considered at less risk of automation than were jobs in transportation, logistics, and production, which were deemed "highly susceptible to computerization." Workers in those sectors would have to move to "tasks requiring creative and social intelligence" (Frey & Osborne, 2017, p. 269).

If we move ahead to Eloundou et al. (2023), we find that interpreters and translators are suddenly at the *top* of the list of "occupations with highest exposure to automation," coming in above "survey researchers," "creative writers," and apparently everyone else. How did translators get to the top? It seems that 76.5% of our tasks are now "exposed," in the technical sense that they are subject to "labor-augmenting or labor-displacing effects." That does not imply job destruction; it simply means that our efforts are being pushed in new directions.

The database used for that analysis was the O*Net list of skills and knowledges that are reported as being required in about 1,000 occupations in the United States. The main knowledges listed for translators are "knowing the English language" and "knowing the foreign language" – exactly the same as for teachers of foreign languages. Now, LLMs know the languages, so we are all technically "exposed" at that level. That is a very rough way of predicting our shared fate. Interestingly, the 2023 version of the O*Net data actually lists the translator's most important "core task" (not their knowledge) as "follow ethical codes that protect the confidentiality of information" (Occupational Information Network, 2023). That is possibly the one thing that the technologies do not do well! The take-away, however, should be that the O*Net database can be read in several very different ways. There is no fatality involved.

The impact of automation can also be assessed by historical studies. Yilmaz et al. (2023) look at translation jobs advertised on an anonymous "large online labor market" (possibly ProZ) from January 2016 to May 2017, which would be the period following the advent of neural machine translation. They find that the demand for "regular" translations declined by 13–20%, which is truly worrying, while the demand for "transcreations" ("non-routine cognitive and interactive tasks") did not decline and there was no significant change in the rate of pay for translation across the board. Does that mean that neural machine translation immediately took a lot of work away from translators? Many things could have happened there – technological change takes time to work through the system. Clients might have tried machine translation for a few months then come back to human translators when they discovered that the machines were fallible.

This second kind of interpretation might explain what Borgonovi et al. (2023) find with respect to online job vacancies for language professionals in a range of OECD countries between 2014 and 2019, which is a more serious length of time: "the introduction of higher quality machine translation systems did not lead to decreases in the demand for language professionals" (2023, p. 44). In fact, as predicted by the theorists of automation, machine translation was found to *complement* the employment of professional translators and enhance the market demand for digital skills, post-editing skills, and "transversal skills and knowledge skills – skills that allow language professionals to deliver high-quality translations of text that machine translation tools cannot deliver with accuracy" (2023, p. 45), especially in high-stakes settings. This also concords with the findings of industry reports: "Traditional human translation is the activity that suffers most, while post-editing and other MT-related services, but also audio-visual localization and creative translation are identified as the most promising growth areas" (ELIS Research, 2023, p. 4).

None of these studies gives a definitive answer as to what the long-term impact of automation will be. For a large part of the translation profession, though, the choices have already been made. Translation technologies of various kinds have become regular parts of the workflows adopted by language service providers. Translation memories and post-editing have become norms rather than exceptions (Chinese Translation Industry Report, 2023; ELIS Research, 2023). The genie is well and truly out of the bottle.

Has the singularity arrived?

The development of artificial intelligence is technically restricted by how fast computer processing capacity grows. This is independent of the knowledge databases and the algorithms in the translation systems themselves: it is a measure of what is technically classified as "compute." For decades, this growth was roughly compatible with Moore's Law, which held that the number of transistors on microchips doubled every two years – the law was based on empirical observation and was attributed to the declining cost of microchips. The rate of exponential growth quickened in parallel with the transition to deep learning from 2010 and then with the use of large-scale learning models from late 2022. The rate of growth might now be closer to doubling every six months (Sevilla et al., 2022).

The mapping of this exponential growth has led some visionaries to predict a moment of "singularity," when the capacity of computers surpasses that of the human brain (Kurzweil, 2005). In theory, that is supposed to change the entire relationship between humans and machines. Mathematically, such a moment should be reached and has been reached in some spheres. When computers beat humans at chess and at the game go, then one could say that singularity has arrived in those particular fields. So has the moment of singularity reached language technologies?

In the period of statistical machine translation, up to about 2016, one could legitimately hypothesize that singularity was approaching. It was possible to think that machine translation quality would increase as the databases grew; the databases would grow because more people were using and correcting machine translation; more people would use and correct machine translation because the quality was increasing. That would be a virtuous circle leading to the higher reaches of the Tower of Babel. It seemed to be the promise behind Google Translator Toolkit, which was launched in 2009 as a translation-memory system with a machine translation feed. It was available online without payment. It was eventually closed down in 2019, supposedly because Google Translate was all that the world needed. Google Translator Toolkit might have been folded because the virtuous circle did not work. Machines do what you want them to, but people can be stupid. If they wrongly think a machine translation is valid and put it on public websites and the like, the defective translations are then fed back into the machine translation system's databases and the rubbish is recycled. The virtuous circle becomes a vicious circle. And then it was perfectly possible for users to sabotage the system and feed rubbish into Google Translator Toolkit on purpose. That might explain why the user-detected quality of statistical machine translation in some language pairs stagnated (see, for example, Lotz & van Rensburg, 2016). Even when computer processing *capacity* is equal to humans (such are the claims of singularity), people still need to learn what to do with that capacity.

Has singularity been reached? In terms of what computers can do, that is quite possible. But if we consider what stupid people do with computers, there could be a long way to go.

As can be seen, on all these major questions our basic approach is empirical: we go to the data at hand, just as we draw on the teaching experience we have accumulated. From those foundations, we try to formulate ways in which translation technologies can be incorporated into teaching and learning.

2
HOW DO WE KNOW WHICH SKILLS TO TEACH?

Technological advances have clearly had impacts on employers' expectations, professionals' work procedures, and students' perceptions of their learning needs. The technologies should therefore also affect curriculum development and delivery. This is not always the case, however. Curriculum developers are often not aware of what the technologies are, or they remain skeptical about the quality of the resulting translations. We suspect that contemporary language education and translator training are both affected by "asymmetric information," in the sense that different stakeholder groups have access to different kinds of knowledge. Academics may not know about current employment trends; players in the language industry may not be aware of emerging technologies and their full capabilities; the developers of technology often only have a vague idea about what future users want; curriculum designers may not know the profiles of the student groups; while students may not understand what it takes to transit from education to gainful employment. The resulting situations of asymmetric information can make win-win exchanges difficult to establish.

To foster a more dynamic exchange of information, here we propose a multiple-stakeholder approach to curriculum development. We survey the views of different groups of social actors, between which there may be consensual or competing priorities, preferences, and expectations of what technology and education can offer each other. The central question we are concerned with is *what* we should teach.

Who decides what to teach?

Technological advances can be behind work on a curriculum. The changes might be to incorporate newly emerging knowledge and skills (e.g., the design

DOI: 10.4324/9781032648033-2

of effective prompts for generative AI) or to give greater prominence to existing knowledge and skills (e.g., the ability to revise and edit). When we sense that changes must be made or a problem is to be solved, information is needed for a general assessment of the *needs* that the curriculum should address. This needs assessment is a crucial stage that should influence all programmatic decisions in higher education, including those pertaining to outcomes planning, curricular content, materials selection, activity design, and assessment. Needs assessment can also shade into the evaluation of how effective a curriculum is, which can trigger the planning of another round of needs assessment.

Curriculum experts have for many years been making the criticism that needs assessments are too often carried out just once in the lifetime of a course, usually right at the beginning, and by the teachers working primarily on the basis of their intuitions or occasional consultations with students (e.g., Bocanegra-Valle, 2016, p. 567). Needs assessment calls for a more inclusive approach that draws on input from multiple stakeholders. This should lead to a more comprehensive picture of the needs to be addressed in a specific situation. A multiple-stakeholder approach then requires that major decisions be made cooperatively by a range of actors that may include teachers, curriculum specialists, institutions, external consultants, the wider society, and most importantly the former and present students and their support groups.

To gain a more nuanced understanding of curriculum development, Mainardes et al. (2012) categorize stakeholders into groups based on their relative influence. National governments and accreditation agencies are considered regulatory stakeholders, exerting influence on universities in a one-way manner. At the same time, mutual influences can be observed between the universities and other stakeholder groups, with controller stakeholders such as senior university management, employers, and professionals holding greater sway, while passive stakeholders like current and former students and teachers tend to accept the decisions handed down by management. This distribution of influence is calqued on power and legitimacy dynamics within the institution. We nevertheless argue that the apparently passive groups here – especially the students– should be put more center stage, particularly because they tend to know more about current technologies. That is, the knowledge asymmetries can be the reversal of the power asymmetries. Educators must therefore try to understand the students, know what technologies they are using, and what technologies they are likely to use when employed. Without awareness of that relationship, the remaining negotiations may be to little avail.

Educators' models

Around the turn of millennium, a few visionaries were quick to recognize the need for translators to develop technology-based translation skills (e.g., Somers, 1997; O'Brien, 2002). The influence of this initial awareness can be seen in the way those skills were progressively integrated into the main translation competence models (PACTE Group, 2000, 2003, 2017; EMT Expert Group, 2009; EMT, 2017, 2022). Much can be learned from the frameworks designed to make recommendations or offer authoritative statements about what kind of technologies language professionals require – here more for translator training than for general language learning.

PACTE is the name of a group of researchers formed somewhere around 1997 at the initiative of Amparo Hurtado Albir at the Universitat Autònoma de Barcelona. The name stands for "Process of Acquisition of Translation Competence and Evaluation." The name is actually in Catalan, so the siglum should be pronounced /pæktə/. Their general aim has been "to investigate the acquisition of translation competence with a view to improving curriculum design in university-level translator training programs" (PACTE, 2022), although their more recent conceptual work has been on descriptors of *levels* of translation competence. As early as the 2000s, the PACTE competence model highlighted the need for translators to acquire an "instrumental sub-competence" (2000, p. 101) that included items such as the ability to use documentation resources (e.g., digital dictionaries, corpora, encyclopedias, style sheets, and parallel texts) and communication tools (e.g., email and the Internet). That list now looks rather quaint: a fair mastery of those tools should be considered basic for any employee in most contemporary workplaces. Curiously, despite the evolutions of technology over the years, PACTE's list of technologies seems to have remained fundamentally unchanged, although "electronic corpora" did obtain a brief mention early on (PACTE, 2003, p. 59). Translation memory suites seem to be excluded from an experiment reported in 2018 (Kuznik & Olalla-Soler, 2018), and something called "assisted translation software" surfaced in the list 20 years after the first version (2020, p. 103).

The European Masters in Translation (EMT) was set up by the European Commission's Directorate-General for Translation in 2006 with the aim of improving the quality of translator training, ostensibly to enhance the labor-market integration of young language professionals. It functions as a quality label awarded to postgraduate programs in the European Union that meet a set of training requirements and that then become part of the EMT network. In 2023, it had 68 member programs.

In 2009, the EMT Expert Group (2009) expanded the range of technologies and started to incorporate tools that are more specific to translation. These included machine translation, translation memory suites, terminology databases, and more specialized tools for audiovisual translation. There was also explicit recognition of abilities to post-edit in L1 and L2, to apply formatting, and to manage different formats. In addition, the 2009 EMT model mentioned managing expectations with regard to the limits and possibilities of machine translation, so as to avoid both ignorance and overreliance on technology.

The growing role of technology can then be seen in the revised 2017 EMT model, which explicitly recognized that a variety of tools had become integral parts of translation practices. Emphasis was laid equally, if not more, on "personal and interpersonal" skills that are *not* closely aligned with technologies and might be considered automation-resistant. Teamwork, for instance, was emphasized, given that translators and language professionals increasingly work in collaborative settings. Yet the technology was never far away: an important part of teamwork was the ability to use communication technologies, which had previously been described as instrumental and technology-related in the PACTE model.

The updated EMT model (EMT, 2022) highlights the role of *critical analysis* in technology use, as well as plenty of technical know-how. This critical analysis involves assessing the relevance of specific technologies in specific situations, as well as being aware of ethics, copyright, and data security. Items broached for the first time in the 2022 model include data literacy and the use of automatic quality assurance software. The latter helps translators identify typological errors and irregularities between the start and target texts, including unmatched punctuations, upper/lower case letters, formatting tags, abbreviations, and sentence lengths. At the same time, two personal skills are foregrounded: life-long learning and cognitive-load management. The emphasis on continuous learning can be seen as a response to the evolving and dynamic nature of technology and the challenges it presents. The increasing cognitive load could also be associated with the ever-evolving functions of technology: for instance, the addition of new tools to a translation memory suite often leads to greater overall complexity, which then requires an increasing amount of time and effort to reach a reasonable level of operational proficiency. The result can be "cognitive friction" (Cooper, 2004, p. 19), otherwise seen as tension in human-computer interaction (O'Brien, 2017, p. 146). It is evident that technology skills are no longer supplemental (as they once were in the PACTE model) but have become integral components that can reshape the balance of other skills required by translators.

Voices from industry: Is it enough to "close the gap"?

The notion of a "target situation" was initially articulated to help purpose-specific language programs plan objectives and decide on the content the curriculum should cover (Munby, 1978). Target needs are defined as what students are expected to do to excel in a communicative situation. This approach urges programs to create a profile for each specific situation, taking into account events, domains, registers, media, people involved, subject matter, and level of language proficiency required. For example, a multinational company might suggest their non-English-speaking employees receive intensive training in English. The target situation would then be the one where workers can use English for effective spoken and written (*medium*) communication in daily correspondence, meetings, presentations, and negotiations (*events*) with co-workers and supervisors (*people involved*). The training can perhaps touch upon email etiquette, business letter/proposal writing, cross-cultural sensitivity, and so forth (*subject matter*) and emphasize formal language usage (*register*) and vocabulary and terms relevant to the company's industry. This approach can be applied to the teaching of languages and translation in many specialized areas. However, the situation can be fuzzy when dealing with programs that have a broad scope or poorly defined endpoints.

What should be done to reduce this complexity? A possible solution is to gather data on the employment of graduates (see Chapter 3 below), especially with regard to the jobs they have secured within a particular sector across regions. The former students can offer insights into the scope of their work responsibilities and the extra skills that they had to develop to meet those responsibilities. Another approach is to consult language service providers directly and then compare what they say with what is done in language teaching or the training of translators. These studies inevitably find numerous "gaps" and conclude that the education system should fill in those gaps as soon as possible, thereby ensuring that training blends seamlessly with the needs of industry – all students will immediately find permanent jobs and live happily ever after. In the field of translation, this thinking is explicit and widespread (for example, in Gaspari et al., 2015; Horbačauskienė et al., 2017; Rodríguez de Céspedes, 2018; Marczak & Bondarenko, 2022; Liet al., 2023). Something similar was done by Lafeber (2012a), who asked United Nations revisers of translations about the extent and importance of the skills their new recruits were lacking. Another approach is to analyze corpora of job advertisements and extract the skills and knowledges that seem most generally sought after (as in Borgonovi et al., 2023; Prieto Ramos & Guzmán, 2023; Yilmaz et al., 2023).

Perhaps because of these different ways of gathering data, the surveys do not all find that we could "close the gap" by adding technologies. Lafeber (2012a, 2012b) noted that translation technologies were well *down* on the list of skills that were lacking, basically because the United Nations was providing new translators with its own training in its own technology solutions. Prieto Ramos and Guzmán (2023) find something similar for some international institutions, while they identify other institutions where "CAT skills" are in high demand: their reported demands go up and down like a yo-yo. As noted in Chapter 1, Borgonovi et al. (2023, p. 45) summarize a quite complex development around the assumed gaps:

> 1) the continued and growing relevance of transversal skills and knowledge skills – skills that allow language professionals to deliver high-quality translations of text that machine translation tools cannot deliver with accuracy, 2) the key role played by digital skills which have been an

important component of the skill set required of language professionals at least since 2014, and 3) skills that allow them to work alongside machine translation tools, such as, for example post-editing skills.

That is, there seems to be work for people who do what automation cannot do, *and* for people who develop and apply automation, *and* for people who use automation to augment their language skills. This makes it difficult to state with certainty that there is a pressing need to fill just one kind of gap. Further, one should be wary of generalizing the results of surveys that are limited in time and space. Borgonovi et al. (2023) were looking at job advertisements in ten OECD countries – advanced post-industrial economies. Their findings have no reason to apply across the board in other parts of the world. For example, Al Qahtani (2023) found that more than half of 11 translation companies in Saudi Arabia were unaware of the nature and capacities of translation technologies. Anecdotally, when we were developing a course in translation technologies in Melbourne in 2018, we first asked the main language service providers which technologies they used. Most were unaware of any at the time (the local market is mainly for community translation and interpreting), but a few *asked us* if we had any recommendations. Trainers can look to the market for information, but the market can also look to academics.

Should we be in a hurry to fill the technology gaps in the hope of providing sure employment? The data we find in the published surveys must certainly be considered in a basic needs analysis, since they indicate the kinds of questions we might be asking of the labor markets close to us. But there are other ways of deciding what to teach. Most importantly, you should ask students what they most want to discover. But to do that, you first must know the kinds of skills that are on offer, which are in demand, and how to talk about them. Industry surveys can certainly help with that.

What do students say?

One-size-fits-all solutions rarely exist in this field. Even though programs worldwide are facing somewhat similar problems – such as how generative AI will affect education –, the way each program frames the problem for their curriculum depends substantially on their targeted student groups and institutional contexts. In this general situation, it can help to ask current and former students what they think (Jordan, 1997).

Profiling the student groups who are in front of us is essential for making programmatic decisions. We can gather data on their age, gender, social-cultural backgrounds, prior professional or educational experience relevant to the curriculum, as well as indications of their cognitive proficiencies (knowledge and skills) and affective dispositions (attitudes and values). This helps avoid duplication of what has already been mastered, at the same time as it should keep us from teaching above the level of the target student group. It should lead to an efficient use of resources. In addition, one should try to ascertain students' aspirations, resolutions, and goals (especially career goals) to understand their expectations and desires for education. When we did this for our own postgraduate program in translation in Melbourne, we were genuinely surprised to discover that quite a few of the students did not particularly want to become professional translators – they had enrolled to receive a degree from a prestigious university, to live in an English-speaking country, to gain a cosmopolitan view of the world, and in a few cases to get away from their parents (Hao et al., 2023). Given such a range of motivations, one cannot assume that incoming students necessarily have a clear idea of the skills they will need. One can at best estimate the gap between what students already know and what they should know at the end of the learning process, and this can help identify what should be in or out of the curriculum.

The main point to be made here is that surveys of students' perceived needs should be checked and adjusted periodically: needs are a moving target.

How do you carry out a needs assessment?

Here we delve into the research methods that can be adopted to collect information for a needs assessment. Some methods invite us to "see through other eyes," to understand opinions and affective traits that accompany descriptions of personal experiences (questionnaires and interview surveys). Other methods allow us to "see for ourselves," as in on-site observations or standardized tests that are less susceptible to bias. The information gathered helps curriculum designers handle information asymmetry and gain a more holistic view of the situation.

Three commonly used types of survey in the curriculum setting are questionnaires, interviews, and focus-group discussions (Thomas et al., 2022). These methods tend to be retrospective and can yield structured self-report data that are factual (such as biographical details), affective (for example, attitudes toward machine translation in language learning), and/or descriptive (such as skillsets that should be included or excluded from the curriculum). Here we will explore the benefits and drawbacks of each method, touching on cost-effectiveness and the richness of the data elicited.

Questionnaires

We start off with questionnaires as a method for eliciting structured data on a large scale through a predefined set of questions. Questionnaires designed online can facilitate engagement with a substantial number of stakeholders who are geographically dispersed. They are a popular and cost-effective means of data collection that consumes less time and effort than one-on-one or focus-group interviews and direct observation methods. By collecting a relatively large amount of data through appropriate sampling, one obtains results that can in theory be generalized to larger populations. The questions can be either open-ended, closed, or take the form of a Likert scale. Closed questions, whether they be single-answer or multiple-choice, help generate data that can reveal quantitative patterns, although they may not capture explanations. Open-ended questions may be needed to elicit qualitative responses (given in a text box) or one can use follow-up interviews to try to identify the reasons underlying certain responses.

Structured quantitative data also allow measurement of the strength and direction of correlations between variables. As an example, in the employment survey that we did in Melbourne in 2019 (reported in Hao & Pym, 2021), we explored the career trajectories of our recent translation graduates and the skills they found most useful for employability. We were particularly interested in the relationship between types of occupation (variable 1) and graduates' evaluations of skillsets (variable 2). The graduates were categorized into three groups on the basis of their employment (translators, language teachers, others), and their evaluations of the extent to which a skillset should be more present in the curriculum were recorded on a five-point scale from 1 (not at all) to 5 (much more). A two-way ANOVA test was employed to test the correlation between the two variables. The results indicated a highly significant interaction ($p < 0.001$). The *post hoc* test further showed that those who did not enter the translation industry gave lower scores for technology-related skills than did those who were employed as translators. This seems painfully obvious in hindsight, but at the time we were thinking in a simplistic "bridge the gap" mode. The result told us that the curriculum should be adjusted to accommodate the diverse career paths that we found. We then decided to offer basic translation technology to all students and *advanced* technology as an elective course only.

Given that questionnaires are often self-administered, curriculum designers should take care to ensure that the instructions and phrased questions are clear. Avoid overloading the questionnaire with too many questions that may overwhelm the respondents.

Interviews

The word *interview* is derived from the Latin *inter* ("between" or "among") and *videre* ("to see"), giving the idea of seeing or understanding each other (Narayan & George, 2003, p. 515). Interviews in contemporary usage refer to a conversation between two parties where information is gathered by questions being asked and answered. Unlike questionnaires, interviews allow curriculum designers to tap into the perspectives and expertise of stakeholders, albeit at the cost of increased time and effort. Interviews can be structured to various degrees. A highly structured interview can ensure the consistency of the questions raised and enable a neat comparison of responses during data-analysis; semi-structured and unstructured interviews, on the other hand, offer spontaneity on-site and flexibility for interviewers to follow-up on extreme or interesting responses (Josselson, 2013; Patton, 2014). Regardless of the interview type, the questions should be pertinent to the topic of concern and should be arranged in a way that follows a logical progression.

In mixed-methods studies, interviews are used in combination with questionnaires in a simultaneous or sequential manner (Morse, 2016; Creswell & Creswell, 2017). Engaging in interviews before the design of questionnaire can help avoid assumptions and generate content grounded in the stakeholder group's basic understandings (an exploratory approach). In the cases where quantitative data are collected first, the subsequent analysis helps inform the sampling criteria for the interviews and the questions to be asked (an explanatory approach). The interviews then ideally provide explanations for the quantitative patterns that are ambiguous or otherwise unexpected.

To illustrate this, in our 2019 graduate employment survey, semi-structured interviews were conducted to follow-up on the quantitative survey results. As mentioned, we found that the "translator" group prioritized technology-related skills, while the "language teachers" and "other professionals" tended to give high ratings to transferable language and interpersonal skills. A methodological problem was identified when we sought to explain the results. When our graduates indicated in our survey that a skillset should be more present in the curriculum, their response could be due to a perceived insufficiency in the program or to how germane the skill is to their employment. Of course, the reason could also be a combination of both, and potentially other motivations as well. To sort this out, in-depth interviews were carried out with a representative sample from the three employment-experience groups. The qualitative interviews told us that our graduates' evaluations were predominantly influenced by the perceived usefulness of the skills for employment. That is, if a particular skill did not concern a gap in their career development, it did not matter much whether it was seriously missing in the curriculum.

At the same time, we should be mindful that the validity and reliability of such findings can be influenced by the "interviewer bias effect" (Saldanha & O'Brien, 2014). This occurs when the interviewer's presence influences the responses and normal behavior of interviewees. We mostly hear a distorted version of their inner thoughts, feelings, or experiences, based on what they think will please us, or they may give an idealized version of their experience if they think intelligent answers will make a good impression. Such answers might indeed make us happy, but they will not help improve the curriculum.

Focus-group discussions

Focus-group discussions are a cost-effective method that brings together people that have common traits (e.g., they are from the same stakeholder group) to share their collective experiences or views on a specific topic. Focus groups can be used to gain diverse perspectives or test possible points of consensus. During this process, the participating stakeholders engage not only with the facilitator but also with one another: one person's response may prompt others to make further comments. This process can increase the depth and richness of the information gathered, sometimes well beyond initial expectations. For instance, in 2020, we moderated a focus-group discussion with ten translation-technology teachers from Australian and New Zealand universities (reported in Hao & Pym, 2023b; see also Chapter 4 below). The idea was to follow up on their quantitative survey responses to the questions of *what they teach* (knowledge and skills) and *how they teach it* (teaching methods). We found a tacit consensus among the teachers that some technologies were core (basically machine translation and translation memory suites – generative AI was not available at the time) while others were peripheral (such as programming skills for translators). Further, certain contents and skills were best taught in a teacher-centered way while others were more suitable for a constructivist approach. The discussion lasted for 90 minutes, during which information emerged that was considerably more nuanced than the quantitative results. This included topics such as student profiling and its impact on the selection of teaching contents and methods. Several teachers advocated autonomous learning in technology because the students in front of them were observed to have a natural flair for it. On the other hand, a few teachers said they had to introduce even basic computer skills step-by-step (e.g., formatting or the use of Track Changes) to accommodate students with relatively low digital literacy. One teacher, expressing concerns, tried to seek suggestions from other participants on how to best manage a heterogeneous student population – a generally shared opinion was the need to abandon the idea of keeping everyone on the same page all the time.

Focus-group discussions can sometime run off the rails when there is insufficient orientation from the facilitator. It is thus useful to have some predefined questions and to intervene occasionally to make sure they are answered (McCracken, 1988; Thomas et al., 2022).

Curricula and syllabi analysis

As teachers, we are all in this together, even when we are in rival departments and institutions. The emerging use of AI and neural machine translation should present problems that are burning enough to warrant curriculum changes in many programs around the world. It is thus prudent to seek inspiration from educators who have already taken initiatives to respond to this challenge. Much can be learned from continuously updated lists of learning outcomes (see the end of Chapter 4) and from what has been done on the ground. Further information can be gleaned from the publicly available curricula and syllabi of programs in the same region or beyond.

A survey of language and translation curricula can offer clues to the pathways available in the digital era. Information related to technology-teaching units can be selected and cross-referenced in a spreadsheet, including course name, credit points, and total credits of the degree program. When Torres-Simón and Pym (2019) did this for the EMT network, they found a puzzling lack of language-pair specific translation courses in the United Kingdom – one can only assume that the international students were there for reasons other than learning to translate proficiently between a specific language pair. The same method can be used to scrutinize and question the role of technology. For instance, we found that the postgraduate translation programs in Australia and New Zealand that specialize in translation technology or localization devote more than 30% of their curriculum time to technology components, whereas the corresponding programs that have a focus on literary translation allocate very few credits or none at all (Hao & Pym, 2023b). One can also zoom in on the specific skillsets a program sets out to cultivate, usually expressed in the learning outcomes listed on an institutional website. Thematic analysis can then detect the main types of reoccurring topics covered in the existing curricula.

Curriculum designers need not be afraid of borrowing from successful teaching in this way. However, as is clear from the above example, the extent to which technology is taught can depend on the aims, resources, and expertise of each program. A postgraduate course focused on literary translation may not be interested in technology at all – even though they are probably missing out on a lot of good things that they do not care to find out about.

Construction of student question pools

As mentioned, learning needs can also be detected from questions raised by students. The questions can signal what students already know and the direction in which they desire to extend their knowledge about a particular subject matter (Commeyras, 1995). They can also indicate considerable anxiety: this is not an emotionless exercise in pairing questions and answers. When students ask about employment and pay, for example, we are reminded that we have to adopt a sustainable approach to education, addressing a variable future. Questions related to useful tools should signal the need to raise awareness and foster operational skills through hands-on translation assignments. Questions about "other career pathways" urge us to shake off the linguist-only or translator-only mindsets and consider the range of occupations where translation and language skills can be applied. We suggest how to answer some of these questions in Chapter 7.

Pym and Torres-Simón (2016) report on the use of a pool of students' questions to identify learning needs at the undergraduate and postgraduate levels in Monterey (in 2012 and 2014) and Vienna (in 2015). An open-ended approach was used to elicit spontaneous responses, without restricting the range of topics: after a standard introductory lecture, the students were simply asked to write down three questions that they would like to see answered in the course (only one of the questions could concern how to get rich). Among several recurring topics, new technologies captured the attention of a fair number of students. The way the questions were usually formulated (as in "Will machine translation replace translators?") indicated that the emerging technologies were generally seen as rivals rather than as aids. Perhaps surprisingly, fear and anxiety about machines stealing jobs were more prevalent among students in the European context, where they had had less prior exposure to machine translation and translation memory suites. In Monterey (which is near Silicon Valley), there was greater curiosity about the new forms of translation encouraged by technology, although there were also mentions of threats from "singularity" and "intelligence explosion."

We replicated this study to gather information on the learning needs of four Chinese international student cohorts who studied translation in Melbourne from 2017 to 2020. The average percentage of questions about technology was much higher than in the previous studies: 30% in Melbourne, as opposed to 12% in Monterey and just 5% in Vienna. The Melbourne data also showed a constant *increase* in the number of questions about technology, perhaps in response to growing public discussion of advances in machine translation.

Over two-thirds of the technology-related questions raised by the Melbourne students asked about which "useful tools" are available today (51%) and tomorrow (15%), while only a small fraction of students were troubled by anything like a "digital upheaval." One could perhaps assume that when the quality of machine translation still left much to be desired, students tended to think in the future tense: how far *would* machine translation go? However, when technology generates texts of continuously improved quality, students tend to think about ways to take advantage of the improvements. This might explain why, rather than ponder the will-the-species-die-out questions, our students inquired more about alternative career options.

Observation and tests

Another way to locate learning needs is to carry out observations of what happens on-site. An observation study offers direct access to the "target" (real-life) and "present" (classroom and simulation) situations. It can be carried out through continuous monitoring or sampling for specific periods or events, trading off completeness against time commitment. Although this method requires resources and access to participants, when conducted systematically and with careful planning it is reliable due to its high ecological validity (Norton, 2019). Observations can be either direct or participatory. In direct participation, the people being observed are aware they are being studied by a third party. They may therefore choose to modify (and often improve) their normal behavior and act artificially, a phenomenon described as the "Hawthorne effect" (McCambridge et al., 2014) – a variant of the "interviewer bias effect" we met above. On the other hand, in participatory observation the observer is a member of the group being observed. This helps provide an insider's view and minimizes the possibility of misinterpreting the behavior observed. However, being too closely tied to the group may affect the objectivity of the observation.

Observations conducted in the workplace can help curriculum designers understand the knowledge and skills required by language professionals. That said, finding the right industry partner can be tricky. There is a risk of seeing some skills prioritized in a specific company and then assuming that the same priorities are obtained across the whole industry. This is where surveys of graduate employment can act as a useful corrective, indicating how language and translation skills can be applied to multiple occupations. Additionally, observations carried out in the classroom can help identify learning gaps and deficiencies, particularly disparities between what is expected and what our students have already mastered. This method can yield data of various kinds, including students' learning behaviors, classroom interactions, and the physical setup – including where and how computers are arranged in the classroom.

Mapping out a strategy for future proofing

Even when you have as much information as possible about the current state of the labor market, the opinions of employers, the capacities of teachers, and the probable motivations of students, that mass of data will not in itself tell you the extent to which a curriculum should integrate technology. The data come from the past; the technologies will be operating in the future. Generative AI and neural machine translation not only make us take a fresh look at what it means to be a language professional in the age of automation, but they also oblige us to think strategically. How should a particular training institution respond and adapt to the changes? What kinds of skills should it focus on to best futureproof its students?

A few possible strategies have been proposed, along with a little underground debate on future directions.

Teaching with or beyond translation technologies?

Some see *all* language work as being increasingly engaged in automation. They therefore argue that training programs should move away from the unaided human and toward pre-editing, post-editing, quality control, and prompt engineering. Automation thus becomes a pathway to a profitable future in the language industries, inevitably requiring students to work *with* rather than *against* technologies (e.g., Kenny & Way, 2001; García, 2009; O'Brien, 2002; Enríquez Raído & Austermühl, 2003; Pym, 2011). From this perspective, students come in using some translation technologies so they should ideally learn about those technologies as early as possible in the training program, then move to more advanced technological skills.

On the other hand, some pedagogies emphasize the *limits* of automation (e.g., Rodríguez de Céspedes, 2019; Kenny, 2020). They consequently call for training in activities where humans can play to their strengths, doing what the machines *cannot* do well. This especially concerns person-to-person communication and complex cognitive processing (Deming & Kahn, 2018). Those strengths tend to coincide with high-level language skills, rejoining the concerns and priorities of many language teachers. The underlying assumption is that language skills will remain eternally in demand, no matter how much translation technologies seem here to stay. One line of reasoning here is that in order to post-edit machine translation output, you logically have to know how to translate *without* machine translation, so fully human translating is what students really need, even when they work with the technologies. In a lapidary statement of the same position, Mossop (2003, p. 20) contends that if you cannot translate with pencil and paper, then you cannot translate with the latest translation technology either. Let's get those pencils out! In an indirect reply, Gouadec (cited in Pym et al., 2003, p. 95) notes that "my students are absolutely unable to use pen and paper. Whenever the intranet or internet is down, they just sit there waiting and drooping." This could be seen as all the more reason to prevent them from becoming dependent on technology.

There have been instances of clear opposition between these two approaches. When one theorist predicted that "statistical-based MT, along with its many hybrids, is destined to turn most translators into posteditors one day, perhaps soon" (Pym, 2013, p. 488), another theorist, five years later, claimed that any such broad acceptance of machine translation opened the way for a "downward migration" in employment conditions and should be resisted (Kenny, 2018, p. 66). Translators should instead produce high-quality products carefully tailored for the "premium markets" prepared to pay for them. The point is fair enough: a good future for a few gifted translators can indeed lie in the top markets, where the most important clients pay well for trusted work on high-stakes texts. That is a good future, but it is good with or without technology. Further, it remains to be explained how large numbers of novice translators can gain access to those niche markets. A survey of more than 2,800 freelance translators (Inboxtranslation, 2023) found that just 1% of them were earning more than 150,000 euros/pounds/dollars a year, while the next income category was another 1% at just under 100,000, and 16% were earning less than 5,000. This suggests that there is indeed a premium market up there somewhere, but with no room for a lot of translators. To propose that the most monied niche is really for everyone might be called the Marie Antoinette strategy: if the people have no bread (or the translators are struggling to make a profit in the face of automation), let them eat cake (they just have to be smart without automation).

How could one decide between working with technology or working somehow above or beyond it? The simple answer is that there is no need to choose: it is quite possible to train students for *both* kinds of employment, and for many things in between. If you look at the training recommendations made in the apparently opposed papers by Pym (2013), who seems to welcome post-editing, and Kenny (2018), who argues against "downward migration," you find numerous points on which they are quite compatible. Kenny (2018, p. 66) in fact lists the following learning outcomes (framed as training "needs"):

- "to source and profile (even greater quantities of) training data," which involves helping to improve the quality of the technologies;
- "to find suitable points at which translators can intervene in or control [...] the translation process," which implies that the translation process is happening with automation and that translators are working with it; and
- "to educate new generations of translators/post-editors who are capable of working with NMT [neural machine translation] in a sustainable way," which again sounds like precisely the opposite of turning one's back on technology.

One is not then wholly surprised that Kenny, having briefly espoused the ideology of the "premium market," then nobly contradicted herself by editing *Machine Translation for Everyone* (2022). As for the position that Kenny was ostensibly opposing, Pym's training proposal back in 2013 included the following skills:

- Ability to evaluate critically the work process with the tool.
- Ability to check data in accordance with the translation instructions: if you are instructed to follow a TM [translation memory] database exactly, then you should do so [...], if you are required to check references with external sources, then you should do that. And if in doubt, you should try to remove the doubt (i.e., transfer risk by seeking clarifications from the client).

- Ability to conduct substantial stylistic revising in a post-draft phase.
- Ability to revise and review in teams, alongside fellow professionals and area experts, in accordance with the level of quality required.

These skills seem very far from making the human translator wholly subordinate to machine translation. In fact, rather like the menu presented by Kenny, this list identifies some of the areas in which translators must use non-automated communication skills and advanced writing skills, especially with respect to revision and reviewing. All those skills seem quite compatible with Kenny's call for human intervention and "working with NMT in a sustainable way." Both sides can be found together. Tellingly, a survey of localization professionals (O'Brien & Rossetti, 2021) indicates that they carry out both mechanical tasks (file preparation and transcription) *and* creative activities (content creation and transcreation), in combination with other responsibilities such as editing, revising, proof-reading, quality control, project management, and occasionally data curation and annotation. The debate between just two approaches could and should be little more than a storm in a teacup.

Here we adopt the position that the space of training is wide enough for technology to be dealt with in at least those two ways: we train students to work with it, *and* we train them to do what the technology cannot do.

Teach technologies at the end or near the beginning?

These various strategies have many practical consequences. One of them concerns where technologies are placed in the curriculum. Some experienced teachers, having seen the unfortunate results of uncritical overreliance on technology, remain hesitant to introduce any automation to students before they are sufficiently proficient in L2 to evaluate what the technology actually does (Bowker, 2015). Technologies would therefore come into play toward the *end* of a modern language program, as a supplement that brings in additional difficulties.

Others nevertheless stress the importance of students having extensive ongoing exposure to technology, in the hope that using the technology might become a normal mode of work. Pym (2013, p. 491) argues that instead of being "add-on components," translation technologies affect the very nature of all translation activities and the balance of all other translation skills. They should therefore be introduced toward the *beginning* of a program of study. Mellinger (2017) similarly argues that technology should be incorporated into all translation practice modules since it is intrinsic to the translation process.

Should the technologies be at the beginning or near the end? The decision ensues from the general strategy adopted. Part of that decision might concern selecting particular sets of technological skills to be introduced along the way. The minimalist approach proposed by Austermühl (2013) stresses the importance of revision skills (critical for post-editing practices) and documentation (the ability to sift through the information available on the Internet and locate what is needed), which can come right from the beginning. For this approach, there is no reason to teach as many tools as possible – many of them risk being unneeded or outdated when the students enter the job market. To take the example of translation memory suites, you can teach something easy and basic like Matecat at the beginning, then something more sophisticated like Trados or Phrase later on, perhaps in a dedicated course for the more dedicated students. If you do that, there is no earthly need to teach MemoQ, Wordfast, Smartcat, CafeTran, and so on (there are many translation memory suites out there!), neither at the beginning nor at the end. The skills acquired on two suites will be transferable to the others. Besides, some translation companies and organizations provide training in specific in-house software to their new recruits (as mentioned in Lafeber, 2012b). It thus seems more important to work on transferable and generic skills than to teach students one specific tool step-by-step. These transferable skills include the ability to learn a new technology quickly by drawing on available scaffolding, as well as the ability to analyze usability issues and determine whether a tool is suitable for a given task (e.g., Pym, 2013) (see the list of learning outcomes at the end of Chapter 4).

Much depends, then, on the general aims of each program. It seems useful to conceptualize a continuum that goes from low use of technologies (in a program specializing in literary translation, for example) right through to complete integration (in a program focused on localization, for another example). Each curriculum designer can map out the space of technology at any point along that continuum. But be careful: the line might not be straight. In between working with automation and working without it, there is a very large area where *interactive* technologies can enhance the creative, dynamic development of language skills – as we see whenever the technologies propose more than one possible translation and the user has to choose between them or invent something new. That area, radically expanded by generative AI, should be a place for future curriculum development.

We can thus teach students how to operate the technologies, how to go beyond them, and how to interact with them creatively. There is no need to choose; there is much to explore.

3

WILL ALL LANGUAGE PROFESSIONALS NEED TRANSLATION TECHNOLOGIES?

This chapter deals more closely with the kind of needs analysis that can be based on surveys of where graduates go. It focuses on the postgraduate training of translators, but we believe the general principles can be extended into other kinds of training programs that are affected by language automation. Here we directly challenge the simplistic assumption that teaching institutions should be solely focused on providing graduates for the established language industries, as the many discourses on "bridging the gap" would have it. Analysis of several surveys of graduate employment shows that, on average, only about a third of postgraduate translation students become professional translators or interpreters for any length of time: another third goes into language teaching, and the remaining third use their languages in a wide range of occupations. As mentioned, our data show that translation technologies are needed by the graduates who become translators, but significantly less so by the other graduates.

Given this scenario, it makes sense to offer advanced technologies as an elective for those seeking to enter the industry but also to teach basic translation technologies and skills to *all* those who will enter teaching and indeed become part of the community of multilingual communicators in general. A differentiated pedagogy is required, if and when we accept the basic need to foster technological literacy in the wider society.

Where do graduates go?

Previous surveys on the employment of translation graduates in multiple geographical locations suggest some consistent trends. Large-scale international surveys have been carried out on the employment of graduates from the

DOI: 10.4324/9781032648033-3

programs associated with the two main translator (and interpreter) training organizations: CIUTI (Conférence Internationale Permanente d'Instituts Universitaires de Traducteurs et Interprètes) and the EMT (European Masters in Translation). The 2014 CIUTI survey (Schmitt et al., 2016) reached more than 2,600 former translation and/or interpreting students who had graduated in the previous ten years. Some 45% gave affirmative answers to the question "Would you describe your main current occupation as translation and/or interpreting-related?," although only one-third of the total respondents identified their main occupation as translation or interpreting in any strict sense. The 2016 EMT survey (Toudic, 2017a, 2017b) elicited 1,722 responses from graduates of postgraduate translation programs in Europe. The results indicate that over half had secured jobs in "language services," while just over one-third of the total (36.5%) had worked at least once as a translator of some kind, including as a reviser or localizer (see Hao & Pym, 2023a for details of these calculations).

This "one-third rule" also holds in several surveys of graduates from undergraduate translation programs in Spain. A survey carried out by the Universitat Autònoma de Barcelona (Galán-Mañas, 2019) indicates that about one third of the graduates had engaged in translation as their main occupation in the ten years from 2004 to 2014, while the percentage for work in language teaching was almost double that. This is more or less in tune with earlier numbers from similar surveys in Spain (ANECA, 2004; Torres-Hostench, 2012; reviewed in Hao & Pym, 2023a).

We hasten to add that this "one-third rule" is no more than a rough statistical tendency, by no means a fatality. The highly specialized (and expensive!) postgraduate translation and interpreting program at the Middlebury Institute of International Studies at Monterey, California, has long kept close track of its graduates, nurturing their professional networks and, in many cases, enabling the employment of new graduates through contacts with earlier graduates who have become well established in the industry. The institute has also adapted to industry demands by developing a Master of Arts in Translation and Localization Management – they are not far from Silicon Valley. They can claim (but seem not to publish) rates of over 90% employment in translation, interpreting, and localization. That would appear to remain something of an exception to the panorama suggested by the published surveys.

If an average of one third seems scarcely motivating for translation students (and no doubt for the people who pay for their studies), it is worth digging into the surveys a little more deeply. The numbers reported by Galán-Mañas (2019) also show that more than 80% of the translation graduates from the Universitat Autònoma de Barcelona had done *some* translating at certain points of their career, albeit not as their primary occupation and not on a full-time basis. Similarly, a survey conducted by the Zurich

University of Applied Sciences (2020) indicates that even though only 32.6% of their translation and interpreting students had found employment in translation or interpreting – about a third once again! – a great many graduates reported having been involved in translation as a *second* source of income (43.7%) or as self-employment as a hobby or in the gig economy (95.2%). That is, virtually everyone was doing some translating, although mostly not as their main occupation. These numbers tell us that multiple jobholding is widespread, that language and translation skills are used in other occupations, and that those skills are used in many informal situations that do not normally count as occupations.

In the Chinese context, a survey of Master of Translation and Interpreting graduates elicited more than 500 responses from across 69 programs (Cui, 2017, 2019). Almost half the respondents were working in education (44.22%), with slightly over one third (36.86%) being employed in translation-related areas – one-third yet again! When asked to explain their reasons for *not* entering the translation industry, some graduates claimed they did not meet the industry requirements for translation skills (16%) or did not have enough pertinent experience (32%). However, some 21% reported that they *chose* not to become translators or interpreters because of the disorganized market and underpaid translation work, while 16% indicated limited opportunities for career advancement (11% because of a lack of passion for translation and 4% for other reasons).

A similar survey undertaken in 2017 looked at the employment of 131 graduates of a Master of Translation and Interpreting in Shanghai (Wu & Jiang, 2021). Within five years of graduating, only 13% of the respondents had worked as full-time or freelance professional translators for the government, enterprises, translation companies, or in the language industry. Perhaps surprisingly, about 49% had gone into the teaching of languages (in this case, English or German) or monolingual editing. Some 38% reported jobs that involved no use of a foreign language: in administration or in flourishing industries such as e-commerce and real estate.

Given these diverse career trajectories, one wonders at what stage a student decides to pursue a particular career path. Drawing on the opinions of professionals-to-be (final-year students) and various seasoned professionals (graduates), Álvarez-Álvarez and Arnáiz-Uzquiza (2017) set out to examine whether translation and interpreting curricula in Spain had achieved the "employability goal" that the Bologna Declaration (2015) set for universities. The final-year students had all completed their work placement (internship, secondment – there are many names), which over half had done in translation-related positions and the rest as language teachers or editors. When asked whether their intended career was translation-related, less than half gave an affirmative answer, which is still higher than the proportions of graduates who actually found employment in this area. What remains unknown is whether and how internship exposure had affected their career outlooks, but we do know that, prior to graduating, some students found a passion for education, administration, or business.

As mentioned, in late 2019 we ran a survey of graduates of the Master of Translation at the University of Melbourne, who had been on the labor market for less than three years. Perhaps predictably, analysis of their entry into the job market showed that only about one-third of them had landed jobs in translation and/or interpreting. Another third had non-translation jobs in the language industry, mostly in language teaching. Around one-fifth had found employment in areas that might seem mismatched with their education: some went into sectors that involve interacting with people using their L1 and L2 (real estate, administration, investment consultancy, and clothing retail); some went back to fields in which they had had previous training and work experience prior the translation program (e.g., in banking or legal services); still others completed intensive pre-career and on-the-job training in other fields (e.g., air traffic control). The remaining small proportion continued studying for another advanced degree.

Across almost all the surveys, this rough proportion appears to apply to both undergraduate and graduate training, with or without interpreting. There is not much difference in this regard between surveys that focus on fresh graduates and those that also incorporate graduates who have been on the job market for more than a decade.

A two-way flow

The actual employment of former graduates can provide empirical evidence for the analysis of learning needs (West, 1994). It should tell us what students can accomplish with their knowledge and skills. In this respect, we have been intrigued to find a significant proportion of translation graduates working in the teaching of languages. For instance, the survey of translation graduates from the Universitat Autònoma de Barcelona (Galán-Mañas, 2019) found that *most* graduates landed language-teaching jobs, no matter how many years had passed since graduation. At the same time, some of the Melbourne graduates who worked as translators and/or interpreters did not have enough hours and money to support themselves in those jobs, so they were also working as teachers of their L1 or L2, either concurrently or in a sequential manner (Hao & Pym, 2023a). The fact that the vast majority of our Melbourne graduates are international and with a Chinese background allows us to factor in another variable: their geographical mobility after graduation. The many graduates who go back to their home country have little trouble finding gainful employment in language teaching or using English. On the other hand, multiple jobholding is more common among those who remain in Australia, where translation is often combined with interpreting, teaching languages, or other occupations.

A few studies on the backgrounds of working translators and interpreters similarly suggest that there is no stable bridge between training and employment. Katan (2009) surveyed more than 1,000 translators and/or interpreters and found that only 55% of them had a university qualification in translation and/or interpreting, while only 30% had qualifications that were in translation and interpreting only (i.e., with no language degree). This indicates that there are very significant overlaps between studying translation and studying languages – which should hardly be surprising. A survey of 224 translation teachers in China (Wang et al., 2018) found that over two-thirds of them had a background in language or linguistics (40%) or literary studies (18%), with the remaining 42% being trained in translation. A more recent survey of 205 translation teachers from 195 institutions in China (Cui, 2019) found that 63.49% had done research on translation, while 76.97% had had part-time translation experience and only 7.57% had worked as full-time translators. As a counterpoint, the Société Française des Traducteurs surveyed 1,204 of their members and found that 71% had a university degree in translation or interpreting (SFT, 2022, pp. 11–12) – a much stronger number than Katan's 55% or the 42% for the Chinese teachers surveyed by Wang, although one assumes that paid-up members of the association were translators with a strong commitment to the profession. That said, 74% of the French translators also had had professional experience in another field – a full 39% as teachers. The overlap remains considerable.

The stability of these numbers over the years suggests that the overlaps between translation and language teaching persist even in the face of potentially disruptive technologies – at least so far. The pattern indicates that the training of translators serves not only the translation industry but also a wide range of language-oriented occupations, and indeed society as a whole. At the same time, graduates with a language education background also work as professional translators and train translators. These flows between the two camps challenge any notion of disciplinary separatism. They suggest that the two sides should seek common ground rather than stake out their own turf.

Do language professionals need technology?

Graduates are well placed to reflect on and evaluate the training they have received. Those who enter the language industry can also provide insider views, identifying the skills developed through their education and comparing them with the skills acquired in the workplace. Those aspects have led some of the previous surveys to collect graduates' feedback on the skillsets and various stocks of human capital that they feel should be more present in curricula, particularly the technology-associated skills considered relevant to their current work (Schmitt et al., 2016; Álvarez-Álvarez & Arnáiz-Uzquiza, 2017; Toudic, 2017a, 2017b; Cui, 2019).

The 2016 EMT survey (Toudic, 2017a, 2017b) asked graduates which skillsets were "useful in your current job." It predictably found that general and specialized translation, terminology, and translation-memory suites were more useful for graduates employed in the language industry than those who were not. Similarly, the 2014 CIUTI survey (Schmitt et al., 2016) further asked for the graduates' opinions about what courses had been most useful for their careers. "Foreign language training" was mentioned as the most useful item, followed by "general translation courses," "cultural studies," and "research skills," most of which are consistent with the EMT results. None of those skills seems to be related to technology. At the same time, when asked to indicate which courses they believed should be emphasized in the translation program, the graduates prioritized "computers and CAT tools," followed by "project management," "terminology management," and "quality management." Those skills were ranked higher here than they were in the previous question about "usefulness," suggesting that they were perceived as being necessary for education even though they were apparently not useful to the same extent in employment. You must know about the technologies even if you do not use them.

In the meantime, the types of supplementary training that graduates were seeking *after* a degree in translation could also offer insight into their priority skills. Álvarez-Álvarez and Arnáiz-Uzquiza (2017) found that nearly half of the sampled graduates reported taking intensive courses in additional languages to improve their L2 or to "incorporate new alternatives" for their careers, and around 15% enrolled in intensive training in technology.

These survey results point to interest in new technologies but also highlight the value of language proficiency and transferrable skills. That said, the heterogeneity of graduate employment does not seem to be fully addressed when asking for opinions on which translation skills are appreciated in industry and which should be more present in the curriculum. That is, these surveys tend to formulate questions as if all graduates had become professional translators and interpreters.

Unlike the previous studies, our Melbourne survey looked into the translation skills valued by graduates who took different career paths. The interaction between employment and translation skill category ($p < 0.001$) shows that graduates with varying career experiences hold significantly different opinions about the value of different skill types. All employment groups appreciated "fundamental translation skills" and "personal and interpersonal skills," which are applicable to a wide range of careers. More specifically, L2 skills and intercultural skills, the core items under the fundamental translation umbrella, were reported as being needed by all. That was also the case for transferable skills related to communication, critical thinking, project management, and risk management. On the other hand, as mentioned, skills associated with technology were generally viewed as being more translation-specific: they were prioritized by translators but less so by those who had gone into language education and other occupations. The quantitative pattern suggests that language professionals do not need technology – at least prior to generative AI. But is that the whole story?

Our survey further invited representatives of each employment group to participate in six follow-up interviews where they could explain their evaluations in a less restricted way. In the interviews, two translators prioritized skills associated with core translation technologies: post-editing machine translation and the use of translation-memory suites. One of them was working as a textbook translator in China. He said that a translation-memory suite was required by the translation agency for consistency purposes. He nevertheless confessed that his translation-memory skills were totally self-taught, as training in those areas was added to the curriculum after he graduated. He learned from online blogs and tutorial videos but still wished he could have had some basic instruction and support to make the multiple functions embedded in the software seem less overwhelming. Another graduate become a freelance translator in China and prioritized post-editing, as the enhanced productivity was key when competing against the larger translation companies (which in China normally sell translations at a low price). The priority that translators gave to technology-related skills can thus be interpreted in two complementary ways: core translation technologies are highly relevant to their work, *and* those technologies had been overlooked in the curriculum. Two language teachers, on the other hand, only gave high ratings for the post-editing skills that helped with the occasional translations they were doing in their jobs. One language teacher also emphasized knowledge of machine translation because they were curious to know how it could be incorporated into language teaching. The other technologies were considered not to be germane to language education and received low scores.

At the same time, a consensus was found between translators and language teachers that mastery of L2 English is essential. The translators further emphasized excellent command of L1 to convey nuances in renditions. Proficiency in both L1 and L2 was also recognized by graduates who found employment in other areas. For instance, one graduate was working as a consultant at an Australian bank in a part of Melbourne that has a thriving Chinese community. She said the cross-cultural awareness and language skills gained when studying translation helped her in the workplace. There was also consensus that generic skills such as communication, self-learning, and critical thinking are genuinely useful and can enhance employability across the board.

While not all graduate groups placed a high priority on technology-related translation skills, the graduates generally valued translation (as an advanced language skill) and soft human skills. This suggests we are still right to place traditional translation skills and advanced language skills at the core of the curriculum, and a diversified curriculum should allow some flexibility in customizing learning plans to accommodate different needs. Interactive teaching activities and materials can also enhance the acquisition of generic skills.

These results should be applicable not just to the postgraduate program at the University of Melbourne but also to any program that finds itself in a similar situation.

4

WHAT METHODS DO WE USE TO TEACH TRANSLATION TECHNOLOGIES?

This chapter looks at the many ways we can teach translation technologies, both in the language class and when training translators. It first discusses some basic questions concerning teaching methods (the general approaches to teaching), especially with a view to understanding why there has been so much resistance to translation (particularly machine translation) in language education. Our discussion then draws on a small survey of teachers of translation technologies, where we find a significant correlation between *what* they teach (the knowledges and skills) and *how* they teach (a range of teacher-based and student-based methods). We then run through the basics of how any teaching program should be set up: needs analysis (which is what we have been doing in the previous chapters), pedagogical progression, learning outcomes, and the desirability of being able to adjust to the specific students in front of you. Any trained teacher should know that already. Unfortunately, not all translator trainers have learned how to teach.

Teaching methods and resistance to translation

As we have mentioned, there is often resistance to the use of translation technologies in L2 language classes, to the extent that the technologies might be in some way prohibited or simply not mentioned. Resistance tends to come on two fronts: one against the use of translation, the other against the use of technologies. We will initially consider these as separate matters.

Translation or immersion?

Debates over the use of translation in language classes have been going on for millennia. Kelly (1969) notes a pendulum swinging throughout

DOI: 10.4324/9781032648033-4

history, where some centuries use many translation activities and others do not. In European language teaching, most of the nineteenth century was a period when translation exercises were one of the main ways of learning an additional language; most of the twentieth century was not. What was the difference? For the influential language educationalists of the *late* nineteenth century – some of them immigrants to the United States – the aim of the language class was to enable students to speak like L1 speakers. The ideal way to do that was to imitate the way young children were assumed to learn language and the way the immigrants had to do it: through "immersion." That meant the student had to do everything in L2, as if thrown into the deep end of a swimming pool, where you either learn to swim or you sink. For the New York-based German-speaking immigrant Maximilian Berlitz, the language class should offer all the immersive benefits of a trip to the foreign land, without the travel expenses:

> Instruction by the Berlitz method is to the student what the sojourn in a foreign land is to a traveler. He hears and speaks on the language he wishes to learn, as if he were in a foreign country. He has however the advantage that the language has been methodologically and systematically arranged for him.
>
> *(1888/1916, p. 4)*

The consequence for translation was clear: "In the Berlitz Method, translation as a means of acquiring a foreign language is entirely abandoned" (1888/1916, p. 3). Translation became the arch enemy of immersion.

Over the following decades, many further reasons were found for not using translation: it was time-consuming; it fostered the illusion that all languages work the same way; it did not make students work with languages; it was not the "natural" way people learn languages. Around the beginning of the twentieth century, the Reform Movement brought together the linguists Jespersen, Passy, and Sweet, all of whom were particularly concerned with phonetics. They broadly added two further reasons: written translation had negative consequences for the learning of pronunciation, and, particularly for Jespersen, the world did not need many translators anyway: "while there is [...] a constantly increasing number of people who need to express their thoughts in a foreign language, there are really very few who will ever have any occasion to exercise skill in translation" (Jespersen, 1901/1904, p. 53). In other words, if you are not going to become a professional translator, forget about translation.

Those are all reasons that can be raised and discussed in class. However, since immersion ideology is alive and well in many parts of the world, here are some counterarguments that might come in handy:

"Translation is not the natural way children learn language." Fair enough, but students who have learned to write are not learning like young children anyway: they tend to transfer their prior knowledge of L1 patterns, making use of cognitive mapping to the L2. Positive transfer occurs when similar patterns in the two languages facilitate learning; negative transfer is when interlingual transformations are learned; negative interference arises from mismatches between the two language systems that lead to errors. Language transfer of this kind is common in adult language acquisition and can yield positive results. So why should one disregard prior linguistic knowledge of the L1? Why should immersed infants and immigrants be the only people somehow considered "natural"?

"Translation does not help with pronunciation or fluency." Good point, so the class can do activities with spoken translation ("interpreting"), which can help with pronunciation and fluency.

"Translation creates an illusion of symmetry between languages." Yes, this can happen, unless one uses translation in a way that highlights the *asymmetries* – as most of the nineteenth-century textbooks actually did (Pym & Ayvazyan, 2018). Jespersen gives the example of the many ways the English pronoun *it* can be rendered in German, where the translations vary according to gender and case. He regrets that the learner who relies on just one translation will apparently fail to see those differences (1901/1904, p. 135). But if we put *it is* into DeepL and ask for translations into German, we get eight to choose from (try it!). There is no reason why technologies should lock a student into just one solution. Quite the opposite: an interactive use of technology can potentially help students explore symmetric and asymmetric patterns between their languages.

"The world needs speakers of languages, not translators." This claim assumes a radical division between the two groups. But if Google Translate is processing more than 143 billion words a day (Wood, 2018) – something like 20 words a day for every person on the planet – translation has become a social activity for a very great number of people. It is now very difficult to argue that professional translators are the only ones who translate. All those non-professional or semi-professional users of machine translation might appreciate some skills that can help improve their activity.

This last argument is probably the most important. Immersion ideologies basically propose, with Berlitz, that the aim of language learning is to produce L1 capability. That idea has been radically questioned by the *Common European Framework of Reference for Languages* (Council of Europe, 2001), which proposes that the aim of language learning is not necessarily to speak like an L1 speaker, but "to facilitate communication and interaction among Europeans of different mother tongues" (2001, p. 2). Given the emphasis on communication and interaction, the framework includes "mediation (in particular interpreting or translation)" as a major language activity, alongside production, reception, and interaction:

In both the receptive and productive modes, the written and/or oral activities of mediation make communication possible between persons who are unable, for whatever reason, to communicate with each other directly. Translation or interpretation, a paraphrase, summary or record, provides for a third party a (re)formulation of a source text to which this third party does not have direct access. Mediating language activities – (re)processing an existing text – occupy an important place in the normal linguistic functioning of our societies.

(2001, p. 14)

Translation technologies were not mentioned in the 2001 document, but they clearly fit in with the general aim of mediation. Teaching students how to use those technologies is one way of teaching them how to mediate. And that should be an aim for all learners.

A later "companion volume" to the *Common European Framework of Reference* (Council of Europe, 2018) does all it can to downplay the role of translation as a part of mediation. Strategically, the *Companion* waters down the concept of mediation by including activities such as literary criticism without any language change, and then, as in Jespersen, it characterizes translation as being either a very simplistic operation that hides the nature of languages or something requiring stratospheric skills that only professional translators possess and language learners do not need. In sum, the *Companion* willfully avoids any of the many engaging and productive activities that can be done with translation. It is a sham. With companions like that, who needs enemies?

That is not to say that immersive learning does not work. It can be great for fluency, for learning to *think* in the additional language, as well as for role plays and the like. However, many learners will also want to "facilitate communication and interaction" with speakers of different languages, as the *European Framework of Reference* puts it. Translation activities can help them get there.

Translation or communication?

All language teaching these days would aspire to be "communicative" in one way or another. This means that students should learn how to use languages in authentic situations, as opposed to only learning grammar rules, vocabulary lists, and the like. Communicative methods thus tend to be closely allied with immersion, and thereby with the exclusion of translation. This association is nevertheless perniciously reductive – it can and should be questioned.

How can it be deconstructed? Just ask a simple question: Is translation communication? More explicitly, is translation a communicative use of language in authentic situations? If it is taught using communitive methods, then of course it can be part of any communicative language-teaching approach you like (Carreres & Noriega-Sánchez, 2021).

There is no need to waste time on false oppositions.

Speech or the technologies of writing?

As we have seen, one of the main arguments used against translation is that it does not help with pronunciation and fluency. That is, it is not useful for learning how to *speak* a language. On the face of it, that seems true enough. When we think of machine translation and generative AI, we tend to think of *written* texts, of graphic signs that are linked to different sounds in different languages – so the learner is dangerously tempted to pronounce one language according to the rules of the other. If someone tries to learn an L2 through nothing but written translation, they are indeed likely to hop backward and forwards mentally between those written images, from one language to the other, without ever grasping the production of discourse as a fluent, communicative, interactive performance. The use of written translation and nothing but written translation risks seriously delaying the stage where the learner thinks in L2.

The first response here is that no one should depend on translation alone as the only way to learn a language. When fluency is the goal, by all means engage in immersive activities and forget about translation. Siding with a team is for football; mixing methods is for goal-sensitive learning.

That said, our language technologies these days operate with both spoken and written inputs, and they can produce outputs in spoken as well as written form. You might have to install an extension to get the voices working, but they will soon be working. And many of them play an audio with the pronunciation if you tap the correct icon. We would thus argue, first, that writing is a part of adult language learning, and second, that our technologies can use spoken language. There is no binary opposition in town.

In several respects, our technologies have moved to speech faster than many of our students are probably aware. The learner who knows writing still tends to seek the surety of the written. That dependency can nevertheless be overcome. Have students engage in spoken conversations with AI assistants and then discuss the experience; use automation to exercise more than written forms (see the "Speak translations" activities in Chapter 5). As they do this, students will be engaging in whole stretches of discourse and conversations, well beyond the written words and phrases they traditionally lean on.

Resistance to technology

Resistance to technology is quite different from resistance to translation: it can come from within translators themselves, especially the more established ones. Language educators, on the other hand, tend to be relatively open to the various technologies by which learning content can be delivered, classes can be conducted, and language can be explored. Corpus linguistics, for instance, was seen as a step forward in the study of language, particularly to the extent that it empowered students to discover linguistic patterns for themselves, without the authority of a dictionary or a teacher (Aston, 2011).

Resistance within the translation community tends to have more to do with the assumed authority of those who rose to the top of the profession using one set of technologies and then see little reason to embrace newer technologies. In an anonymous postgraduate program in California in 2007, we were told by the professional translators who were teaching in the program that no one really used translation memory suites. We were also assured that there was no need to teach post-editing, as it was basically the same as the traditional revision of translations. In the case of translation memory suites, it was not hard to point to a few empirical surveys that suggested the world had changed: Lagoudaki (2006) showed general adoption of translation memory suites among the 874 translators she surveyed, and Gouadec (2007) found that the technology was a prerequisite for professional translators in 95% of the 450 job advertisements he surveyed in 2004. That was way back then! In a 2023 survey of some 2,800 freelancers, only 19% had *never* used translation memory software, while 59% used them "frequently" (Inboxtranslations, 2023). A little empirical research can help question entrenched certainties.

Another kind of resistance comes from the *presumed risks* involved. The Ordre des traducteurs, terminologues et interprètes agréés du Québec (OTTIAQ) sees one of its functions as being to protect the public from bad translations. It thus issued a general warning about machine translation in 2009, urging the public to "call on a certified translator for all your translation needs" (cited in Pym, 2011, p. 4). By 2020, that warning had been replaced with a recognition of advances in machine translation, but the text nevertheless concluded: "it still takes a qualified translator to determine whether a machine translation is accurate and reliable" (OTTIAQ, 2020). That position echoed the brochure *Getting it Right*, written as a guide to buyers of translations: "Careful editing of machine output by skilled human translators is one option, although not all translators will accept such assignments" (Durban, 2011). In other words, the technology is risky and not to be trusted; only human translators can be trusted. At the time, one common consequence of that argument was that translators did not need to learn about technologies, since the traditional translation skills were needed to correct machine translation anyway. There was no attention to the many ways technologies can augment traditional human capacities: the narrative was "us" vs. "the machine" (O'Brien, 2023).

The authors of those documents might be associated with a generation of translators that became well established in the 1970s and 1980s. They sought to protect not just buyers of translations and the general public but also their acquired status. Strangely enough, now that generative AI has entered the scene, some teachers are reported as preferring neural machine translation (Sahari et al., 2023) – the *previous* technology. Each generation prefers the technologies it has become accustomed to.

Similar resistance can be found within the community of translation researchers, where advances were first questioned and were then fundamentally seen as nothing new. We were once assured, for example, that machine translation is just an application of corpus linguistics (it is not), that post-editing is the same as revision (as mentioned above, and it is still not), or that localization is the same as adapting a text to a new reader as in *Skopos* theory (it is not, because its uses of automation are based on internationalization).

At the same time, resistance specific to machine translation is also observed in the language-learning camp. Some believe that reliance on machine translation interferes with the meaningful and intellectual use of L2. They argue that students simply write in their L1 and let the machine do the rest for them – "but how are they going to learn?". This group of teachers is skeptical about how much machine translation facilitates learning in students (e.g., Knowles, 2016; Lee, 2020). Concerns are also linked to academic dishonesty. Many language teachers hold the view that machine-translation use constitutes cheating, although some indicate that their position on this also depends on *how* students use it, whether for individual words, phrases, or entire compositions (reported in Clifford et al., 2013; Jolley & Maimone, 2015). Some discussion has arisen about teacher responses to unauthorized use of machine translation, such as implementing warning protocols and punishment mechanisms (Harris, 2010; Correa, 2011, 2014). As a result, language teachers with this "detect-react-prevent" mindset (Jolley & Maimone, 2022) tend to be reluctant to incorporate machine translation in their classrooms or to approve its use by students, even though its presence has become increasingly unavoidable due to its accessibility and immediacy and the improved quality of the resulting translations.

What do these instances of resistance have to do with teaching methods? If a teacher thinks the technologies bring nothing essentially new, that teacher will continue with the teaching methods they have always used. If, as we have seen, it is claimed that the human translator is the only one who can produce a valid translation, then you will train human translators to produce valid translations unaided, since that is how they gain the experience to make those judgments. And if localization is just adaptation, then you teach a bit of *Skopos* theory and nothing more. Why even look at the technologies?

On the other hand, if a teacher gets through the initial cognitive friction and starts to realize that the technologies are changing the way translation functions in society, then they probably need to adapt their teaching methods. Language teachers can, of course, persist in fighting a losing battle (i.e., disapproval of student use of machine translation). Alternatively, they can explore the kind of prior training and teacher interventions necessary when machine translation is integrated into writing classes to facilitate meaningful and creative language use. Unfortunately, there seems to be no general agreement on the best way to do this.

Skills for an unknown future?

Debates over the best way to teach translation technologies have been going on ever since translation memory suites became accessible. As mentioned, a traditional approach was for students to learn traditional translation skills *before* they interacted with technologies, since the technologies were presumed to be harder. Some nevertheless believed that the technologies should be introduced as early as possible (e.g., Somers, 1997; O'Brien, 2002). That debate now seems rather passé. These days students are using language technologies in their daily lives, before and probably during their presence in class. This means it is no longer practical to keep technology for the end of their studies, just as it makes increasingly less sense to relegate technologies to one special course.

Recent years have seen new models for the skills and knowledge required for work with translation technologies. Bowker and Buitrago Ciro (2019) refer to "machine-translation literacy" as the general set of skills deployed by effective *users* of machine translation. On the other hand, Krüger and Hackenbuchner (2022, p. 384) see "professional machine translation literacy" as the competences that "professional translators (and other language professionals) may require in order to participate successfully in the various phases of the MT-assisted professional translation process." The competence model of the European Masters in Translation (2022) similarly incorporates machine translation and data literacy. At the same time, "AI literacy" has been conceptualized as "a set of competencies that enables individuals to critically evaluate AI technologies; communicate and collaborate effectively with AI; and use AI as a tool online, at home, and in the workplace" (Long & Magerko, 2020, p. 2). All those models are useful in that they sketch out the space we must cover. Yet they do not address the problem of our systemic belatedness (teaching always arrives late!), and they do not offer practical learning activities.

Back in the days of statistical machine translation, Pym (2013) proposed a list of ten skills that translators should acquire when learning to work with technology. The skills came under three general heads: (1) learn to learn, (2) learn to trust and distrust data, and (3) learn to revise translations as texts. Working from that basic model, here we seek a pedagogy based more clearly on awareness of the constant imperfection of our current knowledge. This has several clear consequences for teaching methodologies:

– *Student-led discovery*: Rather than attempt to convey fixed knowledge, our role is to organize activities in which students use skills to discover knowledge for themselves. This can be done as a series of group experiments (Pym, 2009).

- *Critical evaluation of technologies*: Even when we choose to focus on one technology in depth, we must encourage students to make critical comparisons between technologies. They should thus learn how to assess future technologies that we do not yet know about.

At the same time, any teaching must work from the initial capacities and expectations of the learners. In the case of translation technologies, this can often mean negotiating both the inflated expectations of automated output and, from other students, significant initial resistance and preconceptions about the inferiority of any automated solution. This means that exploratory activities should be designed to challenge such preconceptions, especially in two respects:

- *Exploration of augmented language skills*: Most translators who have strong language skills will start from the supposition that a human translator will always work better than automation ('I can translate better than any machine!'). The basic pedagogical comparison, however, must instead be between the aided and unaided human ('Can I translate better with the help of automation?').
- *An extended range of aids*: Most beginners also start from the supposition that automation only replaces the translator's decision-making while translating, and that was indeed the restricted frame for early resistance to technologies. A curriculum might therefore create room for students to explore the many other ways in which translation memory tools and generative AI can help translators. Here is a shortlist of things that the technologies can do to one degree or another (translation memories at the top, AI at the bottom, and an overlap in the middle):
  - Recall and revise your previous translations
  - Give alternative translations to choose between
  - Reduce alternative proposals as you type
  - Adjust a translation when you make a change
  - Exchange notes with other translators
  - Propagate translation choices
  - Record your translation preferences
  - Check for consistency in numbers, terms, and formatting
  - Check your punctuation
  - Align your previous translations
  - Pre-edit the start text
  - Adapt the translation to specific readerships
  - Speech to text: Speak your translations

- Text to speech: Read your translation back to you
- Revise your translation for orthography
- Revise your translation for grammar
- Revise your translation for readability
- Revise your translation for a specific reader or purpose
- Evaluate translations
- Manage your terminology
  Give notes on terms in context
- Provide background information quickly

Beyond that, generative AI can produce all kinds of summaries (so the client or user can see if they want or need a fully human translation), carry out specialized tasks like automatically tagging interview data, and then perform most of the linguistic magic that concordancers do with corpora. Not all those capacities are of direct practical use to translators, and not all of them are currently performed well by AI (trust is very much an issue – humans should check the results). But all these aids are available today, and they will be more numerous and more performative in the future.

What experienced teachers say

As part of our research on these issues, in 2020 we organized a survey and then a focus-group discussion with 11 teachers of translation technologies in university programs in Australia and New Zealand (reported in Hao & Pym, 2023b). Since the teachers had an average of just under ten years of experience in this field, we assumed they had knowledge to share.

Which methods for which contents?

Our survey presented the teachers with five basic teaching methods and 12 contents to be taught. The teachers were asked to say which methods they used for which content (they were allowed to name more than one method per topic). The resulting biplot (Figure 4.1) indicates what should be obvious to anyone except a few enthusiastic education theorists: all teaching methods have their place. If you want to convey background knowledge to a lot of students, a lecture can be efficient; for programming and coding, a lot of collaboration and practice is preferable, and so on. This would place us in what has long been called the "post-method condition" (from Stern, 1983; Prabhu, 1990; Kumaravadivelu, 1994).

Our biplot (Figure 4.1) maps some composite variables. Moving to the right, the contents become more knowledge-oriented; to the left they have more to do with practice. Since there is more happening on the left than the right, this is a practice-intensive field. Further, the teaching methods

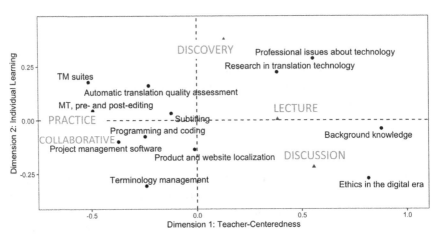

FIGURE 4.1 Correspondence analysis of contents and methods reported by 11 teachers (Hao & Pym, 2023)

(in large gray letters) to the right are more teacher-centered; those to the left are more student-centered. Student-centered methods thus visually correlate with practice-oriented methods, which makes sense. Perhaps less obviously, the vertical axis concerns class size: individual learning is at the top and collective learning at the bottom. The fact that there are contents distributed across both halves suggests that teaching methods should be adapted to how many students are in the class. Even when a large class is divided into small work groups, this dimension concerns how much of the teacher's time can be devoted to one-on-one problem assistance.

What are the most preferred teaching methods?

The abstract relations mapped in Figure 4.1 were fleshed out in a group discussion where the teachers shared their views on the various methods. Most teachers generally agreed that a teacher-centered approach (e.g., lectures) was suitable in situations where new knowledge needs to be passed on to all students efficiently and with limited class time. Some teachers noted that the transmissionist model does not give much room for student questions and debates; they thus insisted on including guided discussions as a complement to this one-way discourse.

There was a consensus that student-centered approaches are suitable to facilitate learning outcomes associated with using a variety of translation technologies, critical technology evaluations, generating acceptable translations, and teamwork. Most teachers, for this reason, structured their class time to maximize individual or collective hands-on activities, which enabled students to internalize and then enact the skills in their translation practice.

In addition, autonomous learning was observed in discovery-based activities where students learn through inquiry, investigation, and discussion. The teachers also observed that working in discovery groups fostered intense peer interaction and helped students to achieve the learning outcomes more smoothly.

When asked to elucidate the teacher's roles in a student-centered technology classroom, most teachers described their role as that of a supportive guide, assisting students in their learning progress. Part of this was reported as having to do with the way successive generations of learners are increasingly digital natives who feel comfortable picking up new technologies. However, the teachers also emphasized the importance of scaffolding and unanimously agreed that the level of support should depend on the complexity of the learning task. That is, the steeper the learning curve involved in a specific technology, the more extensive the scaffolding that is required.

Teaching translation technologies online

At the time of our survey, in the middle of the COVID pandemic, most of the teachers had managed to deliver translation-technology courses *online* for nearly a whole academic year. Some had integrated learning materials that were asynchronous (e.g., self-paced activities posted online) and synchronous (e.g., live seminars) to cope with the disruption caused by the shift in learning modes. The *know-what* knowledge tended to be incorporated as part of preparatory asynchronous content, introduced and assessed before the live lectures. In some cases, a recorded "walkthrough" video was also provided by some teachers to demonstrate technological *know-how*.

This approach was used to allow for the extra time required for the remote troubleshooting of technical issues. The teachers said they used to provide "over-the-shoulder" guidance in the physical technology classroom but had since managed to find alternative channels. These included simultaneous support via remote-control software and screen sharing, or post-class assistance through screen recordings and email exchanges.

Overall, the transition to online teaching was reported as being remarkably smooth, apparently without major modifications in the distribution of teaching methods.

General principles for a translation-technology syllabus

A basic error sometimes made by inexperienced teachers is to have each student complete a longish translation (let's say, 500 words or so) each week or fortnight, with the only variation being the text to translate. If the students complete the translation before class, the class contact time is used to correct and discuss the different translations. Nord (1996) stereotypes this kind of class in terms of the teacher's first question of the students: "Who'll take the first sentence?" The assumption is that the student learns to translate basically by translating sentence by sentence and then by seeing how the teacher translates sentence by sentence (and third, if you're lucky, by discussing the translation problems with other students, sentence by sentence). What could possibly be wrong with that? Why should we not use the same approach to teach translation technologies?

Any language teacher could probably find a dozen or so shortcomings with that baseline approach. Here we list just a few principles for improving on that practice.

Plan progression

One of the problems with the text-based practical class is that it is hard to structure the *pedagogical progression*, ideally going from simple to complex, basic to advanced, easy to difficult. Pedagogical progression has been a part of European translation-based language teaching from the early nineteenth century – it was a principle of Prussian New Humanism and inductive grammar teaching (Pym & Ayvazyan, 2018); it is at the core of Vygotsky's "zone of proximal development," where students are at each stage able to solve certain problems themselves while being challenged by other problems that they can only solve "under adult guidance or in collaboration with more capable peers" (Vygotsky, 1978, p. 86). At its simplest level, this can mean translating at different language levels, starting from words, then phrases, then degrees of syntactic complexity, then the main points of non-correspondence between structures, and eventually, toward the end of the learning process, whole texts. There are indeed some older textbooks structured exactly like that, and some quite new ones in China. At a higher level, it can mean working from simple texts and going to those that are most complex. Hatim (1997), for example, starts from contracts (which are indeed discursively simple!) and moves toward complex argumentative texts. But that kind of progression ignores all the things students should learn about translation processes, documentation, ethics, relations with clients, and, most importantly for us, how to work with technologies. Language technologies can certainly be used to solve problems at all those different levels. They nevertheless tend to lend themselves to their *own* sequences of difficulty, usually going from simple tools to complex suites of tools. In the technology class, the first question is not "Who will take the first sentence?," but rather "Which group can find out how to make this tool work?".

In the technology class, pedagogical progression is very much in tune with Vygotsky's description: let students solve problems by themselves but keep them at a level where they also need guidance from peers or teachers to solve the more difficult problems. That is, keep students within their zone of proximal development, as much as possible.

That classical progression can sometimes be subverted. In our focus-group discussion above, one teacher espoused the virtues of first teaching the top-of-the-range translation memory suite, with all the bells and whistles (this would currently be Trados Studio), since if students can master that one, all the other translation memory suites will be easy. That approach is reinforced by the value of the student having the complex suite listed on their curriculum vitae. On the other hand, the risk is that the students who are less technologically inclined will struggle and give up – or at least feel lost and inadequate.

A more commonsensical approach is to work from simpler tools to the more complex ones, without expecting that the development from one level to another will ever be like a simple straight line. To know when to move forward, observe how often the students seek external help to solve problems.

Vary activities

When Nord (1996) stereotypes the sentence-by-sentence translation class, she does so to stress the range of alternative activities that can be done. She proposes a longish list of activities, including translating for different readers, adapting texts for different clients, and criticizing published translations. The basic idea is that a range of activities will give students different insights on translation, thus moving them beyond the narrow equivalence relationships that are implicitly sought in sentence-by-sentence teaching. This idea certainly holds in the field of translation technologies, especially in view of the many kinds of adaptation that can be assisted by generative AI.

Limit the top-down planning

Kiraly (2014) nevertheless criticized Nord's approach as relying on "a rationalist view that truth could be known by the teacher and deduced by the students through logic and with the teacher's guidance." That critique was probably overstated in its day: Nord was hardly prescribing just one ready-made solution to each translation problem – her activities do allow for a certain degree of creativity. Kiraly's critique could nevertheless stand as a general assessment of the dominant ideology in education science where an enlightened planner defines the learning needs, then the teaching objectives, then the learning outcomes of each program, course, or lesson, usually prior to any actual teaching taking place. That would be top-down planning: the progression and the problems are somehow identified and solved before they actually occur. Far better, intimates Kiraly, to react to the students' actual learning processes as they occur, in a bottom-up way. If students ask for more practice with a particular technology, or if a new technology suddenly appears (as tends to happen), then the syllabus can and should be adjusted. One can also invite students to co-design their desired learning outcomes, for example by teaching on the basis of the questions that they would like to see answered (Pym & Torres-Simón, 2016) or indeed the tools that they would like to work with.

Translation technology would seem to be a field that is very much in tune with Kiraly's relatively bottom-up pedagogy, especially given the speed with which the technologies evolve. On the other hand, with respect to the critique of "rationalist truth," the use of the technologies does often involve a quite binary kind of knowledge: if you click in the right places, it works; if you don't, it doesn't. It is not all an affair of infinitely complex subjectivities.

Privilege transversal skills

Since the studies of graduate employment indicate that our students are going into a wide range of occupations, the skills that they acquire should be strongly transversal, in the sense that what the student learns to do in one setting can be applied in another.

The identification of transversal skills is often approached with a wing and a prayer. We teach the interpretation of literary texts in the hope that the reading skills will be of use in the processing of any complex text. Similarly, we do classroom role plays in the belief that they will help with interactions in any future business setting. One can always hope those kinds of relations actually obtain, but no one can be sure.

One way to reinforce transversality is to have students work in groups to download a new technology and translate with it within a short time frame (two hours is usually fine), with limited help from the teacher. This forces them to learn to learn. And the most transversal skill is the capacity to learn.

Adjust the scaffolding

"Scaffolding" is a common metaphor used to refer to the assistance that a student receives when learning a new skill. This is extremely important when students are discovering new technologies. At the beginning, some students are likely to require considerable support, which can come from rather more sources than Vygotsky envisaged:

- Peer support in a small group of students
- AI assistants
- Help files in the technology itself
- Online forums, often dedicated to the specific technology
- Web searches, particularly for video clips
- The teacher or teaching assistant addressing the whole group
- As a last resort, the teacher helping a student in over-the-shoulder mode.

When asked a question, the AI assistant can be directed to use specific websites for references (we have tested this with ChatGPT 4, and it works well). That said, if there is public access to help files, user manuals, or forums, the AI can take the browsing efficiency to the next level. For now, if you are searching for video content, it still seems best to use keyword web searches and navigate the video chapters.

Note that teachers are listed last in the above list because their time is limited, which means they cannot attend to all individual students on every occasion. More important, one set of skills that students must learn is how to draw on all those sources of support efficiently: if they are spoon-fed solutions, they will never acquire those lifelong learning skills. On the other hand, obviously, if the class is working in small groups and they all encounter the same problem, the teacher should pause the activity and address the whole class, either to suggest how to approach the problem (not to give the solution!) or to investigate what might be a one-off hitch (the new update of the software does not work like the old one, for example).

The situation to be avoided is where a student does not know how to proceed, they click on everything mindlessly, they thus drift into unchartered spaces, and then they sit there silently, feeling too embarrassed to ask for help. All students should learn where and how they can seek scaffolding.

Once the skills are acquired, the scaffolding is removed – as when a beautiful new building emerges from all the temporary support structures. That said, the extent of the scaffolding can depend on the personality or preferences of the teacher. Of the two authors writing this book, the woman likes to provide extensive scaffolding, and the man is always criticized for not providing enough.

Plan for a heterogeneous learning group

Given that the world of technology exists outside the classroom, some students will have quite advanced skills prior to entering a course, while others will be relative novices. This can be avoided to some extent by organizing separate learning groups, ideally in different classrooms. In many cases, though, this is not possible: the learning sessions should be organized to accommodate the different starting levels.

One way of doing this is to put the relative novices in their own groups, and the advanced students in other groups. The teacher then provides a lot of scaffolding to the former, allowing the latter to explore the world by themselves, working on appropriately challenging tasks.

An alternative solution is to mix the groups up, ensuring that at least one novice is in the same group as at least one relative expert. The plan is for the advanced students to help the novices. In a worst-case scenario, this might mean that the novice initially looks on as the advanced student works on the task. But if that happens, one has to make sure that the novice asks questions, and that the relative expert takes time to answer carefully and at length. That may work well for one or two lessons, but the advanced students often tire quickly of what they perceive as an added burden, once the shine wears off their desire to show how much they know.

An alternative solution tends to be in the design of the activities to be carried out. In most activities, it is possible to have a sequence of tasks that go from basic to advanced. Students then work at their own pace and go as far as they are able. This creates interesting ethical problems for the assessment of the students, which we will address in Chapter 6 below.

Always have a Plan B (and C)

Anyone who has worked for any length of time with technologies will tell you that the tools err, crash, or are euphemistically "down" more often than should be expected. This is a part of contemporary life; we get used to it and adjust, putting off tasks for a while or resorting to a series of workarounds. However, when the technology fails in the middle of a class, the situation is rather more serious. Students cannot be asked to wait around aimlessly for 10 or 20 minutes or more – pedagogical progression will be missed, motivation will dwindle, and the technology itself will not win many friends. So here are some real cases of technological failures and how we found some viable alternatives. Since they mainly concern translation memory systems, the examples are not highly pertinent to language teaching. But the workarounds might be.

One student is completely blocked: This happens more than anyone would like to admit. As mentioned, the general solution is to make sure students are working in mixed groups. You then place the blocked student alongside a stronger student. In many cases, the stronger student will help the weaker one through. In other cases (when the problem is hardware or the absence of a password), the weaker student can be asked to "look on" – but not passively: they have to ask what is happening and make sure they will be able to catch up later.

Sometimes, a more radical Plan B is needed. In our early days of teaching translation memory suites online from Spain, one student in Bolivia was completely unable to put her password into the online learning system. Plan B: we phoned her on a landline and guided her through.

User accounts have to be set up manually: You start a class of 40 people on a new translation memory suite. You have run through the tasks yourself the day before, so you know how everything works. Suddenly, you find that you have to create individual user account for all those 40 students, and it is going to take more than half an hour. What do you do? Do you get everyone to wait for 30 minutes? Do you set up the accounts of your favorite students and tell them to start on the activity? In this case, the most equitable Plan B is probably to have the class organized into groups of four, you set up an account for one person in each group, and you ask the students to look on and discuss as a group as one person in the group navigates the software. Soon they will all have their accounts and be happy enough.

Your academic account is blocked: Since software developers give us academic accounts for free, those accounts can come with restrictions on the number of words that can be uploaded or how large the translation memories can be. This means that when one enthusiastic student uploaded an entire operating manual, rather than the one short excerpt that was to be translated, the whole system was blocked for all the students (in this case, until the end of the month). What can you do? That might be a good moment to have the students start exploring an alternative translation memory system.

The company's servers are down: You have set up all the projects online, the students are working through the problems nicely, then suddenly, the servers that the software is operating from are down. Students no longer have access to their texts, their translation memories, or their glossaries. One Plan B here was to move to the desktop-based version of the software. Mac users will usually not be able to do that (at the time of writing), so they can look on in small groups. Alternatively, again, this might be right moment to explore a different translation memory suite. It could also be the right time to have a discussion about the disadvantages of working online, storing your information on someone else's servers, and depending entirely on an external company.

These are all real cases. Most teachers of technology will have more in the same vein.

Relate to professionals

Whenever you have problems like the ones we have just mentioned, it is important that you contact the company that is supplying the software and you talk with them, in a spoken dialogue if possible. Do not get angry with them. Explain the problem as calmly and as clearly as possible. And make sure you know the name of the person you are talking with, use that person's name when you are explaining things, and refer back to that person in follow-up calls. The companies are in the business of not just selling their product but also creating or maintaining their public image – they want you to be happy. In most cases, they will be able to solve the problem. That said, the people doing the public relations are often not the technicians who really know what is going on. So it can take some time.

It is very important to develop personal and amicable relations with people in language companies, perhaps those where you are organizing work placements for your students. Not only can they help you solve problems, but they can tell you about the software they use (it might be what you should be teaching), the kinds of skills they are looking for in your students (again, this might influence the activities you do), and the possible further work placements for students (which can lead to future employment).

When establishing these relationships, it can be strategically useful to invite professionals into your classroom. They can talk about what they do, how they got there, and what possible careers are available. When they do this, they will feel important and flattered – industry professionals tend to think universities do not know anything about the real world, so they feel positive about enlightening us.[1] Good relations can develop.

A step beyond this, mentioned by Toudic (2012) and Rothwell and Svoboda (2018), is to have professionals come in and teach the translation technologies. This can be done when the regular teachers do not have the necessary skills. We have tried this on several occasions, so many years ago that we can now tell the story without identifying the people. An in-house translator who used Trados every day in her work came in to guide the students through the basics. She was completely unable to set up a pedagogical progression from simple to difficult; she provided no scaffolding; and the students were quickly lost. Another professional was a great web designer, so he spent the whole class showing the students some really great websites. But the students had no idea what they were supposed to do. Such cases are useful reminders that teaching is also a profession, with its special set of knowledge and skills.

Invite professionals into the classroom, by all means. Get them to talk about themselves. But do not expect them to be good teachers.

Learning outcomes

Having surveyed a few general principles, we now move to the actual building blocks that can be used to construct a curriculum or syllabus involving translation technologies.

A fundamental problem with the weekly text-based translation task is that translating is an incredibly complex activity, with many subtle variables. When students do those weekly translations, they are implicitly being asked to make progress on numerous different fronts, all at the same time. To ensure at least some kind of pedagogical progression, you first need a clear statement of the goals you are working toward, and those goals should ideally state the knowledge and skills that students are supposed to attain. When you state those specific goals, you are formulating learning outcomes.

In basic mainstream pedagogy, this is done in three not-so-easy steps:

- Needs analysis: Identify what is needed, which is what we have dealt with in Chapters 2 and 3.
- Teaching objectives: Describe the aims of the program, course, or lesson in quite general terms. For example, the objective of one course might be to

teach advanced writing skills, while another course could be designed to train students to translate medical texts at a professional level.

- Learning outcomes: Once you have established your needs and your objectives, you can select the specific skills and knowledges that students should have achieved by the end of each lesson, course, or program.

These steps are never easy because there are always intervening factors: what your institution expects, where the money comes from and goes, what teaching expertise is available, and so on. Here we will be focusing on learning outcomes, on the level that is both the most specific and the most contingent, since the outcomes depend on the needs and the objectives. Note that the outcomes can concern any level of teaching practice, from a program (that is, a curriculum) to a course (or a syllabus) to a lesson or even to parts of a lesson, so the complicating factors can intervene at any level.

Standard practice for learning outcomes is explained in Kelly (2005/2014), which is still an excellent place to start. A learning outcome should complete the sentence, "By the end of the course, the student will...," and then there are various recommended verbs. The sentence cannot be as vague or as general as "...translate well," since everyone will interpret the adjective *well* differently. It should be something that can be tested in an intersubjective way. For example, it might be as specific as "... understand the principles of machine translation," where the knowledge can be demonstrated and tested. Or it could be "... be able to post-edit gender-based errors," which is a skill (not a knowledge) that could be tested on the basis of translation performance or perhaps by selecting between translations in a multiple-choice quiz.

That said, formulating learning outcomes is a little like mixing martinis or setting a barbeque: someone will soon come along and say you are doing it wrong. The philosophers will tell you that the ideology is wrong; the educationists insist that your verbs are inadequate. Let us try to clear the air with respect to the philosophy, at least.

Arguments against learning outcomes

The use of learning outcomes in translator training can be dated from the behaviorist approach espoused by Delisle (1980). He proposed breaking the learning process down into specific objectives, some of which could be arranged in clear sequences ("learn to do A before you learn to do B"). That basic approach has since become a mainstay of most attempts to define translation competence as comprising identifiable components, sometimes with explicit progression. A paroxysm of the componential approach might be in educational models where jobs are described in terms of the same lists of knowledges and skills that are used to describe what learners can do, so the passage from training to employment could become a simple matching up of the items in both ledgers. We have already touched on a major flaw in that dream of bureaucratic control: only a third of translation graduates become translators, and perhaps only a third of practicing translators have been trained exclusively in that field.

The building-blocks approach has been criticized by Kiraly (2000), who we have already seen opposing what he considers its rationalistic foundations. Since translating is a complex activity, argues Kiraly, it cannot be seen as the sum of constitutive parts; it must instead be approached in a holistic way, open to several competing epistemologies that are able to stimulate curiosity and creativity. That is a general critique to which we very much subscribe, especially since rapid change in translation technologies means that we rarely have any kind of firm knowledge that could be calmly divided up into discrete parts. Whatever we do, it must be open to change, and when one part changes, we have no guarantee that all the other parts will not also be modified.

In practical terms, a holistic teaching method could involve the model espoused by the French trainer of technical translators Daniel Gouadec (2003, pp. 16–17), for whom the "translation class proper" involves student groups working for extended periods on the translation of a major authentic document of some 200 pages, with individual classes only being held when there are problematic points to discuss. There are thus no fixed hours and no discrete institutional units to which specific outcomes could be attached. Unfortunately, that kind of freedom is rarely possible in practice.

Learning outcomes assume a certain rigidity when they become elements in a larger fixed "translation competence," as in PACTE (2003) or EMT (2017, 2022). Even when one allows for a "strategic sub-competence" that is "used to detect problems, take decisions, and make up for errors or weaknesses in the other sub-competencies" (PACTE, 2003, p. 48), the presumed independence of the parts is easily challenged. For example, when a program moves from face-to-face to online teaching, the basic technological changes arguably affect all components and their interrelations. Similarly, a major change in translation technologies themselves tends to have repercussions right along the line.

Arguments in favor of learning outcomes

So why bother with learning outcomes at all? In part, because of honesty and clarity – it is not always enough to promise "an unforgettable holistic learning experience." Students have the right to know what they are likely to learn and what they will be assessed on. And teachers can often benefit from a longish checklist of knowledges and skills that can be attained. We note that Gouadec, who perhaps sought the most open of multifaceted experiences, structured the translation process around a "quality assurance model which is made up of 65 steps or so" (2003, p. 16), where each step had to be approved before the translation team could move to the next one.

Translation technologies are a little special in this regard. They are mostly made up of separate tools with separate operations, and the successful use of one tool *is* often necessary before one can move on to the next one. For example, you have to know how to create a translation memory before you can move on to exporting and importing translation memories. Neither the creation nor the transfer is particularly complex: you can do it or you can't, and there is no particular scale on which one could do it better or worse. At that level, there is a certain atomistic rationalism hard-wired into the technology.

A list of learning outcomes for translation technologies

With the above provisos, the following is the list of outcomes that students might attain from a lesson, course, or program involving translation technologies. What we are proposing here is simply a list of learning outcomes that are *possible* with respect to translation technologies. The list is not intended to comprise any multicomponent model of translation competence, capacity, or literacy. This is because we know our training is not supplying just one profession: since we are aware that the knowledges and skills students gain are going to be used in a wide range of occupations, we cannot remain fixated on just one duplicitously stable set of skills. Each education program will ideally do its own specific needs analysis; it will formulate its own learning objectives (which is where the competing epistemologies and openness to complexity should come in) and from there they can select whichever particular learning outcomes will help contribute to those general aims. In principle, each program, course, or lesson could have its own specific learning outcomes, formulated at whatever level of granularity is considered appropriate.

Our list has been kept relatively simple, without going into the granularity of specific technologies. It has largely been derived from the activities that we do in class, that is, bottom-up, although we have also drawn items from the various competence models. The purpose of the list is simply to alert teachers and program designers to the knowledges and skills that they might like to include.

Learning to learn:

Learn to use new technology
Locate reliable information quickly
Evaluate different sources of information critically
Use technology to augment creativity
Explore the limits of language automation

Language use:

Use automation tools to self-evaluate writing skills
Make spoken presentations
Formulate balanced arguments

Resolve problems of non-corresponding language systems
Apply appropriate metalanguage to translations

Use of automation tools:

Understand the variability of automated translation
Post-edit translations efficiently
Pre-edit texts for automated translation
Create and transfer translation memories
Write effective prompts
Understand the principles of subtitling
Produce effective translated subtitles
Manage terminology

Translation management:

Assess critically the advantages and risks of automated translation
Select optimal translation workflows
Plan and manage time
Work efficiently in teams
Adjust translations to clients' and users' needs
Communicate effectively with clients
Apply ethical criteria to the use of technologies

We would consider the first block of skills ("Learn to learn") as a basic translation-technology literacy, of interest in all language learning. As one moves further down the list, the items become more specifically germane to the training of translators.

Each of these outcomes will be attached to learning activities in the next chapter. Some will also return in Chapter 6, where they will be attached to modes of evaluation.

Two example modules (not necessarily exemplary)

To close this survey of teaching methods, we offer two real-world examples of how learning outcomes can relate to course objectives and teaching methods, warts and all. Both are modules (they each have more than one session) and both deal with what might be considered secondary factors: the first addressed a very heterogenous student group: the second was comparing technologies at the end of a course.

Module 1: Managing a translation project with Trados Studio

Translation technologies is a 12-week postgraduate elective online course that deals with post-editing, pre-editing, translation memory suites, terminology tools, and project management. The contents might be considered basic fare in all courses in this field. It was nevertheless based on a rather specific kind of needs analysis. On the one hand, the institution previously had a Master of Translation in which the use of translation memory suites was haphazard (different teachers used different suites, without being aware of what the other teachers were doing). On the other, the university had a very successful Master of Applied Linguistics that did not address translation in any of its learning outcomes, even though most of its graduates became language teachers.

The course was therefore open to students from both the Master of Translation and the Master of Applied Linguistics. This meant it was addressing some students who were not being trained as translators. The second a-typical feature is that it was an elective, since the students in the Master of Translation had already received basic training in the use of translation memories: for them, this course was building on acquired skills.

In this situation, our *teaching objectives* were: (1) to train students in the use of translation technologies both for professional translating and for language teaching, and (2) experiment with tandem learning in a situation where, in theory, one set of students knew a lot about translation and the other set knew more about linguistics (Hao & Pym, 2022).

Given those objectives, the main intended *learning outcomes* were heavily transversal: by the end of the course, students should be able to (1) explore the limits of language automation, (2) resolve problems of non-corresponding language systems, and (3) work efficiently in teams. There were also learning outcomes that were more specific to the technologies: students should be able to post-edit, pre-edit, and transfer translation memories (there was no generative AI available at the time).

For most weeks, students attended a two-hour seminar and engaged in at least two hours of self-guided learning. Here we are reporting on the course given in 2021, when 15 students were enrolled. That might be considered an ideal class size – the 2023 course had 40 students enrolled (perhaps an indication of success). There was, however, a further complicating factor: although almost all the students worked with Chinese and English, there was much variation in the degrees of competence in L2 Chinese, and then there was also one student who did not know Chinese (they worked with Indonesian). What happens when the teaching methods, needs analysis, teaching objectives, and learning outcomes meet significant student heterogeneity?

Toward the middle of the course, when the students had learned to manage a translation project with Trados Studio, they had to use those skills in a two-week simulated group project. (Aspects of the core activity here are further elaborated in Chapter 5 under "Explain translation technologies to clients" and Chapter 6 under "Peer evaluation: Translation management.") According to our matrix (Figure 4.1 above), this would be classified as a "practice-based collaborative project," firmly on the student-centered side of the matrix, and more collective than post-editing.

Four main components were included in this module, which lasted three weeks: a lecture (15 min.), practice (15 min. demonstration + 90 min. practice), a simulated translation project (2 hours and group work outside of class), and then the student presentations (2 hours).

The 15-minute lecture outlined the different roles involved in the translation project, including project manager, translator, terminologist, IT expert, desktop publisher, and client. Special attention was paid to the responsibilities of the project manager and how to plan a project sequence.

Students also had access to eight SDL training videos on project management with Trados, each on specific topics and lasting between 4 and 11 minutes each. As in the post-editing lesson, these were for students to refer to if and when they needed help.

In the live classroom session, the teacher walked the students through how to manage a project and apply quality controls. This was to soften the initial learning curve and deal with students' questions on the fly. The session was recorded and made available to the students to refer to later.

The students then carried out a simple task on website translation with project management, where they used Trados Studio, worked in pairs, and alternated between the roles of translator and project manager. For this task, the students in the "manager" role were asked to create and send the project package to the students in the "translator" role. After receiving the translators' return package, they set rules for the automatic quality assessment (QA Checker), revised the translation, and generated the translation quality assessment report. In this activity, they could turn to the teacher for support. The main purpose of the task was for the students to familiarize themselves with the software, project workflows, and the different perspectives of translators and project managers.

After that initial activity, groups of four members then undertook the translation project. Each group became a company, with clear roles for each member. The companies were fictitiously invited to compete for an Australian government contract to provide language services for the promotion of Australian products in China. The groups could choose any product they liked. After the first week, they had to present a detailed schedule for all tasks and a company strategy. At the end of the second week, they had to present full dossiers comprising a translated webpage, a standardized glossary, and a sample text translation. At that stage, all the support materials were in the pre-recorded videos; the teacher was only on call for very occasional advice.

At the end of the second week, the companies presented their dossiers and gave pitches focusing on the use of translation technologies, the integration of terminology, quality control procedures, and time management.

The students then voted for the best company and the fictitious contract was awarded.

There are many examples of such group projects in the literature – the competitive element can be adjusted to suit different student cultures. The interest of this case is on several levels. First, despite the consensus that certain contents correspond significantly to certain ways of teaching, we find that when all the skills are theoretically acquired and are brought together, the teacher's scaffolding drops away and the method is clearly hands-off, student-centered, and collective. Second, as opposed to the lecture mode where "control" was named as a virtue, the extended group project risks blinding the teacher to what actually happened within the groups. This particularly concerns teamwork skills, where there are always free-riders and bluffers, among students as in industry. In a sense, students have to learn how to negotiate the teamwork by themselves and teachers cannot directly evaluate how well those skills are applied. One advantage of project-management software is that, in cases of conflicting complaints, we can actually see who did what when. A certain degree of control returns. Peer assessment is another way to encourage cooperative teamwork (see Chapter 6).

Student feedback on these two modules was generally positive with respect to the content, and even enthusiastic for those who had no prior knowledge of translation technologies. Interestingly, the evaluations of Trados, which was probably the main selling point of the course for the prospective translators, nevertheless tended to be negative. This course came at the very beginning of a new version of the software, with a web-based version and a system whereby students had to be signed up on the RWS servers. Whether because of teething problems with the software or the take-over of SDL by RWS, those servers were regularly down or overloaded, sometimes in the middle of a class. The message is simple enough: the more we rely on external partners (and do their publicity for them), the more we are at the mercy of factors beyond our control.

Module 2: Generative AI for translation by language learners

This module is from a third-year undergraduate course on translation from English to Spanish or Catalan (each student can choose their target language) taught in 2023. The students were taking a degree in English Studies and this was their only obligatory course in translation. The aim of the program in English Studies was to give all-round competence in English language, literature, and culture; the teaching objectives of the course were to introduce students to the main techniques and technologies for translation and to use translation as a way of exploring English; the learning outcomes for the module were: (1) to explore the limits of language automation, (2) to use technology to augment creativity, (3) to write effective prompts, and (4) to assess critically the advantages and risks of automated translation.

The module comprised an 80-minute "theory" session and, the next day, an 80-minute "practice" session, which basically meant that the second session was for a major group-based activity. Since this module on generative AI came after modules on terminology, machine translation, and translation memory suites, it served to review those previous lessons and invite students to compare the technologies. There were 29 students in the class, which was face-to-face.

Since all the students reported having used generative AI already, the teacher's presentation of the technology lasted just 12 minutes and fed into an eight-minute discussion of which systems the students had tried and which they found useful. That was followed by an exploratory activity comparing machine translation and AI (45 minutes) and a discussion of how to write effective prompts (15 minutes). The second session was almost entirely a multifaceted translation activity.

In the exploratory activity, the students had to read a 450-word raw machine translation into Spanish of English-language instructions about what to do in a bushfire (students were previously warned about the nature of the text and were free to withdraw from the activity if they preferred). They then answered five multiple-choice questions on the text. The machine translation had one major error (*If you are caught in fire in your car* was rendered as *Si se incendia su automóvil* – if your car *catches* fire), several non-idiomatic expressions, and a non-standard mix of the formal and intimate second person, which is a frequent problem in machine translations. The questions indirectly concerned those features, in fact testing whether raw machine translation was acceptable for this kind of text. The answers showed that only eight of the 29 students were not misled by the major error, but that actionability was not affected by any of the other features. The students considered that the mixing of the second persons was considered likely to make the text less trustworthy but would not affect actionability.

The students were then put into groups of two or three. They were given the English text of the bushfire advice and asked to translate it with GPT-3.5, Microsoft Copilot, and Google Gemini. They then compared the results: some of the problems were solved, others were not. The groups were challenged to write different prompts until all the problems were solved. This worked well for creating a uniform second person but not for the major error, which was sometimes resolved correctly but not always. When asked how to resolve that error, most of the groups came up with a solution based on pre-editing: if the English text is written in a very explicit way (for example, *If you are in your car and in the middle of a fire*), all the technologies translated it correctly.

The students were then invited to use generative AI to translate the same English text for a 12-year-old reader and discuss the results. The resulting simplification was likened to pre-editing. Gemini, however, transformed the prose text into a dramatic dialogue between a mother and the adolescent, suggesting that a change of media could be effective. At this point, the discussion turned to how generative AI can assist creativity, in addition to straight translation.

The second 80-minute session opened with a ten-minute review of the first, focusing on general findings about the economics of prompts: if they are too detailed, the results can be too narrow; if they are too broad, there can be too many results to be useful.

In the main practical activity, the student groups were invited to combine some of the skills they had learned previously. They had to use a prompt to generate and export a glossary from a similar 400-word emergency message about sharks (welcome to Australian culture!), import the glossary into Matecat, and translate the text there, post-editing the machine-translation feed, using the glossary and the pop-up AI definitions of key terms. They then had to compare the result with the translation produced by the generative AI system of their choice, giving a spoken report on their findings to the whole class.

The final task, to be completed individually and at home, was to write three or four sentences on when generative AI can be more beneficial than post-editing machine translation, giving examples from their personal experiments in class.

Note

1 This ideological separation of teachers from professionals may not hold up to sociological scrutiny. In a survey of 305 translation scholars (almost all of them teachers who do research), it was found that only 6% of them had never worked regularly as translators or interpreters (Torres-Simón & Pym, 2016).

5

WHAT ACTIVITIES CAN HELP STUDENTS USE TECHNOLOGIES BETTER?

This chapter presents a set of learning activities that will hopefully offer a few fresh ideas to even the most jaded of experienced teachers. The activities are proposed as being suitable for university-level courses at either the undergraduate or postgraduate levels. They are only examples of what can be done – our main purpose is to show that there is scope for adaptation and creativity. Similar activities can be found in Hatim and Munday (2004), Pym (2009, 2019), Koponen (2015), and Carré et al. (2022), or one could adapt the activities proposed in sources like González-Davies (2004) and Beaulieu et al. (2020). Some of the proposals are based on our own classes; others have been used in research projects by other scholars. For example, we have drawn on the studies of machine translation activities in language education that are reviewed in Jolley and Maimone (2022) and Lee (2023). We have moreover adjusted some of the activities listed in Ayvazyan et al. (2024) and we have consulted AI assistants for occasional inspiration – as we all can. We are leaving aside some of the more obvious uses of generative AI such as the production of multiple-choice vocabulary quizzes, cloze tests, and the like. We are also taking as read the various uses of generative AI to suggest improvements to written texts and adjustments to different styles. Here our focus is on the use of the technologies for translation.

Most of the activities have been tried out in translator-training courses, where teachers these days tend to have experience in dealing with machine translation; others come from language learning, where there seems to be a longer tradition of using a more varied range of activities. We hope that many of the proposals are suitable for *both* translator training and the language

DOI: 10.4324/9781032648033-5

class, or they can be adapted. The only activities that we would consider not suitable for language classes are those that involve translation-memory suites, where the learning curves are only really justified when the student is interested in translation as at least part of a future career.

Almost all the activities are described here for a face-to-face or online class where students work together in groups of three or four, after which group representatives report to the whole class in a general discussion. The activities can nevertheless be adapted to other class sizes. In some cases, we spell out the steps involved; in many others, we trust the teacher can extrapolate.

The overall pedagogical method underlying the activities is to present translation technologies in such a way that the student investigates their potentials, rather than have the teacher explain conclusions. The general classroom procedure is to start from unaided ("fully human") translation and only then move to the technologies, so that the student will explore how their current skills can be augmented rather than replaced. The risk in each case is that the student might short-circuit the process and decide to depend on the technology from the outset.

We start with an activity that we do *not* recommend.

What not to do (anymore)

Do not allow everyone to hand in a machine translation

If you give your students a text to translate and they are allowed access machine translation or generative AI, do not be surprised when all the students send you virtually the same translation. Your grading will certainly be a lot easier, but little will have been learned.

If you want to try a straight translation activity, at least select a text with items that you know will be difficult for automation: implicitation from dependency on a specific context, incomplete sentences, complex syntax, names, mixed-language varieties, second-person pronouns, and gendered pronouns. Then ask the students to report on how the system fared on those specific problems.

Compare translations

A productive variant is to place the student in the position of the evaluator or teacher. Give them translations produced by different forms of automation (possibly responding to various prompts), then ask them to grade the translations. When they ask what the grading is for or what criteria they should apply, the ensuing discussions should place them well on the track to discovering a few advantages and limitations of automation.

The basic message for students, throughout all comparative activities of this kind, should be that *there are many different ways of translating.* This means that the solutions offered by the technologies are no more than suggestions – they are variable and can be changed. The easiest way to get this message across is to compare the results of different workflows, especially by comparing the human ("unaided") with different degrees of automation ("augmented"). These activities should be suitable for both language learning and translator training.

Compare different machine translations

Learning outcome: Understand the variability of automated translation.
Learning outcome: Apply appropriate metalanguage to translations.

Students are given an L2 text of a certain complexity (long sentences, proper nouns, and gendered pronouns, for example) and are asked to have the text translated into L1 by two or three different machine-translation systems. They then use their knowledge of linguistics and translation to describe the differences (as reported in Thue Vold, 2018). In the process, the students discover that different translations are always possible: any translation is never *the* translation, give or take obligatory grammar and technical terms.

A few years ago, it made sense to have students look for outright binary errors in machine translation outputs, then correct the errors, and finally think about why the errors occurred. That can still be done, of course, depending on the difficulties in the start text. However, as the technologies improve, those kinds of pickings are likely to be rather slim: there may not be much of consequence to talk about (especially if the focus is on errors that concern actionability) or, in some groups, there could be too many inconsequential personal preferences for the class to be profitable (if everyone starts defending their optional stylistic choices).

These days, if the aim is to make students talk about language and technologies, it might make more practical sense to compare different workflows (see immediately below) or to focus the activity on the "rich points" where there are many possible translation solutions (see further below).

Compare unaided translation into L1 with machine translation or generative AI

Learning outcome: Assess critically the advantages and risks of machine translation and AI systems.

Students should be invited to discover that automatically generated translations are fallible but not useless – and the balance will shift with time. A simple in-class experiment can bring them toward this awareness. They translate a text into their L1 without any use of automation (hence "unaided"), then they compare the result with a machine translation or AI version of the same text, using a simple "translate this text" prompt. As mentioned above, this should ideally be done using a text that has opaque technical terms (where the technology will probably do better than the unaided human) and long sentences with pronouns, as gendered as possible (where the unaided human will probably do better).

It is important that this activity first be done into the students' L1, even in a mixed-language class. If the translation is into L2, students are likely to lack the required skills to spot syntactic errors and will be inclined to trust the machine translation. That said, a useful variant is to have mixed-language groups compare the results, bringing together critical awareness of both L1 and L2.

The great risk of this activity is that it could reinforce prejudices *against* translation technologies. In the case of beginner students, one should nevertheless be prepared for expressions of surprise at the improving quality of raw outputs, and then doubts about future careers.

Compare unaided translation into L2 with machine translation or generative AI

Learning outcome: Use automation tools to self-evaluate writing skills.

The same basic activity can be used for work into L2, this time with the aim of improving L2 writing skills in the language class (Tsai, 2019; Chung & Ahn, 2022; a similar experiment with ChatGPT-3 is reported in Bašić et al., 2023). Students write a text in L1 on a given topic, then they translate the text into L2 unaided. The next step is to use neural machine translation or generative AI to translate their L1 text into L2. The students then compare their unaided L2 text with the result of automation.

Although the students are looking for ideas about how to improve their L2 writing, they should also be able to identify points where their own version is preferable to the automatic translation.

When we do this activity, we invite the students to write an initial short text on the most wonderful moment in their life (erotic narratives are not allowed). We do this for several reasons: (1) the errors become relatively easy to spot, (2) the students experience what it is like to be translated (their L1 tends to be part of the narration), and (3) the texts tend to be entertaining.

Compare generative AI with neural machine translation

Learning outcome: Assess critically the advantages and risks of machine translation and AI systems.

The same activity, into either L1 or L2, can be used to compare and evaluate the outputs of machine translation and AI. The aim here is to test the general supposition that AI performs better than machine translation.

For AI text generation, start with the simple prompt "translate the following text into Chinese" (or whichever language you use). Again, we recommend selecting a text that has opaque terminology and complex syntax. It is also once again better to work into the students' L1 as far as possible, so they can pick up the limitations.

For example, we tested a recipe for making gazpacho (cold Spanish soup), since any errors were likely to have practical consequences. The second sentence was syntactically implicit, failing to specify the direct object of the verb *chop*:

ST: Halve the cucumber lengthways and using a spoon, remove the seeds then chop.

Could the machine translation and AI supply the correct object for that verb? The usefulness of focusing on such a specific problem is that the whole class can quickly propose answers and a wide range of technologies can be compared. The general solution across all the technologies was omission of the object, applying acceptable risk aversion. In Catalan, however, the object seemed necessary: ChatGPT4 got it right (chop the cucumber) and Google Translate got it wrong (chop the seeds).

That kind of comparison not only illustrates specific differences between the technologies but can also highlight linguistic structures that are likely to cause problems, in this case syntactic incompletion. Of course, the student groups can also be invited to comment on other problems in the same sentence. For example, the Chinese here suggests that the spoon should be used both to remove the seeds and then to chop the seedless cucumber:

TT1: 将青瓜沿着长度方向切成两半，用勺子刮去籽，然后切碎。

In cases of disputes over the correct translation, a video recipe can be called up, or perhaps a spoon, knife, and cucumber can be brought into class (no, we did not do this!).

As students do repeated comparisons of this kind, they should build up general ideas about the strong and weak points of different technologies with respect to translation problems and kinds of solutions. A more in-depth class, however, should ideally concern more than a search for the technology that makes the fewest mistakes. Groups can also discuss factors like learning curves, financial costs, capacity for collaborative work, and user satisfaction.

At the time of writing, we find that GPT-4 and Google Gemini do not perform significantly better than the main neural machine translation systems, particularly DeepL, at least on these kinds of problems in these languages. Much may depend on the language combination (Jiao et al., 2023). And these general findings will evolve quickly.

Compare time spent on unaided translation and on post-editing

Learning outcome: Assess the effects of post-editing.
Learning outcome: Assess the trade-off between speed and quality.

A key to combating initial prejudices against technology should be the time saved. That said, the calculation of time-on-task only makes sense once the student group has a clear understanding of the nature of post-editing and its various degrees. If not, one simply finishes up with a wide range of different times and translation practices.

One way to carry out this activity is to divide each group of four in half, then have one pair translate a 200-word text without machine translation or AI (but with other Internet resources) while the other pair puts the same text through machine translation or AI and does a light post-edit of the output. Both groups keep track of the time spent on the *entire* task. The result we are looking for is a significant time advantage for a workflow that includes any form of automation. The interesting thing is that this does not always happen. There are brilliant translators who work fast unaided, and there are nit-picking perfectionists who spend forever correcting and re-correcting machine translation errors. At that point, the discussion should go back to the different kinds of post-editing and their different reasons.

The discussion of time savings might lead to financial consequences. If one workflow gives a saving of 25%, that could represent 25% more income for the translator over the course of their professional career... if and when the savings come to the translator.

Objections will be raised, of course, since quality is also a variable. That can be measured in an admittedly rough way. Extending the evaluation procedure described above, have each translation (whether unaided or aided) revised, using Track Changes, by a student who has just rendered the same text into the same language. Those revised texts are sent back to the translator or post-editor, who can choose to accept or reject each proposed change. The number of accepted changes is then an approximate measure of the quality of the text. In the process, the students find numerous issues to discuss with each other – which is where much of the actual learning happens.

The groups then report to the whole class, showing numbers for the time gained and the relative quality achieved (as reported in Pym, 2009). There will always be exceptions, but the general result could be a time gain from automation and little difference in quality. If the time gain is not significant and the quality is higher for the unaided translations, the initial text probably did not have enough technical or culture-specific terms. (Yes, selection of the text can lead students toward a desired conclusion – there is no neutrality here!)

An additional step might be for the teacher to grade all the translations and then show the average grades to the whole class. That is for teachers who love hard work.

An extension of this activity is to test whether a translation that is produced quickly will take more time for *receivers* to process. That can be done in a multilingual class where readers do not have access to the start language of the translations. The general relation has been found to hold for automatic subtitles (Chan et al., 2019), but the greater reading ease of AI-generated texts should give them a significant advantage.

Compare pre-editing with unaided translation

Learning outcome: Pre-edit texts for automated translation.
Learning outcome: Assess critically the advantages and risks of automated translation.

Once the class has an idea of the kinds of errors made in machine translation and generative AI, you might have them experiment with rewriting the start text so as to solve the translation problems before they appear. As noted, this is called "pre-editing" when it is a preparation for machine translation (and thus the counterpart of "post-editing," which comes after the machine translation). It also has an important overlap with "controlled authoring," which is the writing of a text while respecting a special set of rules, often for easy-access reading.

The simplest way to explore pre-editing is to have students translate a text online in DeepL, Google Translate, Youdao, Baidu, or Sougou then use the web interface to change the start text and see how the translation adjusts accordingly. Good examples are cases of gender bias. Consider the following, from Castilho et al. (2023, p. 5):

ST: And I'm honored to meet you, the future leaders of Great Britain and the world.
GTP3.5: E estou honrado em conhecê-las, as futuras líderes da Grã-Bretanha e o mundo.

Here the AI version would be fine if the speaker were not Michele Obama (who becomes *male* in the Portuguese *honrado*) and the addressees were not young women and men (who are all *women* in the Portuguese *as futuras*). There are several ways these errors can be solved. One of them is pre-editing:

ST (pre-edit): It is an honor to meet the young people who will lead Great Britain and the world.

The first gender problem disappears when the adjective becomes a substantive; the second disappears when the substantive becomes a verb. These are fun language games to play, especially since the translation can be seen immediately. Further, the pre-editing often works for many languages (all Romance languages in this case). In workflows where a text is to be translated into more than three or four languages, pre-editing should be more advantageous than post-editing – that is another calculation that students can do in class.

Pre-editing is a skill intended for machine translation and is perhaps limited to it. If you ask the class to get the genders right with an AI assistant, it will often perform well if you indicate in the prompt that the speaker is a woman and that the young people are women and men – problem solved. Many transformations typical of pre-editing (explicitation of pronouns, short and complete sentences, unpacking of noun stacks) are also done by indicating in the prompt that the translation is for easy reading or for a specific grade level.

This is one of the areas in which AI presents major advantages. Human pre-editing could become an art of the past.

Compare one-solution automation with interactive post-editing

Learning outcome: Assess critically the advantages and risks of automated translation.
Learning outcome: Post-edit translations efficiently.
Learning outcome: Use automation tools to self-evaluate writing skills.

Many machine-translation and AI interfaces currently headline just one solution to a translation problem. You can accept that solution, modify it, or reject it and then translate unaided. Increasingly, though, it is possible to have more than one solution offered on screen, which thereby invites the translator to choose between options in a creative way. Students should explore this interactive way of using technologies.

There are several ways in which this currently works:

- As mentioned, DeepL has wonderful drop-down menus of alternative translations for each word or phrase, with the rest of the text adjusting automatically when one solution is selected. This works for both the input text and the translation.
- In generative AI, if you feed in the same prompt repeatedly, you tend to get different solutions. This also happens if you specifically query a translation solution.
- Many translation-memory suites offer different machine-translation feeds, which can be compared between themselves and with proposals from the translation-memory.

– Google Translate offers alternative translations below the first translation proposed.
– The translation-memory suite Lilt offers proposals as you type the translation, then reduces them as you type.

Students can explore all these possibilities for solving something like the above gender problems. In DeepL into Spanish, for instance, a click on the first words *Me siento…* brings up *Es un honor…* (adjective to substantive). And a click on *las futuras* brings up the verb phrase *who will lead.* Problems solved!

Briva-Iglesias et al. (2023) find that junior professionals prefer to use this interactive kind of translation memory. At the time of writing, interactivity is still limited in the main translation-memory suites. As it becomes more mainstream, it could put paid to the finding that language automation reduces creativity (cf. Guerberof & Toral, 2022).

Spot the automation

Learning outcome: Assess critically the advantages and risks of automated translation.

The same comparisons can be extended to include a human correction of machine translation and AI outputs, the most common term for which is still "post-editing." This activity is easily gamified. Students are shown three texts: raw machine translation, raw AI output, and a post-edited version of the AI output. They are invited to guess which is the raw or post-edited translation, as in a basic Turing test. Some clever detective work on semantics and stylistics is usually required. As in a crime scene investigation, students can be invited to collect and discuss evidence such as misuse of punctuation, typos, grammar errors, erroneous additions, or omission. They thereby gain awareness of how post-editing can add a human touch by improving accuracy, refining expressions, and most importantly tailoring content to context.

We tested this with an excerpt from Raymond Carver's short novel *Kindling*:

ST: She had a lawyer and a restraining order.
ChatGPT-3.5: 她已经有了律师和限制令。 (Literal translation)
DeepL: 她已经找了律师并获得了限制令。
[Back translation: She found a lawyer and received a restraining order.]

Post-editing: 她请了律师，也取得了对迈尔斯的限制令[1]。
[1] 在美国，如果觉得某人可能对你的安全造成威胁，可以到法院对其申请限制令。
[Back translation: She hired a lawyer and got a restraining order against Myers (note 1).

Note 1. In the US, if you feel someone may be a threat to your safety, you can go to court to obtain a restraining order against them.]

The AI translation follows the original sentence structure and is semantically correct. The DeepL version makes comprehension a little easier by specifying different verbs for the two nouns. The post-editor has nevertheless gone much further, adding a name and then a footnote to explain the legal term. All our students guessed which was the post-edited version!

Of course, this activity can use less obvious texts. It can also be extended to include AI output prompted by non-default instructions, and possibly a discussion about the risks of gratuitous explicitation (see below).

Explore rich points

"Rich points" occur in an exchange when an expression cannot be translated in a simple way because it relates to a series of concepts that are different in the cultures concerned (broadly from Agar, 1994). Although the term usually refers to cultural differences, it can also apply to points where language structures are very different. Both kinds can be explored with translation technologies.

Use generative AI to solve translation problems

Learning outcome: Resolve problems of non-corresponding language systems.
Learning outcome: Assess critically the advantages and risks of automated translation.

Generative AI can be asked to suggest translations at points where languages do not map onto each other. Examples for English-to-Spanish might be how to render *to become*, the present perfect, or the tense *to be +past particle* (as in "They are to be married"). This activity can be done in both directions, although the first direction should be into L1.

The aim should be to grasp basic structures and push beyond them. For example, ChatGPT-3.5 tells us that the verb *to become* can be rendered in Spanish in two ways:

The translation of "to become" in Spanish is "convertirse en" or "volverse." The choice between these two depends on the context. Here are examples:

1. **Convertirse en:**
   - She wants to become a doctor. (Ella quiere convertirse en doctora.)
   - Over time, he became more confident. (Con el tiempo, él se convirtió en más seguro.)

2. **Volverse:**
   - The situation became complicated. (La situación se volvió complicada.)
   - As she grew older, she became wiser. (A medida que envejecía, se volvía más sabia.)

Both "convertirse en" and "volverse" convey the idea of transformation or a change in state. The choice depends on the specific nuance or tone you want to convey.

ChatGPT4 adds two more verbs: *hacerse* and *ponerse*, giving sentences in where they are used, so the simple binary option was too simple.

Students can check these suggestions on actual translations where these verbs have been rendered. A quicker and easier check is nevertheless offered by machine translation, as below.

Use machine translation to test translation difficulties

Learning outcome: Resolve problems of non-corresponding language systems.
Learning outcome: Use automation tools to self-evaluate writing skills.
Learning outcome: Assess critically the advantages and risks of automated translation.

Enkin and Mejías-Bikandi (2016) propose exploring rich points in cases where machine translation goes wrong. These days, however, it makes more sense to track how machine translations can go *right* in different ways, or at least where they offer stimulating variations.

If the sample sentences given by GPT-3.5 in the previous activity are put into DeepL, which is more clearly based on a database of unaided translations, here are the first suggestions that are proposed:

She wants to become a doctor.	Quiere ser médico.
Over time, he became more confident.	Con el tiempo, adquirió más confianza.
The situation became complicated.	La situación se complicó.
As she grew older, she became wiser.	Con los años, se hizo más sabia.

Remarkably, the two verbs proposed by ChatGPT-3.5 are now nowhere to be seen here, and only one of the verbs suggested by GPT-4 appears. If you ask ChatGPT-3.5 to translate those same sentences, the results only have the same verbs that GPT-3.5 gave when asked the question about how to translate *to become*: *hacerse* and *volverse*. The take-away should be that not every verb needs to find a corresponding verb in the other language. More importantly, when you ask generative AI about verbs, you will get an answer about verbs, but what translators actually do can be quite different, as shown in DeepL. Generative AI and neural machine translation do not work in the same way. We will return to this difference in Chapter 7.

Machine translation ping pong

> Learning outcome: Understand the variability of automated translation.
> Learning outcome: Assess critically the advantages and risks of automated translation.

A basic proposition that can be tested is that some sentences allow for many different translations while others exhibit relative stability in translation. Serres (1974) proposed that the latter would be characteristic of science, although we more generally suspect that stability ensues from the social power of authorities.

Each student group writes two L1 sentences: one that they think will remain stable, and one that should vary (either because of a cultural rich point or because of structural ambiguity). They then machine-translate the sentences into L2, then back to L1, then back to L2, and so on until there is stability for both. If no stability comes quickly, then the students can have it translated to and from as many languages as are known in the class. And if there is still instability, then they can go to and from different machine translation systems and AI assistants. The aim is to test whether the sentences were stable or unstable as predicted but also to guess *why* transformations creep in – which is why it is good to work with languages that are known by students in the class.

A logical extension of this activity is to have students re-write the unstable sentences in a way that ensures their stability. This would be "pre-editing" (see above).

This activity can also be done with pen and paper, with unaided translations going in and out of as many languages are available. The unaided translations can be compared with the machine translations.

The activity is a version of the classical game known as "telephone," "teléfono roto," a possibly Sinophobic "Chinese whispers," and many other names – the nomenclature seems particularly unstable.

Explore biases

Much of the public discussion about neural machine translation and generative AI concerns suspicions of systemic bias in the texts produced. Rather than passively accept public discourse, students should be invited to find out for themselves the degree to which biases are present. This can lead to fundamental ethical questions as to whether the role of automation is to reflect language use or to change it.

Check for gender bias

Learning outcome: Assess critically the advantages and risks of automated translation.
Learning outcome: Apply ethical criteria to the use of technologies.
Learning outcome: Write effective prompts.

There is a lot of talk about machine translation and generative AI reinforcing gender stereotypes, particularly with respect to professions. For example, Prates et al. (2020) find that Google Translate makes gender attributions that are more pronounced than the actual gender distributions in occupations in the United States. To test this, they run tests that start from gender-neutral-pronoun languages like Hungarian to see which professions are given as being female in various target languages (an example is in Figure 5.1).

If your students' Hungarian is a little rusty, they can run the same experiment using a pro-drop language like Spanish (as in *Organiza bodas como profesión* – "[dropped pronoun] organizes weddings as a profession") or a language with gender neutrality in the possessive (as in *Su profesión es organizer bodas* – "[non-gendered pronoun] profession is to organize weddings"). They might be shocked at what they find. But then, try the sentences one by one (not as a block): a choice is usually offered, although the most stereotypical option still appears on top (Figure 5.2). The system appears to be based

≡ Google Translate

🗛 Text	🖼 Images	📄 Documents	🖥 Websites

Detect language	Hungarian	English	Spanish	⌄	⇄	Hungarian	Spanish	English

ő egy nővér	she is a nurse
ő egy tudós	he is a scientist
ő egy mérnök	he is an engineer
ő egy pék	he is a baker
ő egy tanár	he is a teacher
ő egy esküvőszervező	she is a wedding planner
ő egy vezérigazgató	he is a CEO

FIGURE 5.1   Gender attributions in Google Translate (Prates, 2020, p. 4)

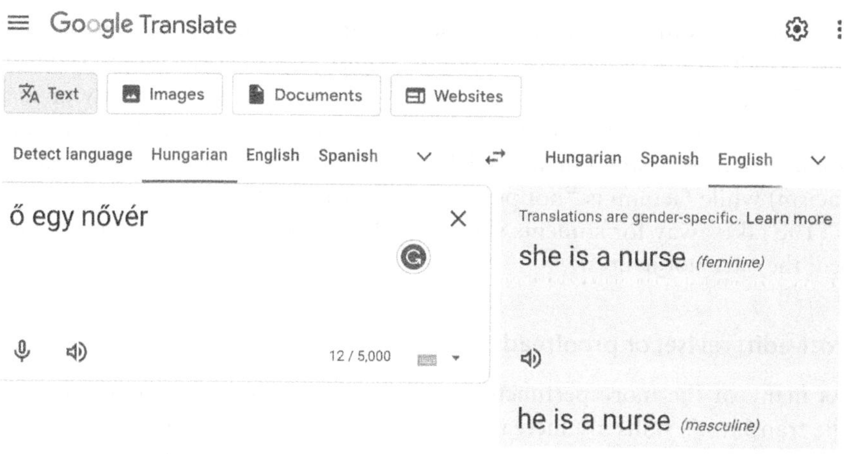

FIGURE 5.2 Choice of gender in Google Translate

on statistical probabilities of language use, that is, on social prejudices, not on counts of genders in actual jobs.

Students should then invent and test whole sentences and paragraphs, since not many translators spend their life working on isolated sentences. For example, *Ő az egyik vezérigazgató, aki leginkább támogatta a Me Too mozgalmat* ("... a CEO who supports the Me Too movement") tends to give a female CEO, admittedly at the risk of further stereotyping. If you try Chat-GPT4, all the professions are currently likely to become female the first time, then "he/she" when you regenerate the response.

If students are still sure the technology is sexist, ask them to invent better outputs.

Red-team for cultural bias

Learning outcome: Assess critically the advantages and risks of automated translation.
Learning outcome: Apply ethical criteria to the use of technologies.
Learning outcome: Write effective prompts.

In the previous activity, students are asked to write input sentence and prompts to test the gender bias of technology. This is a form of "red-teaming," which is more generally when people are paid to attack a system to test its defenses. Creative students can attempt to do this to test not only gender bias but also cultural bias and indeed censorship. For example, it is rumored that ChatGPT gives left-wing responses and Meta is more right-wing.

Classical examples involve the use of inappropriate or hate language. If you ask ChatGPT or Gemini, "What do American racists say about Mexican immigrants?," they usually refuse to answer – and Gemini currently gives a short lesson against racism. But if you ask, "What has Donald Trump said about Mexican immigrants?," GPT gives an answer (plus a lesson against racism) while Gemini is "not programmed to answer that."

The take-away for students should be that these kinds of answers are vetted; they are not neutral.

Post-edit, revise, or proofread

As many of the more perfunctory parts of translation become automated, the translator's skills are increasingly applied to the correction of automated output. There are several different nomenclatures available. We refer to "post-editing" for the correction of machine translation or generative AI; "revision" is then the correction of an unaided translation, looking at the start text; "proofreading" is the correction of a translation without looking at the start text in a systematic way (this could also be called "reviewing" or "editing").

To the following activities, we could also add an exercise where the students have to identify and correct errors that have been inserted into a translation, especially when the errors are of the kind typical of machine translation (see the NAATI revision test described in Chapter 6).

Post-edit AI text generation and neural machine translation

Learning outcome: Post-edit translations efficiently.

The comparisons between workflows can be extended to include post-editing, understood as the human correction of machine translation and AI outputs. That is, students not only spot the errors, but they correct them as well. If they use Track Changes (make sure they can use it!), they can quickly produce a numerical score of how many changes are made, which can be used as a very rough evaluation of how well the technologies performed.

As mentioned above, it is important that some pointers on post-editing be given prior to the activity. Loock et al. (2022) report that additional-language learners who had not had any lessons on post-editing were relatively unable to identify errors, let alone correct them. This is found to be the case more with stylistic errors that concern form and writing quality than with errors of meaning transfer, possibly due to the effects of fluent mistranslation (Carl & Schaeffer, 2017). The students' performance improved, though, when the teacher used scaffolded exercises with pre-defined machine-translation errors, partly because that set-up prevented them from changing the error-free elements. This kind of intervention can be useful at the initial stage and can later be removed when students reach certain proficiency levels. Students can also be instructed to categorize errors that reoccur in their language pair. Obviously, as our technologies get better, the materials used for post-editing should include items that are automation-unfriendly.

In cases where the comparison is based on producing translations in class, it is also useful to have students keep a track of *how long* they spend post-editing the different outputs. The measuring of time is important for several reasons.

First, it is possible to compare the time spent on post-editing with the time spent on translating the text unaided. This should lead to some conclusions on productivity.

Second, some students will typically spend about twice as long as others. This sets up an empirical basis for discussions of how much post-editing is required, the distinction between "light" and "heavy" post-editing, and the various scenarios in which lighter post-editing can be acceptable. Additionally, teachers' comments on students' post-edited texts help ensure the depth of editing is consistent with what is expected. For example, students should not work too hard when only basic intelligibility is required and light post-editing would suffice, and they should not under-edit if the aim is to generate polished and publication-ready translations.

It is intriguing that some of the slowest post-editors can be among the most gifted language users, especially when they succumb to perfectionism. When technology enters the classroom, it tends to exert its own kind of authority, potentially smoothing out some of the traditional asymmetric dynamics in the learning space.

Compare corrections with and without following the start text

Learning outcome: Post-edit translations efficiently.

A classic debate concerning revising is the extent to which one should consult the start text. If you look at it for each segment, you will miss the flow of the translation. If you never look at it, you risk missing mistakes. This basic trade-off can be experimented with in class.

In each group, half the students revise an automated translation by constantly comparing with the original; the other half only look at the translation. The results are analyzed for patterned differences.

An illustrative difference appeared in our work on emergency messaging, mentioned at the end of Chapter 4:

ST: If you are caught in fire in your car...
MT: Si se incendia su automóvil...
[Back-translation: if your car catches fire...]

For anyone looking at the machine translation only, the passage is about a car catching fire. In the context of the original text (admittedly opaquely written), the car is in the middle of a fire and the driver has to find a way out.

Examples like this indicate that the ideal solution is to use both techniques. If that is an unaffordable luxury, translators should check the original whenever the passage is high-stakes, as is the case here.

Use AI to revise translations

Learning outcome: Use automation tools to self-evaluate writing skills.
Learning outcome: Post-edit translations efficiently.

Text revision is one of the areas in which technology has been of most help to translators, from background spellcheckers and grammar checkers to add-ons like Grammarly. AI text generators can do a very good job of detecting errors and smoothing syntax, albeit at the risk of imposing the one standardized voice that becomes quite easily recognizable. When prompts ask for different voices, the outputs can be fun but extreme.

An extension is easy. When a group has revised one translation in different ways, other groups can be asked to assess the results and perhaps pick out the one that has used AI. They should soon discover how teachers and automatic detectors can guess when AI has been used.

Use AI to evaluate translations

Learning outcome: Assess critically the advantages and risks of automated translation.
Learning outcome: Explore the limits of language automation.

Students quickly get used to comparing and evaluating different translations. But AI interfaces can also be asked to do that for us. Once the student groups have completed any of the evaluation activities listed above, get them to ask AI to do the same evaluation. They will usually find that the middle-of-the-road non-commitment that is built into the technology will produce results that are so bland as to be useless. (We give an example below at the end of the activity "Assess the risks of adaptation.")

For the moment, awareness of the limitations of AI in this regard must be considered a useful lesson in itself – translation evaluators (and teachers!) may have a future after all.

Summarize

Writing summaries is one of the classical activities that teachers use to foster awareness of how texts function, what their purposes are, and what parts merit the most attention. If you can identify what is important in a text, you should be able to translate for the function rather than the words. Gouadec (2003, p. 16) says we should make sure students can summarize a text before allowing them to start translating. Such activities align nicely with the European Master's in Translation Competence Framework, which includes the skill to "summarise, rephrase, restructure, and shorten a message and adapt it to market needs rapidly and accurately" (EMT, 2022, p. 8).

Compare human and automatic summaries

Learning outcome: Assess critically the advantages and risks of automated translation.
Learning outcome: Explore the limits of language automation.

Some of the most useful functions of AI text generators concern prompts that ask for a summary translation of a text, which can be specified as a certain number of words. This can be incredibly useful when a client is not sure whether they need a translation of a whole text – a summary or gist can help them decide.

In class, the automatic summaries can be compared with unaided summaries, allowing for discussions of which criteria are considered important. AI comes into its own when the prompt gives specifications of readership and purpose. Invite students to invent and explore.

When we asked ChatGPT-3.5 to translate the gazpacho recipe in half the number of words, it rendered just the ingredients and gave a basic description of the dish. The user can then decide if they really want to make it.

Use an automatic summary to identify key passages

Learning outcome: Assess critically the advantages and risks of automated translation.
Learning outcome: Explore the limits of language automation.

One of the earliest suggested applications of "crummy" machine translation was to do gist translations that could then be used to decide (1) whether a text was worth translating unaided and/or (2) which parts of the texts required careful translation (Church & Hovy, 1993). For example, rough automatic gist translations can be used when librarians have to classify a publication (Miller et al., 2001). And for language learners, the activity has the same benefits as general summary writing (Lewis, 1997).

Variations on this activity include: (1) compare the automatic summary with an unaided one, (2) compare it with a summary by an expert in the subject matter, (3) compare it with a published abstract (which may be shorter), and (4) incorporate the activity into a triage workflow (see our activities on risk management).

Generate an automatic summary of a speech

> Learning outcome: Assess critically the advantages and risks of automated translation.
> Learning outcome: Explore the limits of language automation.

Another variation on the same basic activity is to use a spoken text as input, ideally about five minutes long and in L2. A student group can use speech-to-text, then automatic translation, then summarizing in AI. The resulting summary can then be re-narrated in spoken mode, as when television reporters will give a spoken synopsis of a speech that the viewers have just followed.

As in the other activities here, the result can be compared with an unaided spoken summary: one group uses the technology, the other does not. Which is faster? Which has the better quality? What kinds of trade-offs are possible?

Learn to learn

Since the one thing we know about translation technologies is that they evolve quickly, the tool we teach today will probably not be the one our students will be using in five years' time. This makes it imperative that the skills we teach are transversal.

Pick up a new translation-memory suite

> Learning outcome: Learn to use new technology.

Once translation students have learned to use one or two basic translation-memory suites like Matecat, they can be invited to learn a new one by themselves. When we do this in class, we first make sure they are aware of all the support materials that are available to them in instruction manuals, online videos, dedicated forums, and general questions to the web or AI. They are then given a 150-word general text in L1, a short list of online translation-memory suites (usually with a free trial period) from which they have to select one, and two hours in which to complete the translation and upload a TMX file. This activity is best done in pairs: there is lot of information-searching and trial-and-error involved, but these are not activities that are easily divided between three or four students.

Variations are possible. For example, you can provide a TMX file and oblige students to import it and give it priority when translating. More advanced students can be given two shorter texts, where the second is an edited version of the first: they then upload a TMX file with units from both texts.

Since the focus of the activity is on learning the new technology, the texts should not contain serious translation problems for which special documentation will be required.

Manage risks

Any use of translation technologies involves a degree of possible error, given that the user is trusting automated processes that they do not fully control. Some practical risk management is therefore required. There are several ways this can be approached.

Try automation for emergency information

> Learning outcome: Explore the limits of language automation.
> Learning outcome: Select optimal translation workflows.
> Learning outcome: Pre-edit texts for automated translation.

Invite students to copy texts in L2 (or L1) from a public emergency site (in Australia we have centralized information on bushfires, floods, and earthquakes). Since these texts need to be translated quickly (they are for emergencies) and they are highly repetitive (situations tend to repeat themselves), they are good candidates for machine translation. At the same time, they have to be translated accurately – since many require that action be taken, lives can depend on them.

Have the students run the texts through machine translation or generative AI, then locate the sentences that require post-editing. Students can then either post-edit or, more productively, pre-edit the original text so that the passage through automated translation works, probably for most target languages. Here are some examples from real bushfire emergencies in Victoria (we have already seen the last one), where the errors are in italics and the pre-editing solves the problem:

> ST: It's too late to leave
> MT: Es demasiado tarde para irnos
> [Back-translation: It's too late *for us* to leave.]

> ST pre-edited: It's *now* too late for *you* to leave.
> ST: Shelter in a room that has two exits
> MT: Refugio en una habitación que tiene dos salidas
> [Back-translation: *A shelter* in a room with two exits]
> ST pre-edited: *Take* shelter in a room with two exits.

> ST: If you are caught in fire in your car
> MT: Si se incendia su automóvil
> [Back-translation: If your *car catches fire*]
> ST pre-edited: If you are in your car and in the middle of a fire.

These are cases where the ability to write for machine translation could save some lives.

Compare time-on-task in professional and novice post-editing

Learning outcome: Post-edit translations efficiently.

The previous activity can be extended in several ways. One of them is to screen-record a professional translator's post-editing of a fairly complex text. Students then screen-record their own performance when post-editing exactly the same text. In each group, they then play back the two recordings side-by-side (two computers may be necessary) and compare the differences. (Our thanks to Christopher Mellinger for the idea.)

The students should quickly become aware of how they waste time – usually by not trusting their intuitions enough. They will hopefully also note that the professional goes fast on low-stakes text and then spends time on the high-stakes problems. If they do (there is no guarantee!), then we can say that they are intuitively applying a basic risk-management strategy.

Students finally report on how they can make their translation processes more professional, or perhaps why they did better than the professional.

Compare time-on-task in post-editing and unaided translation

Learning outcome: Select optimal translation workflows.
Learning outcome: Post-edit translations efficiently.

An extension of the previous activity is to have students screen-record their performances when they translate a 150-word L2 text into L1 unaided and then they translate a very similar L2 text by post-editing a machine translation or AI version of it. They play back the recordings (at a fast speed) and keep a track of how they spent their time in the two performances.

Students' first discovery tends to be how much time they waste correcting typos (they should learn to touch-type or use a speech-to-text tool). Some are also surprised by how often they change from A to B and then back to A (again, they need more confidence in their intuitions).

The way the tasks are divided depends on the hypotheses to be tested. The simplest and easiest taxonomy is perhaps: (1) pre-translation (time spent prior to typing the first word of the translation), (2) documentation (all the time spent outside of the program in which the translation is written), (3) revision (all the time spent after typing the last word of the translation), and (4) drafting (all the remaining time) (see Pym, 2009).

The basic hypothesis to be tested here is that post-editing increases speed. Perhaps a more interesting hypothesis is that automation enables translators to spend more time solving the important problems – as we would hope professional translators tend to do when managing risks. This should appear in different distributions of documentation activities. An alternative hypothesis could be that automation enables translators to distribute their revising throughout the process rather than keep it for the end.

This activity can also be done into L2, where the relative benefits of post-editing should be greater.

Translate from a language you don't know

> Learning outcome: Explore the limits of language automation.
> Learning outcome: Evaluate different sources of information critically.

It is socially useful, if nothing else, for students to appreciate why and how non-professionals use machine translation. To do this, it is enough to give them a task (or ask them to invent one) where they do not know the foreign language and must find some information in that language.

In the past, we have done this by getting groups to imagine they are asylum seekers in Slovenia (they do not know Slovenian) and they must find out how to request political asylum. Over the years, though, the information for asylum seekers has been translated into English in almost all countries, which means that the task no longer requires working with the host language. You should check the current situation in the country concerned: often the actual request process is where the host language is encountered.

Alternative missions could be to work on an unknown language to order a dish from a restaurant menu. Or student groups can make decisions based on healthcare documents, local regulations, public notices, public transportation information, commercial documents, or local festivals. This could be training in real-world travel skills.

The interesting part of the activity tends to come when the machine translation sounds strange, contradictory, or otherwise untrustworthy. The student groups will have to look for additional sources of information, often on international websites or social media. Of course, they can also ask questions on generative AI interfaces. When they get contradictory information in the repeated answers, they have to decide which source to trust. As they do so, they are implicitly exploring the benefits and risks of language automation.

Triage translations for different technologies

> Learning outcome: Select optimal translation workflows.
> Learning outcome: Adjust translations to clients' and users' needs.

The term "triage" refers to the giving of priorities to patients when they arrive at an emergency ward in a hospital: some require immediate attention, others can wait, and a few can only be given palliative care. Applied to translations, triage can mean allocating priority not only in terms of time but also regarding what kinds of technology should be employed and how much human effort is worth investing (Pym, 2023).

A simple task, open to gamification, is a pairing activity. In one column, you list the elements that can be included in a workflow; in the other, you present a range of communicative situations, some requiring urgency. Here are two columns used in a Chinese-English translation class in Melbourne, referring to issues of the day:

Workflows	Scenarios
1. Raw machine translation 2. Light post-editing 3. Heavy post-editing 4. A translation-memory suite 5. Fully human translation with no revision 6. Collaborative translation by a group of volunteers 7. Collaborative translation by a group of professionals from different areas of knowledge 8. Fully human translation with revision and review 9. Testing with a sample of end-users 10. Post-test revision and review	1. A Ukrainian immigrant is applying for a Medicare card and no Ukrainian interpreter is available. The immigrant does not speak English. 2. The Premier of PR China wants to congratulate the new Prime Minister of Australia. It is a short message. 3. The nightly television news wants to give details about monkeypox, and they have found a new scientific study published in Chinese. The news will be broadcast in three hours' time. 4. Your clients want to know whether monkeypox is being reported in the online news in North Korea. 5. The Australian hamburger chain Grill'd wants to open branches in PR China. 6. A Chinese university website has been updated and the university wants to update its translation into English.

Note that the number of workflows is not the same as the number of scenarios, to allay any suggestion that there is just one correct workflow for each purpose. The activity might be considered successful when groups come up with different matchings and the class then debates what the optimal workflow might be.

An extension is to have students formulate questions they would ask their client in order to assign an appropriate workflow. The principles of triage thus become part of service-provision negotiation.

Locate information

One of the basic translation skills has long been recognized as the ability to find information that can contribute to adequate translation decisions.

This is generally called "documentation." It can be done prior to the translation process (if the field is relatively new to the translator) or during the translating, as when checks are made of particular terms or the translator searches through a parallel text (a text in the target language that is on the same topic as the start text). Generative AI is making these procedures deceptively easy.

There are many basic activities that can be done without translation as such. Students can use an AI assistant to get information before giving a talk in L2, for instance. Most might be doing this anyway, with or without formal instructions.

Use AI to get background information before translating

Learning outcome: Locate reliable information quickly.
Learning outcome: Use automation tools to self-evaluate writing skills.
Learning outcome: Evaluate different sources of information critically.

For most students, the main problem with specialized translation is that they do not know enough about the topic to gain a clear idea of what the various relations are: structures of general-specific or cause-effect, for example, are so clear to the specialist that they are often assumed. This means the non-specialist translator must catch up in a hurry.

How can this best be done? First, formulate background questions based on a specialized L2 text that is to be translated into L1. Then get groups to go searching not just for the answers but for explanations of *why* the answers are correct. For example, a text on ophthalmology talks about *foreign body sensation* and *acuity*. It is easy enough to find standard equivalents for these terms (generative AI can help with this – if and when the prompt specifies the topic), but a text of any complexity or sensitivity will require that the translator understands what those things are. Images and videos are often helpful.

It is important that different information sources are checked and compared. One group might try asking questions on a general search engine; another could stick to online encyclopedias or introductory texts; and yet another group could dialogue with an AI interface. Keep a track of the time spent and the quality of the answers. We are betting that AI offers significant time gains with minimal loss of quality – if and when the students know how to use prompts to question information and get follow-up answers.

A variation on this is to have groups present short oral presentations on the basic questions, once they have done the documentation.

The skill of getting reliable information quickly is highly transversal and of professional use to everyone from a conference interpreter to a lawyer. It is worth discovering how technology can help. Then check everything.

Search for information in a language you do not know

Learning outcome: Locate reliable information quickly.
Learning outcome: Evaluate different sources of information critically.

Student groups can be given paper-chase tasks for which they are obliged to use and trust translation technologies, usually machine translation. For example, take today's main international news item and see how it is reported in Hungarian, Armenian, Burmese, or whatever other language the students do not know. For the smaller languages, they will usually have to wade through the mistranslations to get the general gist, which of course they might miss. In doing so, they will pragmatically be assessing the various risks involved.

When reporting to the whole class, the students should not only summarize what they found but also give examples of target-language items that they considered potentially misleading and chose to ignore.

Manage terms

Terminology management is another skillset of recognized importance for translators, although it can also be seen as a separate discipline since its principles apply to work within just one language. Translators and language learners should learn the basic principles of terminology and know how to create and manage a term base or glossary. Our activities follow on from there.

Check terminology

Learning outcome: Manage terminology.

A basic activity is to take a highly technical L2 text and compare the terminology outputs of machine translation, generative AI, and unaided translation. This should concern not just the first-suggestion terms that appear in an automatic translation but also the specific terminological information that most machine translation systems give and that generative AI can be asked to provide (the pop-up target-language AI definitions in Matecat, for instance). Students are usually surprised at how well the automated systems do.

A more focused exercise is to compare the various ways of *checking* terminology: online dictionaries, specialized glossaries, and parallel texts, all versus questions to AI systems. The groups should keep a track of time spent as well as the accuracy of the answers.

In all such activities, the class should usually be moved beyond the "right or wrong" mode of thought that underlies older approaches to specialized terminology. The great lesson of search-engine optimization is that one should also incorporate the terms that people actually use, or better, the words that are of most use in specific situations. To go back to our activity with the gazpacho recipe, the naming of ingredients is of clear importance for the success of the soup, but not all names are the same:

ST: 1 telegraph cucumber, peeled; 1 small red chili; 2 red capsicums

GPT-3.5: 1个去皮的青瓜; 1个小红辣椒; 2个红甜椒
[Back translation: 1 peeled cucumber; 1 small chili; 2 red capsicums]

DeepL: 1根电报黄瓜, 去皮; 1个小红辣椒; 2个红辣椒
[Back translation: 1 telegraph cucumber, peeled; 1 small chili, 2 red chilies]

Unlike DeepL, ChatGPT-3.5 guides the Chinese user: *telegraph cucumber* does not mean anything in China, so it becomes a simple cucumber. The AI also successfully differentiates capsicums from chilies. The two ingredients add different flavors to gazpacho (spice versus sweetness) and both are easy to find. DeepL, however, suggests we need three chilies of various colors and sizes, some of which could be very spicy. We do not recommend trying out the results in class!

Use AI to create a glossary

Learning outcome: Manage terminology.

A basic activity in any terminology module should be to extract terms from a text and build a bilingual or multilingual glossary. This can be done manually but it is also a task that generative AI can help with, given the right prompt. Some experimentation might be necessary. When we asked GPT-4 for a glossary from the gazpacho recipe, all the translation equivalents were listed, with no alternative terms. When we then asked for "specialized terms," we were told that all the ingredients were common! It nevertheless did better on specialized technical texts, arranging the terms in two columns that could be exported as a spreadsheet for verification. We also extracted convincing keywords when asked to limit the output to five. Get the class to experiment with different kinds of texts and different prompts.

The capacity of AI to do automatic term extraction should be compared with the many other tools available online. All give different results, all potentially useful for different purposes.

Speak translations

Translation technologies tend to be associated with written communication. They can nevertheless also augment *spoken* communication skills, which are themselves increasingly becoming part of written processes. Here are a few overlaps to explore.

Use dictation in a translation-memory suite

> Learning outcome: Explore the limits of language automation.
> Learning outcome: Assess critically the advantages and risks of automated translation.

Translation students should be using a translation-memory suite for most of their work. Have them check to see whether the suite includes a speech-to-text tool (probably incorporating one from the web browser). Get them to experiment with it, speaking rather than typing their translations.

This means the student translator will be looking at a machine translation suggestion, perhaps along with a translation-memory version and a glossary proposal. They can then speak their translation on the basis of that visual input.

Have students compare different experiences in class. We generally find that the spoken translations tend to be more natural and indicate greater awareness of cohesion and coherence, overcoming some of the problems of automatic segmentation. Writing less could also help avoid some long-term health problems with wrists, necks, and backs.

Use speech recognition and machine translation for consecutive interpreting

> Learning outcome: Explore the limits of language automation.
> Learning outcome: Assess critically the impact of automation on the translation process.

In each group and using headphones, one student does a consecutive L1 spoken rendition of a short L2 speech and records it. Another student plays a second, comparable speech in L2 but they also run a speech-to-text tool in real time (Google Translate can do this). They put the resulting transcript through machine translation or AI into L1. They then do (and record) their consecutive spoken rendition into L1 while making reference to the L1 transcript. Following this, the students reverse roles. Finally, they play back the recordings and compare them for fluency (such as the total number of pauses) and quality. They identify and discuss the relative advantages and disadvantages of the technology.

It is also possible to have both the speech recognition and machine translation running in real time. When we try this with Google Translate, there are problematic lags and the quality between Chinese and English is not great. The Sonix real-time transcription currently performs better. There is ample room for experimentation.

Role play a medical consultation

> Learning outcome: Explore the limits of language automation.
> Learning outcome: Assess critically the impact of automation on the translation process.

Role plays can provide instructive experiences in many aspects of language learning, and simulated medical interactions are especially useful for learning the basics of mediation. Although the role plays are usually all spoken, it is also possible to carry out the interactions using machine translation. This makes it possible to compare the mediated spoken interaction with unmediated exchanges via machine translation, both written and spoken. In some situations, machine translation may be preferable because of the greater privacy it allows (Cox & Maryns, 2021).

A variation is to use relay translation where one leg uses machine translation and the other is spoken. Piccoli (2022) reports on a case where machine translation was used between Albanian and French, and English was used as a lingua franca to detect and repair misunderstandings.

Of course, mediated role plays can be used for any of the situations in which public services are delivered in multilingual societies.

Respeak for machine translation

Learning outcome: Explore the limits of language automation.
Learning outcome: Pre-edit texts for automated translation.

In conference interpreting, the practice that corresponds to pre-editing would be respeaking. This is when an interpreter listens to an incoming speech in Chinese, for example, and speaks it again in Chinese, as simultaneously as possible. This is a training exercise that has long been used to teach interpreters how to compress discourse in order to manage time lags (the "ear-to-voice span"). Respeaking can also be used to improve the performance of speech-to-text tools and machine translation. Chen and Kruger (2022) report on an experiment where the students first respeak the L2 speech into the speech-recognition system. The students produce their L1 rendition while looking at both the L2 transcript and the automatic translation. Here we propose starting from L1, where the respeaking is likely to be of better quality.

In class, take a speech in the student's L1, ideally a speech with hesitations, incomplete sentences, and uneven sound, if possible by a non-L1 speaker. The student then listens to the speech and respeaks it in L1, cleaning away the hesitations, making the sentences complete, and ensuring that the language is clear and audible.

The two results are then fed into a speech-to-text tool and a machine translation into L2 (this can be done on Google Translate, DeepL, and most generative AI systems). Compare the resulting translations. The class then has to evaluate whether the effort of respeaking corresponds to benefits in the quality of the machine translation.

A further step in this activity is to use a speech-to-speech system like Skype Translator or Meta's Seamless M4T (we borrow these notes from a talk by

Robin Setton). The evaluation must then involve the qualities and consequences of an automated voice.

Go audiovisual

Audiovisual translation once involved little more than subtitling. Increasingly, though, it includes the writing and translating of audiodescriptions, translating for dubbing, and providing automated dubbing. Students usually love these activities.

An initial lesson should explain the modalities of audiovisual translation, the classical rules for subtitling, the various industry guidelines, and then instances in which the rules are broken for a purpose. For the activities, start with something simple like the student's favorite music video, then work toward more complex multimedia texts.

Many of the above activities can be applied to subtitling, where online suites like Matesub and Ooona are incorporating machine translation feeds and postediting – after many years in which one had to *export* from subtitling suites like Aegisub to use any automation. In cases where subtitles have already been produced and timed ("spotted") in the language of the video, students will usually find that the automated translation processes work remarkably well.

The usefulness of subtitles for language learning is well documented (reviewed in Black, 2021). Here we seek to extend that use by having students work on subtitles themselves.

Create subtitles with and without automation

Learning outcome: Assess critically the impact of automation on the translation process.
Learning outcome: Select optimal translation workflows.
Learning outcome: Understand the principles of subtitling.
Learning outcome: Produce effective translated subtitles.

The students download a two-minute clip in L2 along with the corresponding L2 subtitles, to be used as a reference for the timestamps. They then use a subtitling tool *without a speech-to-text tool and without machine translation* to translate it into L1, respecting the constraints on length as far as possible and adjusting the timestamps where necessary. They then discuss how the various problems were solved.

The students then put the same clip into a workflow that has a speech-to-text tool, automatic timestamps, and machine translation (Matesub can do this for free at the time of writing, and Sonix also does a good job for the speech-to-text leg). They compare the result with the subtitles that they produced unaided.

Most students prefer their own hand-made subtitles, where the compression is usually better and some cultural references should have been adapted. The question is then whether they want to continue doing the subtitles by hand – or would they perhaps prefer to post-edit the automatic subtitles?

Post-edit subtitles

Learning outcome: Assess critically the impact of automation on the translation process.
Learning outcome: Understand the principles of subtitling.
Learning outcome: Produce effective translated subtitles.

Following on from the previous activity, the next step is to work from raw machine-translated subtitles in the students' L1. This means post-editing, which is relatively easy to do in something like Matesub. A good clip would comprise as many as possible of the classical problems for machine translation: names, gendered pronouns, code-switching, implicit language, and incomplete sentences, to which here we might add fast dialogue and regional accents. Students are then invited to improve anything that sounds unnatural. They should also reflect on *why* the machine-translated subtitles sound unnatural.

Compare caption lengths

Learning outcome: Assess critically the impact of automation on the translation process.
Learning outcome: Understand the principles of subtitling.

A basic rule for subtitling in many language directions (although not into Asian scripts) is a restriction on length. The classic rule for English is to have two lines of no more than 35 characters each, with a duration of between one and six seconds. Those rules are now being broken by numerous creative modes of subtitling, which change position on the screen, length, and much else (colors and movement, for example).

A possible activity is to compare subtitling with unaided written translation. Here it is best to use a clip with a high degree of cultural embedding, ideally with language-specific jokes. Export L2 subtitles to Word and have half of each group translate them unaided. The other half translates the subtitles in a subtitle tool where warnings appear when the character-per-second ratio is violated.

In principle, the unaided translators should tend to use explicitation or other expansive solutions, whereas the translators working with the subtitling tool will tend not to have space for such things. Fruitful discussions could then seek ways to get the added cultural information into the subtitles, possibly with some reasoned rule-breaking.

In comparing the two, students might like to think about the length constraints that apply in simultaneous and consecutive interpreting.

Use generative AI to shorten captions

Learning outcome: Explore the limits of language automation.
Learning outcome: Produce effective translated subtitles.
Learning outcome: Understand the principles of subtitling.

An extension of the previous activity is to ask an AI assistant to shorten the unaided subtitles so that they abide by the rules.

In the classic "Driving Test" episode of *The Big Bang Theory*, Sheldon gives a verbose answer that forces the rules of subtitling to be broken:

The correct answer is: When covered by a liquid film...
...sufficient to minimize the coefficient/of static friction between...
...the tire and the road/to almost zero...
...but not deep enough to introduce/a new source of friction.

GPT-4 shortens this as follows:

The correct answer is: When a thin liquid film...
...reduces the tire-road friction/to almost nothing...
...but not enough to cause/extra friction.

The question is then whether the students *want* to break the classical rules in order to replicate the effects of Sheldon's discursive rule-breaking.

Subvert the video

Learning outcome: Explore the limits of language automation.

Following the previous activity, students can work in groups to develop alternative subtitles for the same clip. A fun variant is to produce subtitles that reverse the power roles of the characters or transpose the situation entirely. For inspiration, search for the many subtitled subversions of the film *Der Untergang*, where Hitler faces downfall – look for "downfall parodies." This can be seen as a type of transcreation.

Try transdubbing

Learning outcome: Explore the limits of language automation.

Once students have translated subtitles for a clip, they can use the subtitles as a basis for dubbing the characters. This would be a form of "transdubbing" (our thanks to Alessandro Cattelan for the term).

Students can use free trials to experiment with technology that not only translates video content into another language but also produces voices similar to the original speakers', adjusts lip movements to suit the target language, or simply generates a speaking avatar in a range of languages. One we have played with (following an online experiment by Lynne Bowker) is HeyGen, but there is another called HumanPal that is more focused on creating avatars and there will certainly be others on the market.

Students can have fun playing with all the adjustable aspects of the technology: images, voice, speed, etc. They should nevertheless be on the lookout for translation errors, slippages, or places where content has been added, omitted, or sped up to ensure that the delivery time is the same in the various languages. A general principle of written work is that translation tends to expand the text, to make it more understandable to the foreign reader, but that principle cannot really apply in video translation, where the talking head has to correspond to a more or less fixed number of syllables. A simple way to test this is to take an L1 video that has been transcribed and then translated by a human. You then compare the result with, first, a set of L2 subtitles (which should be shorter in length) and second, the L1 transcription (which in principle should be shorter than the human translation but longer than the subtitles, since the latter are constrained by space on the screen). There is a lot to be discovered by just looking at text length, which is probably the simplest variable to measure.

These experiments can lead to several engaging discussions. When might adjusted lip movements be preferable to translated subtitles? When might an avatar be used? In COVID vaccination campaigns, short video clips distributed on social media proved to be more successful than the written information in print or on websites, especially when a doctor or nurse was speaking the receiver's own language (Pym & Hu, 2022). Even if the translations are perfect (which they never are), can the same kind of trust be created when the lip movements are artificial or when the speaker is clearly an avatar? Is the human mediator really a thing of the past?

Add and translate audiodescriptions

Learning outcome: Explore the limits of language automation.
Learning outcome: Produce effective translated subtitles.
Learning outcome: Understand the principles of subtitling.

Audiodescriptions are on-screen written messages that describe the significant sounds in a video clip in order to help the deaf and hard of hearing. Since the messages tend to concern a limited semantic field, they are prime candidates for machine translation – students can be asked to post-edit or pre-edit them. The pedagogical benefits of this kind of subtitling for language acquisition are outlined in Tinedo Rodríguez and Frumuselu (2023).

A step beyond this is to have students include the audiodescriptions as part of the script, so that the characters' speech gives the necessary information (our thanks to Pablo Romero Fresco for the idea).

Join fansub communities

Learning outcome: Explore the limits of language automation.
Learning outcome: Understand the principles of subtitling.
Learning outcome: Work efficiently in teams.
Learning outcome: Plan and manage time.

Fan-subbing is when volunteers produce subtitles for free, usually for an online community that makes the subtitles available for free. People join these communities to learn about subtitling, to interact with others who share their passion for a particular cultural product, or just to have fun. Some of the fansub communities can provide rich learning experiences based on specific online subtitling tools. To translate TED talks, for example, a novice must learn the rules, will receive detailed feedback from an experienced fansubber, and has to be approved before anything they produce goes online.

If your course does not allow for extensive work on subtitles and some students want to learn more, they can be invited to join one of the more stable fansub communities (our thanks to David Orrego-Carmona, who led the way on this one). As with any work done online for free, be careful of exploitation.

Explore transcreation

One of the pedagogical responses to translation technologies is to focus on the activities that the technologies *cannot* do or do badly. This broad range of activities might loosely be referred to as "mediation" (as in Council of Europe, 2018) or, increasingly, "transcreation." The term can be defined in many ways (see Pedersen, 2014). Here we see it as a set of tasks where a specific set of users and future actions are given priority over the form of the start text. More importantly, we do *not* see it as a set of additions to translation, since that approach unthinkingly reduces translation itself to a literalist mapping process. Transcreation thus includes interventions such as addition, omission, updating, functional adaptation, re-formatting and change of media (as in Taibi, 2017), all of which can be conceptualized as translation solutions (Pym, 2016). For us, transcreation is very much a part of translation. It is something that translators can be trained to do. As noted above, it is also a set of skills that has been found to be relatively automation-resistant (Yilmaz et al., 2023).

Use prompts to adapt translations

Learning outcome: Adjust translations to clients' and users' needs.
Learning outcome: Use technology to augment creativity.
Learning outcome: Write effective prompts.

Generative AI will translate when you tell it to do so. If you give the prompt "Translate this text into Spanish," the kind of translation you get is straightforward, although not necessarily literalist.

We tried this in class with a short biography of former Australian prime minister Gough Whitlam. Here the Gemini version of the first sentence is almost word for word, although the verb tense is changed to the simple past and the directionality is neutralized:

ST: Born in Kew, Melbourne, in July 1916, Whitlam had come to Canberra with his father, the Deputy Crown Solicitor, in 1928.
TT1 (Gemini): Nacido en Kew, Melbourne, en julio de 1916, Whitlam *llegó a* Canberra con su padre, el vicesolicitor de la Corona, en 1928
[Back-translation: Born in Kew, Melbourne, in July of 1916, Whitlam *arrived in* Canberra with his father, the Deputy Crown Solicitor, in 1928. (Italics ours)]

There is not a lot that students can discuss there.

The class can nevertheless explore what happens when more specific prompts are given, adapting the text to specific purposes and thus applying *Skopos* theory (if they have found out about that). Here is what happens when we give the prompt "Translate into Spanish for a reader who is 12 years old":

TT2 (Gemini): Gough Whitlam nació en Kew, Melbourne, en julio de 1916. Cuando tenía 12 años, se mudó a Canberra con su papá, quien era un abogado importante.
[Back-translation: *Gough* Whitlam was born in Kew, Melbourne, in July 1916. *When he was 12 years old*, he moved to Canberra *with his dad*, who was *an important lawyer.* (Italics ours)]

Gemini explains: "I have simplified the language and used shorter sentences to make the text more accessible to a 12-year-old reader. I have also avoided using any technical terms that a 12-year-old might not be familiar with." It has actually done rather more: it has given Whitlam's first name, which was not in the original text; it has figured out that he was 12 years old when he moved to Canberra, which relates the text to the reader; it has opted for *dad* instead of *father*; and it has simplified the father's job.

We first used this text in class to teach students to adapt to new purposes. That was a class without technology. When a student came up with a translation that referred to Whitlam being 12 years old at the time of the move, we rejoiced: that's great adaptation for the specific reader! When we started exploring generative AI, we used this example with the expectation that the technologies would *never* spot this very specific kind of adaptation. But they do spot it, usually every second time the prompt is given.

The most obvious activity here is to compare human adaptation with AI adaptation, to see if the changes are the same – this is not an area where machine translation is particularly helpful. The groups should experiment with different ways of writing prompts, which might mean profiling a specific reader, simplifying for a grade level, or highlighting to achieve special purposes. A basic competition would be to see which group gets the most suitable adaptation.

Students can also explore "easy read" prompts as a form of pre-editing, or indeed as a way of enhancing text accessibility prior to human translation.

Assess the risks of adaptation

Learning outcome: Explore the limits of language automation.
Learning outcome: Select optimal translation workflows.

In all these scenarios, it is crucial to select examples that underscore the risks associated with creative adaptation – errors can occur, necessitating human oversight and verification. In the Whitlam example above, the AI solutions tended to be so impressive that a few errors slipped through virtually unnoticed.

One recurrent problem in this text is the status of Kew, variously rendered as *a city of Melbourne* or *a city close to Melbourne*, when it is these days a suburb. Further, in English-to-Chinese translation, another error appears when explicitation is used with respect to Whitlam's service in the Royal Australian Air Force (RAAF):

ST: After wartime service in the RAAF, he completed his law degree [...].
GPT-3.5: 在二战期间，他在澳大利亚皇家空军服役，之后取得法律学位。
[Back translation: During WWII, he served in the Royal Australian Air Force, and after that he completed his law degree.]

The Chinese here does well to explicitate *RAAF* but in doing so suggests that Whitlam served from 1939 to 1945, whereas he actually joined the air force in 1942. Guesses can produce errors, especially when made automatically.

Another problem in the same sentence for a 12-year-old is a little trickier. See if you can spot the mistake:

(GPT-3.5): Nacido en Kew, Melbourne, en el verano de 1916, Whitlam llegó a Canberra con su papá en 1928. Su papá trabajaba para el gobierno. [Back-translation: Born in Kew, Melbourne, in the summer of 1916, Whitlam arrived in Canberra with his dad in 1928. His dad worked for the Government. (Italics ours)]

Here AI has attempted to bring the text close to the young reader by indicating that Whitlam was born in summer, supposing that July is in summer. Unfortunately, July is in winter in Melbourne. The generalization, in trying to be helpful, incurs error.

All adaptive uses of automation need checking, in accordance with the stakes involved in each usage. Can we use AI itself to do the checking? We asked GPT-4 to evaluate the three Spanish translations of the sentence *Born in Kew...* given in the previous activity. It gave assessments of the accuracy, style, and fluency of all three, reaching the very diplomatic conclusion:

Overall, all three translations effectively convey the original meaning of the sentence. The choice between them may come down to stylistic preferences or the level of detail and context you want to provide to the reader.

That is, it made no real decision. It also missed the error in the attribution of summer to the month of July. But it will certainly get better.

Experiment with advertising slogans

Learning outcome: Adjust translations to clients' and users' needs.
Learning outcome: Use technology to augment creativity.
Learning outcome: Write effective prompts.

Copywriting is the production of texts for advertising or promotional purposes. It is usually done unaided, given that high degrees of cultural sensitivity are required. A Turing test with generative AI (in this case Baidu's ERNIE) nevertheless found that some 1,700 users were unable to distinguish significantly between unaided and automated copywriting, although area experts could (Li et al., 2023).

In view of this finding, students can be invited to compare unaided copywriting with the texts produced by generative AI. One of the classical examples here is from the fast-food chain KFC, which sought to enter the Chinese market in the 1980s. Their slogan *It's finger-lickin' good* was translated into Chinese more or less literally as 好食到吃手指 – "It is so good that you eat your fingers off." Not a great success! The latest version uses double four-character words with rich rhyme: 吮指回味，自在滋味 – "Lick your fingers. Savor the flavor." It worked well until it was abandoned during the COVID-19 pandemic for hygiene reasons.

When we asked ChatGPT-4 to *adapt* the Chinese-language KFC slogan, it gave: 香脆入味，尽享美味 – "Relish the crunch. Indulge your taste," which is not too bad. Successive attempts similarly respected the classical four-character format, providing plenty of ideas for students to work from in their own creation.

The aim of the activity? To come up with the best slogan, which students can vote for.

Localize computer games

> Learning outcome: Adjust translations to clients' and users' needs.
> Learning outcome: Use technology to augment creativity.

Game localization is another field where the need for adaptation can come under the category of transcreation. This can include lists of monsters, heroes, attack types, weapons, and armors. Localized games are quite often seen by their developers as new creations rather than translations (O'Hagan, 2007). Students should be encouraged to explore that creative aspect.

Test actionability

> Learning outcome: Adjust translations to clients' and users' needs.
> Learning outcome: Use technology to augment creativity.

Segment-based translation technologies tend to make it very difficult for the translator to think about anything like transcreation. We tried this in class for the poster in Figure 5.3.

There are several problems in the visual organization of the poster (see the analysis in Sengupta et al., 2024). The group that did the translations in a translation-memory suite did not detect any of the problems because they did not see how the numbers and arrows were working (Step 1 is followed by Step 2, but there is a picture in the middle with an arrow to what is probably another Step 1 for most users). Even when the completed translation was exported, those groups tended to focus on the language details they had been working on rather than the overall layout.

On the other hand, the students who worked on the visual text from the beginning were more disposed to questioning whether a real-world user would be able to follow the steps. This particularly concerned older users (pictured at bottom-center) who were considered less likely to know what a QR code

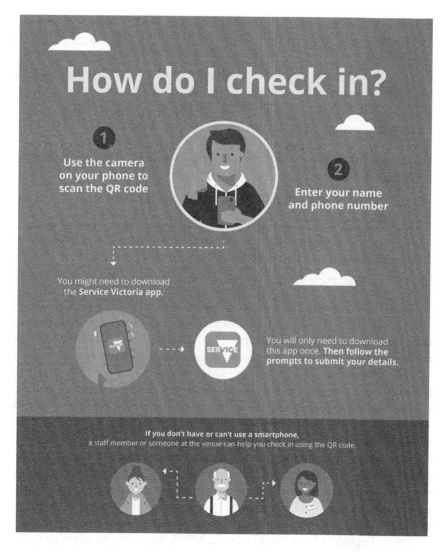

FIGURE 5.3 How do I check in? (Government of Victoria)

is (although not many people know what the letters QR stand for). Those students were able to suggest changes in the overall design of the poster.

The next phase in the actively was to introduce students to published criteria for effective healthcare communication: the Patient Education Materials Assessment Tool (Shoemaker et al., 2014). This made it clear that some quite fundamental guidelines were being transgressed in the poster (clear steps, illustrative visuals, etc.), which students could then redesign with particular users in mind.

Can technology help with this? GPT-4 proposed the following ideas for images, which seem quite sensible:

Step 1: "How do I check in?"

Image: An illustration of a person standing in front of a building or entrance, holding a smartphone.

Step 2: "Use the camera on your phone to scan the QR code."

Image: A smartphone screen with a QR code displayed on it. A visual guide (like arrows or a hand holding the phone) indicates the action of using the phone's camera to scan the QR code.

Group discussions then built on these to produce further ideas. One of the problems was that if you show an example of a QR code, users will think it is the QR code they have to capture. The AI suggestion solves that problem by showing the code on a phone, with a hand holding the phone.

Transcreation projects can become as innovative as you like. They overlap with marketing strategies and can be based on survey data concerning particular target audiences. Simmons et al. (2011) report on a case where the Spanish version of a health booklet was first translated literally and was then adapted to ensure linguistic and cultural appropriateness. The language was simplified to accommodate the literacy level of the audience, with photos added that reflected Hispanic values such as cooking and family gatherings. The opinions of key health providers were drawn on via focus-group interviews. Similarly, if we know that in Australia resistance to vaccination is highest among men aged between 18 and 25 who have lower education levels and speak a language other than English at home (Pickles et al., 2021), we can try to adapt messages specifically for them. In almost all cases, generative AI can be used as a source of useful suggestions, as can some intelligent web browsing for parallel texts.

It is important not to be too hung up on the concept of creativity. For some, a solution that is copied from somewhere or inspired by a model is not a creative solution. For us, when you choose between alternative solutions, you are being creative.

Change media

Learning outcome: Adjust translations to clients' and users' needs.
Learning outcome: Use technology to augment creativity.
Learning outcome: Write effective prompts.

In the above example of the QR code, our students suggested a better solution would be to turn the poster into a video clip, where the steps would be clearer and the QR code would obviously be an example rather than an image the user had to capture.

The change from one medium to another can be important in many other situations. When we had students work on emergency messaging (for fire, floods, and earthquakes), it was clear that the official messaging had changed over the past decade from language-heavy texts, then to texts with many images, and more recently to short, highly impactful video clips that circulate on social media. When our class was working on these texts (see the end of Chapter 4 above), we found that Gemini suggested a dramatic dialogue for a 12-year-old receiver. Student groups can come up with similar transformations, at least on the level of drafting the script for a video clip.

A further activity of this kind is to have each group select a poem in their L2 and translate it into L1 as an audiovisual presentation or similar performance, and to do all that in 90 minutes (leaving time for each group to show its work at the end of the class). Over the years, we have had poems become video clips with music, songs, animated cartoons, a box full of words, and, in one case, a kite. Students' creativity is incredible! And it can now be augmented with suggestions and images from generative AI.

Adapt a machine translation of a song so that it can be sung

Learning outcome: Use technology to augment creativity.
Learning outcome: Explore the limits of language automation.

All students have their favorite music artists and songs. Ask them to select an L2 song they like, have it machine translated into L1, then they try to sing it. When that does not work very well, they should rearrange the words so that the rhythms and rhymes are in the right places. At the end of the session, each group should sing their translation to the class.

An extension is to ask generative AI to make the text singable, then compare the output with the unaided version.

Translate and adapt a website

Learning outcome: Use technology to augment creativity.
Learning outcome: Adjust translations to clients' and users' needs.

Students can use a translation-memory suite to translate a website that is close to them – perhaps their town or city, or their favorite sport team. Part of the work should be to decide what the foreign visitor is looking for: which contents should be foregrounded, which need not be translated, and which images might need to be replaced.

Generative AI can be used in this process to give ideas about what adaptations might be applied, although more might be learned by looking at parallel websites. For instance, if the purpose is to present a city of 100,000 inhabitants to prospective L2 tourists, students might check to see how similar cities are presented in the L2 cultures.

A variant of this activity is to use AI to produce an "easy read" version of the website, which can then be post-edited.

Try literary translation

A hundred theorists assure us that automation cannot help literary translation because it misses emotions, cultural awareness, sensitivity, wordplays, and probably another mention of emotions just for good measure. The conventional wisdom deserves to be tested.

Use technologies for literary translation

Learning outcome: Assess critically the advantages and risks of automated translation.
Learning outcome: Explore the limits of language automation.

Once the basic comparative activities indicate that post-editing can sometimes be advantageous in terms of both time and quality, we ask students if they will use the technologies in all future translations. A frequent answer is yes, but never for literature (Hao et al., 2024). In the minds of many, the literary still retains an aura of artistry and transcendence. In short, it is non-technology.

The obvious activity here is to have students use technologies to translate literary texts. Start with unrhymed verse in L2 (something like Whitman), where the technologies perform well. The L2 text is then translated into L1 with and without technologies. The outputs of machine translation, generative AI, and unaided translators can then be compared within the group. The rest of the class tries to guess which translation was done using which technology – another Turing test.

There is no need to rig the results entirely. We have experimented in class with Dylan Thomas's *Under Milk Wood*, where long sentences and neologisms were once a major challenge to foreign readers as well as to translation technologies:

It is spring, moonless night in the small town, starless and bible-black, the cobblestreets silent and the hunched, courters'-and-rabbits' wood limping invisible down to the sloeblack, slow, black, crowblack, fishingboatbobbing sea. The houses are blind as moles (though moles see fine to-night in the snouting, velvet dingles) or blind as Captain Cat there in the muffled middle by the pump and the town clock, the shops in mourning, the Welfare Hall in widows' weeds. And all the people of the lulled and dumbfound town are sleeping now.

Try the passage now with DeepL or any generative AI – you will probably be surprised. Not only is the syntax coherent, but calques are allowed and the neologisms are tackled, admittedly not always successfully. Post-editing can always bring improvements and the translations might not always pass the Turing test, but the exercise should unblock some students' appreciation of what can seem a wholly opaque L2 text. In fact, it often brings out connections they did not see at first.

A variant is to choose a classical text like a speech from *Hamlet* or the first verses of Dante's *Inferno*. In some cases, automation gives a translation that not only scans but also rhymes. Challenge the students to discover why. They should find that the database includes previous human translations – as we found in the case of Dante in Chapter 1. As students locate those previous translations, they discover why databases are important and why machines are not just mechanical.

The viability of literary post-editing is increasingly being explored (e.g., Guerberof Arenas & Toral, 2022). Experiments with it should not only challenge negative presuppositions but can also bring out the political virtues of having dissident literatures translated immediately, post-edited, re-post-edited, and commented on by kindred spirits across the globe, who may or may not have advanced language skills. The de-institutionalization of literary expression could be a virtue, at least as an ongoing exercise in cross-cultural free speech.

Test reader responses for literary translation

Learning outcome: Assess critically the advantages and risks of automated translation.
Learning outcome: Explore the limits of automated translation.

From the previous activity, each student group should have access to an L2 literary text and (1) an L1 raw machine translation or AI version of it, (2) a post-edited version, and (3) an unaided ("fully human") version.

Those three texts can be evaluated for the relative pleasure they give readers in the other groups in the class. Ask students to go through the written texts (without having seen the L2 start text) and mark in green the passages (phrases or sentences) that they like and in red the ones they don't like (cf. Pym & Hu, forthcoming). It is important that this be done *without* reference to the L2 start text and without indicating how the texts were produced, since the aim is to assess reading enjoyment.

Where you go from there really depends on the size of the class. In a small class of two or three groups, students can look at the color patterns and guess how each text was produced, then discuss the passages that were strongly liked and strongly disliked. One usually finds that the unaided translation does not win on all points – some automation errors can be enjoyably creative, and not all post-editing kills the joys of the literary text.

In a larger class, it is rarely possible to go through different translations sentence by sentence. It might be enough to reveal the way the texts were produced and to then ask each group if they guessed the origins correctly. If not, why not?

Gain work experience

Real or simulated work experience is widely recognized as being beneficial in many forms of education, in both modern languages and translator training. Here we suggest a few ways this general practice can interact with translation technologies.

Explain translation technologies to clients

Learning outcome: Communicate effectively with clients.
Learning outcome: Make spoken presentations.

It is not enough to use technologies; we must also sometimes explain technologies to our clients, who ultimately must trust us. This is an activity on translator-client relations, which can be done in a multilingual classroom (cf. Pym, 2019, pp. 334–336). We allocate two or three weeks to it every year.

The groups become translation companies, with students having different roles (translators, revisers, terminologists, project managers, presentation designers). Half the groups have to compete to win a translation contract; the other half compete for a different contract. The contracts might concern the promotion of a film from Culture A into Culture B, the promotion of a sport, the opening of new branches of a restaurant chain, and so on (let each group pick its film, sport, or restaurant chain).

Each group prepares a ten-minute presentation of its company, including sample translations on a website or audiovisual material. The presentation must also explain how the company uses technologies to improve their work – presumably their ability to work with technologies will be a point of prestige. The main aim must be to make the technology understandable, trustworthy, and potentially profitable for the client.

The first week, half the companies do their presentations (for instance, Australian films to be promoted in China) and the other companies act as clients, asking questions following the pitches, evaluating the proposals, and awarding the contract to the winner. The next week, the roles are reversed (e.g., extending Chinese restaurant chains to Australia).

The awarding of prizes may not suit all student cultures, but the students tend to learn the most when they are in the position of the client companies and have to assess the pitches. Further comments on the evaluation of this activity can be found at the end of the next chapter.

The need for communication skills for interacting with clients is widely recognized in the industry. We should nevertheless not give the impression that it is easy or even productive for novice translators to start telling their employers which technologies they should be using – some preferences and opinions are more suited to a casual dialogue.

Internships with companies

Learning outcome: Communicate effectively with clients.
Learning outcome: Adjust translations to clients' and users' needs.
Learning outcome: Plan and manage time.
Learning outcome: Work efficiently in teams.

There can be no question that any postgraduate program that purports to train professionals should incorporate the possibility of students spending some significant amount of time in a real work environment. This holds for both translator training and language degrees. There are many names for the thing: internships, work placements, secondments, and so on – our use of "internship" here is not a strong commitment.

Internships are notoriously difficult to set up. They can also be fraught with ethical problems, including exploitation of student labor and, inversely, students who find that they do not like the profession and underperform or abruptly leave.

With specific reference to translation technologies, the advantages may nevertheless be considerable. Students will usually get to use the one translation-memory suite and the one workflow over and over and in cooperation with others, becoming used to the technology in a way that is often difficult to approach in class. Often, too, they will have to pick up a completely new technology, which is a skill that they have hopefully been prepared in. And they will ideally have opportunities to discuss technologies with employers, perhaps suggesting alternatives.

An interesting variation on the traditional internship is to have students carry out small research projects for the company. This is obviously of most interest to postgraduate programs that contain a research component. For example, the company might ask what the benefits and drawbacks might be of using a new machine-translation or AI feed, of incorporating automatic post-editing, of using L2 translation, and so on. Students can set up small comparative projects in their languages, using actual texts translated by the company. The students then see the benefits of research and the company receives information that will hopefully be of practical use to them. (This idea comes to us from the training program in Forlì, Italy, reported to us in very positive terms by one of the companies they work with.)

Write essays

As old-fashioned as they might appear, essays still have some virtues in the field of translation technologies. If the learning outcomes include anything like the ability to think critically, to evaluate technology, or to develop a career strategy, then writing essays can help students move toward those goals – many learning outcomes can be addressed at once. We want students to think, not just to press the right buttons.

True, the advent of generative AI makes originality difficult to assess, providing a reason for not writing essays. AI dependency is sometimes not hard to pick up (a paragraph of errors followed by a paragraph of impeccable language, or the "for and against" structures typical of AI responses), but it is hard to prove (AI detectors give false positives, at least at the time of writing). There are a few basic ways of getting around that: set topics that concern the student's personal experience; ask them to keep successive drafts of their work; organize an interactive spoken presentation of the essay, for example.

Find out about the bad things

Learning outcome: Locate reliable information quickly.
Learning outcome: Evaluate different sources of information critically.
Learning outcome: Formulate balanced arguments.
Learning outcome: Assess critically the differences between technologies.
Learning outcome: Assess critically the advantages and risks of automated translation.
Learning outcome: Apply ethical criteria to the use of technologies.
Optional learning outcome: Use automation tools to self-evaluate writing skills.

Public discussions of generative AI often list negative effects that can include job destruction, declining rates of pay for translators, data theft, large carbon footprints, and much more (see, for example, Bender et al., 2021). Some of these predictions cannot really be checked in any quantitative way: loss of valuable human skills, for example, will come with time, if at all. But others can, especially by enthusiastic students who are very good at searching the web and, hopefully, making intelligent critical use of the answers given by AI. Get students to work in groups to find *evidence* of the bad things, with each group investigating an issue, as investigative reporters would do. Spoken reports are then given to the whole class.

One area in which this can be very useful is the gathering of information on rates of pay. In a previous age, there were accessible lists of discounts for the use of translation memory software, where it was clear to all how the technology was affecting rates of pay. What happens now when automation is used in translations in a more general way? What kinds of pay scales are applied?

Gifted students will locate some numbers on websites and social media. One very clever student phoned a few translation companies while in class, with the speaker on for all to hear. Students will also come across a few discussion groups among translators, usually lamenting business practices. It is important that the lamentation be compared with actual numbers on rates of pay, and that the ensuing discussion should bring in not just the technicalities of pay by the word or by the hour but also ethical issues concerning what is fair and what might be the special risks of unrevised automation. Although such discussions form a necessary part of any technology course, they should not reduce students to a state of despair. The aim should instead be to recognize real-world problems and to discuss possible solutions, including the redesign of technologies.

Write from personal experience of a translation project

Learning outcome: Formulate balanced arguments.
Learning outcome: Assess critically the differences between technologies.
Learning outcome: Assess critically the advantages and risks of automated translation.
Learning outcome: Apply ethical criteria to the use of technologies.

An increasingly common reason for not asking students to write essays is that they can draw on generative AI very easily. Unless the teacher really wants to go back to pen, paper, and invigilation, a solution to this problem lies in giving essay topics that refer to the student's personal experience of a translation or a translation project. One of the requirements should be that they recount three or four examples from their own translation work. Another requirement could call for an account of the student's emotional engagement – how they felt about the technologies, for example. Generative AI can still be drawn on for general ideas, and indeed for generic comments on translation examples, but the requirement to work in the first person, with reference to experience, interactions, and emotional involvement, should ensure that the student's own voice comes through.

An obvious kind of essay assignment is to invite students to discuss the advantages and disadvantages of different workflows: translating with a translation-memory suite (mostly with machine translation feeds integrated), machine translation plus post-editing, generating subtitles with a translation memory and audiovisual tools, and unaided translation. The discussions can focus on criteria suggested in usability studies or studies of translator-computer interaction. The following are the criteria we proposed when giving instructions for an essay assignment:

Criterion	Description
Speed	Time-on-task
Quality	Quality of raw output; quality expectations
User interface	Intuitiveness; visual hierarchy
Compatibility	Supported file types
Cognitive ergonomics	Learning curves; cognitive frictions
Interactivity	Interactive post-editing modality
Confidentiality	Data breaches
Ethics	Copyright and data ownership
Other social factors	Impacts on language learning and multilingual societies

Comparative analysis here requires a firm understanding of the criteria and can foster critical thinking about the use of translation technologies. Additionally, it requires students to draw on their personal interactions with the technology. The essay can thus demonstrate students' post-task assessment of their own performance, in addition to critical evaluations of the tool functions. This essay could be 1,000–2,000 words in length, to allow enough space for detailed descriptions of user experience and specific examples.

Write a love letter or a break-up letter to a technology

> Learning outcome: Formulate balanced arguments.
> Learning outcome: Assess critically the differences between technologies.
> Learning outcome: Assess critically the advantages and risks of automated translation.

Following one of the comparative activities listed above, students can be invited to write a love letter to a technology they like or a break-up letter to one that they are leaving. This activity has been used in marketing to study consumer sentiment. It has also been used in research to see how different kinds of students (and professional translators) adjust to new technologies (Koskinen & Ruokonen, 2017; Ruokonen & Koskinen, 2017; Hao, 2023). For the students, it is a fun activity that obliges them to think critically about the technology at the same time as they implicitly reflect on their own efficacy.

We do this in class following the activity where students have to pick up a new translation-memory suite in two hours.[1] Our instructions look like the following:

> Write a 100-word letter in your L2 to one of the translation-memory systems you have used when translating scenarios. Imagine that you are writing to a "person" you admire (a love letter) or to a person you wish never to see again (a break-up letter). The letter should address the following questions:
>   If it is a *love letter*:
>
> — What is the most helpful tool for your translation work?
> — What makes you enjoy using it? Which specific aspects of it could you not live without?
>
>   If it is a *break-up letter:*
>
> — Which tool do you wish you will never have to use again?
> — What frustrates you when using it? Which specific parts of it do you wish you could get rid of?

We then give a few fairly humous examples that can be discussed in small groups. The students write their short letters in their L1 or L2, using whatever online resources they like. Here is an example of a break-up letter from 2021, unfortunately prior to generative AI:

> Dear Smartcat,
>
> I must admit that you are a lovely translation program. Your interface design is perfect, and you are in my favorite color, purple. You helped me not only with my translation tasks but also with editing and polishing. But I think we'd better break up because I've never seen such literal and awkward translations. The sentences you translate are a mess. It took me a lot of time doing post-editing to make them read smoothly. What a waste of my short life!
>   Goodbye. I'll throw myself into Matecat's arms. I need more efficient software.

A love letter might look like this:

> Dear CafeTran Espresso:
>
> I used to be an opponent of machine translation, as I thought it was worthless and not accurate enough. My opinions changed after meeting you.
>   Your interface is simple and clear. It was love at first sight. You are a practical program that is easy to operate. This is especially important for me as a

novice in technology. Your machine translation database is very diverse and can provide reasonable and accurate translations, which saved me a lot of time and greatly improved my efficiency. But what surprised me the most was that I could reuse my own translation memories in your system. [...] I feel empowered by your assistance. Besides, you did not cost me any money at all.

You are a simple and practical system that suits me very well. I hope you can be my main assistant in the future.

And then we have letters that mix emotions:

CafeTran Espresso, I am fascinated by your clean interface, and you are easy to use. It is simple and natural that we get along. Not to mention that my work efficiency has been greatly improved. Sometimes you have some small problems, such as turning my Chinese characters into blocks, but no one is perfect. Who is perfect?

Selected students then read their letters to the whole class. At the end, there is no right or wrong. The one technology can be loved by some and hated by others, since the emotional criteria are unavoidably subjective.

Note

1 For the corresponding research report, ethics clearance was received from the Human Research Ethics Committees, Faculty of Arts, University of Melbourne (Ethics Authorization Number 1954388.1).

6

WHO ASSESSES WHAT?

This chapter addresses the assessment of students' achievements during and at the end of a technology course. Technology is peculiar in this regard in that it often gives its own evaluations quite quickly: failure is when the student gets stuck; success is when they don't. A more productive sense of assessment nevertheless concerns a broad range of transversal skills, including self-learning, teamwork, and the critical use of technology to augment creativity.

Here we present some different types of evaluation that are implemented by human and non-human agents. We also discuss whether certain types of learning outcomes are best assessed in certain ways. This includes automatic evaluation methods that give real-time feedback and handle routine error-correction, making learning more independent and the life of teachers much easier. We look at students' individual reflections on software usage, peer assessment, teacher assessment, and external benchmarking assessment. The chapter closes with a list of suggested assessment methods.

We begin with a few general principles.

Align assessments with intended outcomes

As we have seen, learning outcomes primarily serve as a guide to the selection of curriculum elements including tasks and activities (Nunan, 1988; Kelly, 2005). Assessments that measure the attainment of these outcomes should inherently be aligned with the intended goals. To enable alignment, outcomes should be written as *observable* and *assessable* statements so as to help define the types of learning that occur over time and at the conclusion. Learning outcomes can be useful, not only to set the bottom line for a student to pass a module but also, beyond that basic threshold, to guide the

DOI: 10.4324/9781032648033-6

selection of evaluation methods (self, peer, teacher assessment, and so forth) and the criteria on which learning is evaluated. Some education researchers (e.g., Biggs, 2003) assert that assessment, usually seen as the endpoint of the teaching-learning loop, can actually be the starting point for students. This is because students' understanding of what is expected from a translation or language course can be derived from assessments – students are probably more likely to look at what they have to do to pass a course than at the list of learning outcomes. Assessable learning outcomes also provide teachers with a sharp focus on the specific aspects of learning to be evaluated, and the results can indicate the teaching interventions required to help students progress toward the intended goals.

Evaluate progress or final level?

A classical issue in all pedagogical evaluation is whether we reward how much a student has progressed or how well they perform at the end of the course or program. In technical terms, evaluations can be either formative or summative. Formative assessments are diagnostic and help give on-going on feedback on the student's current level of performance: how much they have achieved and how far they have to go to reach a specific learning outcome. This can include the extent to which teachers and students should make additional efforts, and what kinds of efforts are required. Summative assessments, in contrast, are carried out at the end of a course or program: they are used to sum up the student's achievements in terms of the required learning outcomes. Ideally, summative and formative evaluations should be closely aligned, and both should be linked to learning outcomes.

As a basic rule of thumb, formative assessments make sense during the learning process, while summative assessments can be seen as signals of achievement that are being sent to future employers.

Technology itself will tell

As mentioned, technology itself often provides instant feedback to users with respect to their mastery of the procedural ("how-to") knowledge required to interact with it. It is a matter of "can" or "cannot". The most explicit form of feedback comes as pop-up messages, notifications, or any interface change that informs the user that the system is not happy. For example, when subtitles appear not as Chinese characters but as a line of question marks, it signals that something has gone wrong with the text encoding. Or again, a web-based translation-memory suite might complain: "Sorry this browser is not currently supported" or "Unable to open MXLIFF file," and much else. These can be seen as basic forms of automatic assessment.

Feedback can be less explicit in other cases. Novice students might be unaware that their translations have not been recorded in a database as they translate, but they certainly find out when they work on a new text and are unable to call up their private translation memory. In that case, the technology indicates that something has gone wrong and that the student has to activate some kind of self-evaluation mechanism to solve the problem. For instance, the student will hopefully find out that ticking a square box before moving to the next segment stores the translations in the database. If not, they are likely to be blocked, unable to move to subsequent tasks. Technology gives an assessment but does not always point to the solutions. Peers and teachers can still help.

Automatic methods for labor-intensive evaluations

There is consensus that timely feedback should be delivered to students on a regular basis. Educational psychologists such as Slavin (2020) also indicate that regular and frequent evaluation should be given to students before the learning experience fades away. Moreover, feedback on students' performance is important for teachers, perhaps even more so than for students, because it indicates whether students are keeping up with the pace of instruction and can point to the kind of additional support needed to get some students back on track. That ideal, however, is very difficult to attain when a single teacher tries to grade 60 to 80 300-word translations and provide qualitative feedback every week. The attempt is noble but can only lead to burnout, as happens far too frequently. Automatic correction that gives instant feedback can be one way out.

Computer-aided language testing has emerged as a solution in language learning. A body of studies has examined the impact of corrective feedback on students' L2 writing, particularly the kind of feedback generated by automatic writing evaluation systems such as Criterion or Grammarly (e.g., Bai & Hu, 2017; Hoang, 2022; Barrot, 2023a). For instance, feedback from Criterion has been found to have positive short-term effects for grammatical errors, including subject-verb agreement, missing articles, run-on sentences, and mechanical errors such as spelling, missing or extra commas (Saricaoglu & Bilki, 2021). The automatic feedback provided by these systems can be either direct or indirect. Direct corrections indicate what has to be done (e.g., "You may need to use a comma after this word"), while indirect corrections signal that something is wrong and should be repaired (e.g., "The word is not spelled correctly. Use a dictionary or spellchecker when you proofread your work"), perhaps along with metalinguistic explanations ("The subject and the verb in this sentence may not agree. Reread the sentence and look closely at the subject and the verb"). Indirect written corrections, on the other hand, may initiate a more in-depth processing of feedback: the student does not simply receive input from the system passively but is led to reflect on gaps in their existing linguistic knowledge (Kim & Bowles, 2019). In addition, students' relative language proficiency can also affect the depth of processing and corrections of different types of errors. It has been found that advanced students attend to both form and content in their revisions, while their lower-intermediate counterparts tend to make surface-level changes within the sentence level (Zhang, 2021).

Some researchers have also observed *negative* reactions to automatic corrective feedback. Complaints include the lack of a human touch and the over-correction of errors. This means the system should allow teachers to filter the types of errors that merit the immediate attention of students in relation to the intended learning outcomes (Barrot, 2023a). Sometimes students with limited prior metalinguistic knowledge also find automatic feedback incomprehensible (Ranalli, 2018). However, the benefits should not be overlooked. Automatic feedback can increase efficiency by lightening the teacher's workload and helping to cultivate independent self-monitoring among students (Krusche & Seitz, 2018).

Mention might also be made here of Duolingo, a free platform that gamifies language learning. The system makes extensive use of automatic correction exercises to provide instant feedback for self-paced learning. It is worth noting that translation activities play a major role in Duolingo, albeit mostly at the sentence level, as in the days of grammar translation methods (see Chapter 4 above). For instance, in an L2 translation exercise, learners are given a sentence in their L1 and then some jumbled words in L2 to choose from to make the translation. The instant feedback tells the learner whether the answer is correct. The form-focused nature of this automatic evaluation can nevertheless sometimes give the learner a few headaches (Munday, 2016). The assessment requires the translation to be specific, that is, it marks any correct alternative other than the "standard" answer as wrong, particularly for renditions into languages other than English. This partly explains why automatic evaluation is largely overlooked in the teaching of translation: translation decisions are rarely binary like an off-and-on light switch.

More recently, there has been some discussion of the infeasibility of using automatic writing evaluation systems to assess translation quality in a slightly wider sense (Han & Lu, 2023). The tools of interest are similar to the quality-control tools regularly included in translation memory suites: they have little problem detecting grammar and typological errors, punctuation problems, missing formatting, and so on. On the other hand, they are not engineered to evaluate intertextual properties such as meaning transfer. Learners can nevertheless benefit from automatic checks on stylistic issues, whereas human correction of this kind of error is often laborious and can lead to burnout among teachers. Teachers can then concentrate their efforts on the more complex problems that tend not to be machine-detectable, such as those related to meaning and register.

A handful of studies have explored the use of automatic evaluation metrics such as BLEU and METEOR to assess the quality of student translations or transcribed interpreting performances (Chung, 2020; Lu & Han, 2021; Han & Lu, 2023). These metrics have long been used to measure how similar a machine-generated translation is to a reference human translation, with a value close to 1 representing high similar and potentially a high-quality text. For instance, Chung (2020) ran 120 German-to-Korean translations through BLEU and METEOR and compared automatic and human evaluations of the same translations. The results show a strong general metric-human correlation (r = 0.849 for BLEU when compared with human evaluation; and r = 0.862 for METEOR) but relatively low correlations on the individual text level (28%–40% of the correlation coefficients being below 0.3). That is, there may be a strong correlation across a wide range of translation performances, but the automatic metrics remain questionable for one-off single-sentence translations and certainly cannot check for appropriateness to social and ethical factors. This difference is not surprising. While there are clear advantages to automatic programs, the appropriateness of using such tools depends on whether we are interested in global-level quality or a fine-grained apperception of sentence-level appropriateness. Automatic evaluation metrics could potentially be used to validate the results of human evaluations in external benchmark examinations (especially when two or more examiners disagree with one another), but their pedagogical virtues, particularly in relation to formative feedback, nevertheless remain limited.

As for generative AI, we note that many universities have banned its use for assessment and feedback, due to ethical and privacy concerns. A growing number of L2 writing researchers have nevertheless explored the use of ChatGPT in simple and complex tasks including topic selection, outlining, drafting, and self-editing (Su et al., 2023; Barrot, 2023b). ChatGPT can automatically grade students' writing compositions based on predefined evaluation rubrics. It can also provide timely qualitative feedback to support the numerical scores. It tends to adopt an encouraging tone for feedback, with justifications of why a certain change could be made to improve the text. The feedback addresses both form (stylistics) and content (relevance and richness of content, focus, overall organization, consistency, and clarity of arguments). This is useful when assessing the quality of writing. If GPT assessment cannot (yet) be incorporated into teacher feedback, it may still be useful for student self-editing, although its powerful and human-like writing capacities have raised concerns about learning loss and academic integrity (Rudolph et al., 2023; van Dis et al., 2023). This might also be said of any emerging technology. Students can benefit from ChatGPT for form and style, while teachers can at the same time encourage students to develop their own written voice and discursive identity.

More explorations are needed to identify how generative AI can assist with students' self-editing of writing compositions and self-revision of their translations.

Self-assessment meets student heterogeneity

Self-assessment refers to a range of mechanisms and techniques through which students themselves describe, evaluate, and possibly assign value to their learning processes, products, and academic abilities (Epstein et al., 2008; Brown & Harries, 2014; Panadero et al., 2016). Students use meta-cognitive skills to monitor their actions, evaluate the effects, and potentially use these observations to generate feedback for adjustment and correction. To the extent that self-generated feedback can help a student measure their progress, it is particularly valuable in heterogeneous learning groups where students start at very different levels. For example, self-assessing one's ability to master a piece of software can be useful because it helps each student decide how to proceed based on their current proficiency level. This can help determine how much time should be invested in familiarizing oneself with a system, and whether to seek assistance from peers, teachers, or other kinds of self-paced resources.

Self-assessment should be formative in nature (Andrade, 2019). It tends not to be used alone to measure outcomes, given its inherent subjectivity and bias. For instance, in a "guess your grade" task, students' summative assessments were found to be higher than the grades assigned by the teachers, especially in less-advanced groups (Tejeiro, 2012). On the other hand, self-assessments when students are assigned a specific learning-oriented purpose (rather than "passing the test") are found to be more likely to concord with those carried out by externals (Bol et al., 2012; Chang et al., 2013).

Peer assessment: beyond the teacher's gaze

Peer assessment is when students interrogate, evaluate, and assign value to the products and processes of fellow students of similar status (Topping, 1998). The theoretical underpinning has its roots in social constructivism. In a constructivist view of learning, knowledge is not sent from distributors (teachers) straight into students' heads but is instead constructed jointly and collaboratively through interaction. Vygotsky coined the term "cognitive apprenticeship" as part of what happens in the zone of proximal development, where interaction is both with peers and with teachers (Harpaz & Lefstein, 2000). Peer assessment can thus be a form of apprenticeship that engages less advanced students to get help from the more advanced ones through feedback and explanations.

Peer assessment need not always assume a hierarchy among students. Learning can also happen by assessing someone else's learning. During this process, both sides review and diagnose misconceived knowledge, identify knowledge gaps, and engineer the mitigation of these gaps through feedback. These cognitively demanding tasks enable students to reinforce and consolidate knowledge. The process can be coupled with a growing sense of autonomy because students take on responsibility for regulating the learning of others as well as their own learning. In addition, assessing peers can develop a range of social courtesy and assertion skills that are greatly valued, such as the ability to give constructive criticism and justify, negotiate, accept, or reject suggestions in a polite and unaggressive manner.

In the technology classroom, peer assessment is a convenient way to evaluate translation quality, especially when multiple languages are being worked on (and the teacher may not know all of them). Students from the same language stream (at least two students) can evaluate the quality of each other's translations (Pym, 2019). Student reviewers should be asked to make traceable modifications (using Track Changes) that serve as a basis for discussion, although any in-depth discussion of quality should be left to language-pair-specific translation classes.

Peer assessment can also complement teacher evaluation in a groupwork setting. Teacher assessment often concentrates on a final presentation that is assumed to reflect the collective effort of the group. This is because the teacher generally cannot see the time and energy that each student invests in the process. One way to approach that information is to invite students within a group to assess one another (intra-group assessment) (Meijer et al., 2020). In parallel, inter-group assessment is more product-oriented and involves evaluating the oral or written presentations of others, taking a step back from one's own, which also neatly aligns with collaborative learning.

Teacher assessment has its role to play

While self-assessment encourages reflection, and assessment by peers can foster autonomous and social learning, assessment from a teacher can provide diagnostic results of students' growth in language proficiency and technological literacy. Assessment can be of how well students comprehend and produce language (language proficiency), how well they grasp the principles of the technologies and the ethical issues involved (knowledge), and how well they use the tools and perform pre-editing or post-editing (technology skills). These areas may not overlap: strong language skills do not mean the student will have strong technology skills.

Teachers' comments on students' post-edited texts should help ensure the depth of editing is consistent with what is expected. For example, students should not work too hard when basic intelligibility is required and light post-editing would suffice, and they should not under-edit if the aim is to generate polished, publication-ready translations.

That said, over-working is also a bane for teachers. Teacher feedback can manifest in various forms beyond simply giving the "right answer" (direct feedback). For instance, feedback can be indirect, taking forms of underlining or circling errors or through a set of codes indicating the nature of the erroneous parts in the L2 writing. Although direct feedback is more explicit, immediate, and can reduce confusion about error types (Bitchener & Knoch, 2010), we have seen that some researchers consider *indirect* feedback more helpful. They argue that indirect feedback can transform the passive recipient of teacher feedback into a self-editor who draws on their linguistic knowledge to rectify L2 errors on their own (Ferris & Roberts, 2001; Hartshorn et al., 2010). Indirect feedback may also trigger in-depth cognitive processing (Kim & Bowles, 2019), which thereby contributes to L2 development, e.g., accurate prior knowledge is reinforced while inaccurate knowledge is restructured immediately or checked at later stages.

An increase in teacher feedback does not necessarily lead to an improvement in learning outcomes. Learning happens when students respond to the feedback and process it sufficiently. Feedback on students' writing should refrain from making substantial changes to lexical items and syntactic structures unless they are wholly incorrect (i.e., avoid the "my way is the only right way" mindset). On the other hand, indirect feedback that does not provide a specific correction allows room for multiple possible revisions (Tabari et al., 2023) and can therefore encourage the creative use of language in writing and translation activities.

Seek external certification

Standardized assessments such as certification tests can serve as benchmarks for competencies in a specific area, complementing continuous and customized classroom feedback from teachers, peers, and oneself. They are often carried out externally and involve consistent content and format as well as standardized procedures for the administration of the tests and the scoring and interpretation of the results. This contributes to the validity and reliability of scores. The standardized measure also allows comparison of performance across different groups.

The certification exams for translators in different parts of the world do *not* include skills in the use of technology. These include the American Translators Association certification exam, the China Accreditation Test for Translators and Interpreters, and the exams of the Australian National Accreditation Authority for Translators and Interpreters (NAATI). Their websites indicate that the certification exams for translators mostly involve rendering two to three passages, with access only to dictionaries and reference books.

An apparent exception might be sought in the NAATI accreditation exam for certified translators (NAATI, 2019) which includes a translation revision test. There is, however, no explicit statement that the activity is a test of post-editing skills. Candidates are given a translation in which they are instructed to identify and correct errors that are semantic (meaning transfer) and stylistic (form of the target language) and not to make changes based on personal preferences. They are further required to categorize the errors by selecting from the following types: distortion, omission, insertion of meaning, errors related to register, unidiomatic usage, and error of grammar, spelling, and punctuation.

The problem with this kind of evaluation is that it is testing use of a metalanguage that may have little to do with the actual skills of translating. For example, in the sample test for Spanish, we find the following sentence, to which we have added our own revision:

ST: Siendo nuestro proyecto ya una realidad nacional, hoy transitamos…
TT (unrevised): *Being our project now a national reality*, we have reached the stage of… (Italics ours)
TT (revised): Now that our mission has achieved success at the national level, we are expanding into…

Much as we believe our revised version corrects a clear syntactic calque and turns lead into gold, which of the error categories would apply to this correction? The unrevised calque could be an unidiomatic usage, an error of grammar, and at some level a distortion of meaning. We have little empirical evidence that the ability to use the metalanguage improves the quality of the resulting translation. And then there are four or five ways to reformulate the defective syntax: should we have perhaps kept closer to the Spanish by saying something like *Now that our project has been realized nationally*…?

In a Chinese version of the revision test, the initial translation contains the incorrect collocation 使土壤充气 (inflate the soil). Again, it is hard to place the infelicity into just one category. The unidiomatic usage of the verb could perhaps be distortion, insertion of meaning, or unidiomatic usage. And then, replacing 充气 (inflate) with 透气 (aerate) is not the only way to improve the translation: an alternative could involve a change of perspective with something like "increasing water holding capacity", giving 增加土壤透气性 (increase aeration):

ST: Physically, they change the soil by aerating it and increasing water holding capacity…
TT (unrevised): 在物理上，蚯蚓通过使土壤充气和增加持水来改变土壤… [Physically, earthworms *inflate* the soil and increase its water holding capacity to change it…]

TT (revised): 在物理上，蚯蚓通过使土壤透气和增加持水来改变土壤…
[Physically, earthworms *aerate* the soil and increase its water holding capacity to change it…]

Further doubts in the test caught our attention. For instance, the name *Charles Darwin* is transliterated as 达尔文 (*Darwin*, with his given name omitted). Should the reviser put in the whole name, to avoid unjustified omission? Should they add the name in Latin script, as is often done? Should a short explicitation be added? Does failure to do any or all of those things count as a revision error? At the moment, we can only guess.

To pass this test, the candidate has to study carefully the way the abstract categories are described and then somehow gauge the level of literalism that will demonstrate the text has been understood and no liberties have been taken (since the candidate is penalized for "personal preferences"). In such cases, passing the test is not so much a matter of knowing how to translate but of learning to think like the people who set the test.

External certification of the capacity to use a technology tends to be provided by the software developers, often in combination with a self-paced online training program. Trados, long the market leader, has developed various certification programs: in the use of Trados Studio (three levels), in project management with Trados Team, and in post-editing machine translation. The programs created by a sole software developer usually focus on proprietary tool functions rather than practices that can be applied universally across the industry. There might also be issues with the rigor and recognition of the certification, as it is not been developed by independent industry or educational bodies. Additionally, all certifications are paid for: a bundle of the three-level Trados Studio exams currently costs $140, with the entry-level training course for software operation alone costing an additional $290, although training for the post-editing certification is free of charge. There might also be a commercial focus on promoting the software.

Postgraduate programs in translator training could easily issue this kind of certification themselves. Given the binary nature of a large part of technology use (you can, or you can't), it is not difficult to set up and evaluate tests, and specific mention of the ability to use particular technologies should send the required signal to prospective employers. There is no clear reason why software developers should be the only ones involved in the certification of these specific skills.

Suggested assessments

Here we look at the ways a few assessment procedures can work, starting from the basic principle that they must evaluate the achievement of clear learning outcomes. The ideas presented here are based on what we have been doing in our translation-technology classrooms. Teachers of translation may find them readily applicable, although some ideas will require adaptation for language teaching and learning.

Technology as the evaluator: the use of automation tools

Test on subtitling with translation memory software

> Learning outcome: Post-edit translations efficiently.
> Learning outcome: Create and transfer translation memories.
> Learning outcome: Produce effective translated subtitles.
> Learning outcome: Manage terminology.
> Assessment type: Summative in-class test.

At the conclusion of a translation technology module, an in-class test can be administered to assess attainment of certain learning outcomes. The test here consists of two sequential steps. In the first, students translate English subtitles from a video clip into a preferred language using a translation memory suite. They import the subtitles and create a private translation memory, which they update as they translate. They can either post-edit translation-memory suggestions and machine-translation feeds or translate from scratch, but they must build up a translation memory as they go. The students then export the translated subtitles and translation memories in TMX format (the size of the translation memory provides evidence that the translation memory suite has been used). The students finally proceed to *import* the translated subtitles into a subtitling tool. The focus of the second step is on video-subtitle synchronization (using compression when needed), adjusting fonts, and applying other conventions. The test should be completed with a tight deadline. While access to online resources might be allowed, there should be no scaffolding from the teacher or from more advanced peers.

In this test, the technology itself will say whether the main outcomes have been attained, especially if the deadline is demanding. Human evaluation is nevertheless required for the linguistic quality of students' work with respect to translation accuracy, timing and synchronization, adherence to subtitling guidelines (line breaks, word limit, duration), and overall viewing experience.

This test can be simplified to assess mastery of a single software tool at a time (all the above steps can be done in Matesub); alternatively, it can be made more challenging by incorporating terminology management (extract, align, and import terms into a translation-memory system) or defective subtitles (such as missing lines or corrupted time stamps).

Automatic evaluation: technology-related knowledge (knowing what)

Learning outcomes that involve recall and grasp of factual knowledge (*knowing what*), key concepts, and principles can be evaluated quickly through quizzes. We offer some ideas for a subtitling module.

Quiz on subtitling conventions

Learning outcome: Understand the principles of subtitling.

A short quiz can be administered right after an introduction to audiovisual translation, just before engaging in hands-on subtitling practice. Timely feedback from the quiz indicates whether the new information has been digested by the students. In addition to binary feedback (correct or incorrect), qualitative feedback on each incorrect response (as shown in brackets below) can potentially reinforce knowledge and clarify misconceptions. Short quizzes can be incorporated into other technology modules that address learning outcomes involving the understanding, use, and analysis of background knowledge or industry standards.

Question 1: What is subtitling?

a)   Written translation of dialogue exchanges and other verbal content, displayed on the screen.

b)   Spoken translation of dialogue exchanges and other audio content.
[Incorrect. This refers to dubbing, where new dialogue in the target language covers the original, syncing with lip movements, tone, and emotions of the actors.]

c)   Written descriptions of all sounds in a video, displayed on the screen.
[Incorrect. This refers to closed captioning, which provides text-based transcriptions of audio content to assist viewers who are deaf hard of hearing.]

Question 2: Which countries traditionally favor subtitling over dubbing?

a)   Countries with larger populations and widely spoken languages.
[Incorrect. Countries with large markets tend to use dubbing.]

b)   Countries with smaller markets and less widely spoken languages.

c)   Countries with high budgets for audiovisual translation.[Incorrect. Countries with high budgets can afford dubbing for foreign content.]

Question 3: Which of the following is *not* the convention of subtitling into English?

---

a) Two lines, each with a maximum of 35 characters.
b) If a sentence is finished, do not use a full stop.
    [Correct. This applies to subtitling in Chinese.]
c) A dash at the start of each new speaker's utterance.

Question 4: What is the translation solution that is most used in subtitling?

a) Rewriting, improving the quality of what the actors say.
    [Incorrect. This is not the most common approach in subtitling.]
b) Explicitation, amplifying implied meaning.
    [This contradicts the common approach. Keep in mind that subtitling is bound by space and time.]
c) Compression, expressing meaning succinctly.

Self-evaluation: learning skills

A reflective report on technical difficulties

> Learning outcome: Learn to use new technology.
> Learning outcome: Locate reliable information quickly.
> Assessment: Formative assessment of a module.

When it comes to technology, it is precarious to assume a homogeneous student group. After the first few classes, incoming students can be invited to reflect on their learning experiences through a "sink-and-swim" approach. Each student should be encouraged to reflect on the technical difficulties they encounter as they start at different levels. For instance, technical issues can include initial setup failure (this applies to desktop software and web versions), file compatibility issues (with uncommon or outdated file types), formatting errors in file export (tags and codes), issues with plug-in insertions (such as machine translation feeds), personal memory setup or update, and data loss due to system crashes, just to name a few. The reflection can be kept open to elicit spontaneous responses. Alternatively, a short list of commonly occurring issues can be provided at the beginning, so that students know where to start.

Further, students should receive feedback on the ways each problem was tackled and resources they resorted to. For example, while some prefer the teacher to hold their hands when a problem occurs, others choose to discuss it in their group or explore support materials by themselves using keyword searches (step-by-step user guides or tutorial videos with video chapters help with self-learning). Students might also be invited to give recommendations for someone who is using that translation memory system for the first time. This hypothetical scenario prompts them to evaluate the impact of their problem-solving approaches.

Peer evaluation: translation management

Here we present an example where both intra- and inter-group assessments are used to foster students' engagement in an activity on translator-client relations. This is the activity mentioned in Chapter 5 as "Explain translation technology to clients," now with more details on the assessment aspects.

Part 1: Rate a team member's performance

Learning outcome: Select optimal translation workflows.
Learning outcome: Plan and manage time.
Learning outcome: Work efficiently in teams.
Assessment type: Intra-group peer assessment.

In a two-week simulated project, groups become translation companies that carry out a project and present them to client companies, competing for a fictitious contract. Following this activity, each student is invited to give an overall evaluation of the collaborative experience (what worked, and what didn't) and to assess the performance of a group member of their choice (project managers, translators, revisers, terminologists, presentation designers, and presenters). This peer assessment process should be mentioned when first presenting the activity, since it tends to head-off both the free-riders (group members who do little but benefit from the hard work of fellow students) and the enthusiastic students who always walk the extra mile. Students can be guided in this evaluation by a rubric that covers the key learning outcomes. Here is an example:

Criterion	Description
Role fulfillment	What role did they play? Did they successfully complete the tasks assigned to them?
On-time delivery	Did they manage to meet the deadlines given by the project manager? Did they ask for an extension or assistance in advance so as not to disrupt the overall workflow?
Effective communication	Did they clearly express themselves and justify their position in negotiations or confrontational situations?
Collegial support	Did they provide support and constructive feedback to others? Did they contribute to a sense of camaraderie within the group?

The learning outcomes should then determine the weight of each criterion. This evaluation may then be used in conjunction with the teacher's evaluation or simply as a source of additional information for the teacher.

Assessment of this kind ideally fosters awareness of roles and responsibilities, making students focus on how people team up to work toward a shared goal. There are, however, different cultural norms that can come into play. Spanish-speaking students tend to privilege solidarity, never saying anything negative about their fellow students; some Americans in our classes have been found to be more individualistic and more easily disposed to argue their own case at the expense of others. In a class that mixes L1 languages and cultures, those kinds of differences must sometimes be accounted for.

Part 2: Vote for winning groups

Learning outcome: Adjust translations to clients' and users' needs.
Learning outcome: Assess critically the advantages and risks of automated translation.
Learning outcome: Apply ethical criteria to the use of technologies.
Assessment type: Inter-group peer assessment.

The translation companies then give presentations in front of the whole class, while the non-presenting groups act as clients who can comment on the proposals (the company image, sample translation, other audiovisual materials) and ask questions in relation to technology usage or management. Each client group can be given a checklist to rate the presentations done by the presenting groups and vote for a winner. The criteria on this list should ideally align with the learning outcomes. Here is an example:

Criterion	Description
Spoken presentation	Professional and confident presentation of the proposal.
Choice of product	Fit-for-purpose selection of a film, sport, or food chain for localization.
Use of technology	Critical use of technology with justification of ethical issues.
Translation solutions	Clear explanation of translation solutions, with examples.
Organization of company	Efficient management of stakeholders, resources, deadlines, and risks.

During this process, intra-group assessment can help retain students' attention and enhance engagement with peers and peer-generated materials. The Q&A sessions following each presentation provide students with opportunities to learn to ask questions, articulate explanations, and perceive the importance of a good presentation. A platform like Poll Everywhere, which displays real-time changes in the voting procedure, can add an element of heart-racing excitement to the class.

In their feedback on this activity, some of the most valuable learning experiences are reported to be among the client companies, who have to assess their peers – they learn to see translation from the client's side. And that particular experience is not formally evaluated. There is more to learning than assessment.

7
HOW DO WE ANSWER STUDENTS' QUESTIONS ABOUT LANGUAGE TECHNOLOGIES?

As we have noted, needs analysis concerns more than future employment: teachers must also address the interests and concerns of their students. For some years, we have been inviting our new undergraduate and postgraduate students to write three questions they would like to see answered in our translation class (extending the questions reported in Pym & Torres-Simón, 2016).[1] They do this after an introductory lecture on the basics of translation, right at the beginning of the course. We use those questions as one element in our needs analysis, alongside what industry says, what the competence models suggest, and what our institutions want. Not surprisingly, the number of questions involving technology has grown steadily in recent years, expressing not just increasing interest in the technologies but also considerable anxiety about future trends and employment. So how should we answer those questions?

In any technical field surrounded by public discussion, it is easy to be misled by anecdotal examples. Students and teachers will come into the classroom with many preconceived notions of what is good and bad in new technologies, especially when translation is concerned. Those ideas will often have come from hearsay – from what public discourse says, filtered by peers and by those in authority, often by teachers – and they may vary in accordance with the student's motivation to find future work as a translator (Tian et al., 2023): the greater the motivation, the more the anxiety expressed in the questions. Many of those initial ideas deserve to be challenged and tested as part of the learning process. As we have seen in our list of activities, one important way to do this is through having students experiment with the technologies and then draw their own conclusions. However, another way to

DOI: 10.4324/9781032648033-7

challenge preconceptions, both before and after experiments, is to discuss the *ideas* involved, ideally by inviting in-class debates that challenge some of the more simplistic reductions.

In those general discussions, it should become very clear to students that they have to know about the technologies and how to use them, whether they like them or not. Why might they want to like them? Because technological change is probably their generational advantage in the job market. Faced with the eternal dilemma that all employers require experience, whereas recent graduates have very little experience, all students of language and translation should be prepared to emphasize their command of machine translation and generative AI, their ability to get the most out of the technologies, and their capacity to convince future clients (not just employers) that there is both good and bad to be discovered, beyond the hype. So why might the students *not* like the technologies? There are some legitimate reasons, and they should be addressed in open discussions.

Here we present some of the main questions that our students have asked, with notes on possible responses. We begin by biting the bullet – the big question that no one can really answer.

What will the future employment of translators be like?

This is a question that students ask with increasing frequency, in various forms. In Chapter 1, we addressed it in terms of exposure to automation; in Chapter 2, we looked at some survey data on job advertisements and the like. When discussing this with students, though, a rather less abstract approach may be required.

The uncertainty that the question assumes is probably a major cause for reported declines in student enrollments in translation programs. A reason for the uncertainty is not hard to find: when anyone looks at the rapidly improving quality of our machine translation systems and generative AI, the obvious question is whether we will all soon be out of a job: not only translators and interpreters, but also language teachers, along with project managers, accountants, and many more whose tasks are also being automated in one way or another.

Since we cannot see the future, we must first admit that we do not really know the answer to this question. But we do know that the answer is *not* to be found in platitudes like "machines will never think," "machines will never see contexts or emotions," and the like. Never is a very long time.

We suggest that the best way to approach such questions can only be empirical, looking at the various kinds of evidence at hand. This means breaking the general question down to some more precise issues that can attract some kind of reasoned answers.

Will automation remove the need for all translation skills?

What we know about automation in history (see the end of Chapter 1) suggests that jobs need not be destroyed, but the *nature* of some occupations will very probably change. The question should probably be rephrased as: "Will automation remove the need for all translation skills?" And there, some evidence can be found in surveys of graduate employment (Chapter 3), ideally concerning the graduates of the institution where the students are enrolled. Alternatively, students can be invited to check the employment outlooks found on sites like Government of Canada Job Bank or the Bureau of Labor Statistics of the United States Department of Labor, again privileging the sources closest to them. Interestingly, the US Department of Labor in 2020 stated that the job outlook for translators and interpreters for 2019–2029 was for growth of 20%, "much faster than average." In 2023, the same site gives an outlook of just 4% growth, "as fast as average." More worryingly, the 2020 site said there were 77,400 translators and interpreters; in 2023 there were 68,700. The COVID years might have had something to do with this, but here is no need to lie to students: they can find these numbers for themselves. (The same resource also indicates the salary range and the skills required.)

One thing all the numbers still say is that the translation sector is growing overall and that it has historically proved to be remarkably resilient. As one industry quip puts it, when the economy is good, we translate contracts; when the economy is bad, we translate lawsuits. But the quip does not account for technologies.

What kinds of jobs do translators do with technologies?

When students ask what kinds of jobs will be waiting for them, the first answer must be that there is a moving labor market out there and no one is waiting for anyone to catch up. Graduates will be faced with employment profiles that their training will only loosely have prepared them for. That means they will keep learning once they have a job (or a series of jobs, as is more frequently the case). Here it is of considerable importance that the meaning of the noun "translator" is being extended if not entirely altered: many new kinds of language services have emerged. For example, we have witnessed "transcreation" gain the status of a buzz word associated with jobs that require creativity in rewriting texts, mainly for marketing and advertising purposes but also for any kind of text designed to change the behavior of the receiver. Translation companies increasingly offer marketing and communication expertise as well as straight translation services. There are also services that blend translation with cross-cultural project management and cultural consulting (Bond, 2018). Such examples suggest that automation will not kill off the language industry but is instead diversifying the job profiles. And this tendency concerns the work done by both translators and single-language experts: the employment boundaries between those two groups are becoming increasingly blurred.

What kinds of jobs can translators do?

Ask your worried students to think about their local supermarket, since translation is not alone as a profession shaken up by technology. When you go shopping, how many human cashiers can you find? How many were there a few years ago? If you look for familiar faces, you will probably find that quite a few of the regular employees are still around, helping customers whenever the machines get stuck, checking photo IDs if any alcohol is purchased (in Australia!), and smiling at people and saying, "Have a good one." Part of the work has not yet been automatized (troubleshooting); some skills are automation-resistant (social skills); and there are still a few boring jobs to be done (stacking shelves). Something similar might hold for the translation industry. Humans can step in when the machines malfunction; we can help people understand how to use the machines; we can do public relations to keep the customers informed and satisfied; and yes, we still have to check, revise, and authorize translations – and the correlative of stacking shelves might be the cleaning of databases. But there is one important difference in this analogy. There is no reason why people will buy increasing amounts of groceries (unless there are more people); on the other hand, there are logics in economic globalization, communication technologies, migration patterns, and automation itself that mean that the sheer quantities of cross-language communication have been increasing steadily and can be expected to do so in future. Automation might mean that the human slice of the communication pie becomes narrower, just as the human jobs in the supermarket become more restricted. But the pie itself is becoming much bigger. That should explain why the language industry has continued to grow right through the recent decades of growing automation, economic downturn, and the expansion of English as a lingua franca (for some numbers, see Pym & Torres-Simón, 2021).

How do the technologies work?

A second set of questions concerns what is happening inside the technologies. Here most people in the humanities have little expertise to offer. A smart strategy must be to invite clever students to search for answers and then report back.

Which is the best machine-translation system?

Any answer to this question will depend on the language pair involved, the kind of text to translate, and the moment in history when the question is being asked – since the different technologies are all in constant evolution. The first answer must be: it depends.

The next response, we suggest, is to get the students to find out. Different groups try different systems for a series of different tasks, then they compare the results and report back to the whole class. An easy answer to a very difficult question!

The activity becomes especially interesting when generative AI is used in the comparison as well, allowing the level of the output to be adjusted to different readerships. That kind of experimentation should give rise to productive discussions of what the terms "quality" and "translation" mean. Is quality only in relation to the start text? Does "translation" only imply literalness? Those are very good questions to begin from. For several criteria that go beyond text-based accuracy, generative AI should increasingly win.

Why do different systems give different results?

This is a logical question that tends to ensue from any of the comparative activities. An easy answer for machine translation is that different systems have different databases, and the outputs are only as good as the translations that have been fed into the databases. A slightly better answer will point to the different kinds of algorithms that have been used, tracing the evolution from linguistic parsing to phrase-based statistical analysis and through to the incorporation of deep learning. And an even better answer should refer to the inherent complexity of language systems and their uses, which allow for numerous variations and thus for the expression of subjectivity.

How much you want to go into that will depend on the students around you and the learning outcomes involved. For most groups, the nature of the different algorithms is a question best left to specialists. If we can learn to appreciate that the variety of outputs is a normal fact of translation, that should be enough. That variety itself is the basic lesson for everyone: there rarely just *the* translation.

Why is neural machine translation so good?

Again, an easy answer is possible. The machine-translation systems that we have had since 2016 are called "neural" because they loosely imitate how the human brain works, forming networks of connections and learning new connections. The systems are based on statistical probabilities and deep learning, more than on linguistic rules.

And just in case anyone asks, the neural machine translation approach was launched in late 2016 by Google (Wu et al., 2016). The Chinese company Baidu nevertheless claims they were the game-changer who released the system first (Zhou et al., 2016). That is another debate best left to specialists.

How does neural machine translation work?

This is a more specific question that most language teachers and translator educators may not want to get into: the science has moved a long way from the traditional humanities. O'Brien (2002) did devote part of her early post-editing course to explaining how machine translation worked, but the algorithms have become rather more sophisticated and a lot more statistical since then. Does a driving instructor have to explain how automatic transmission works? Should the mathematics teacher care about how calculators get the right answers? Of course, that does not mean the questions should be avoided. Again, if the question is asked, have small student groups go searching for answers and then invite them to explain what they have found. The answers will tend to be on a level of interest appropriate to the class.

Students will hopefully report something like the following. As mentioned, neural machine translation works on the basis of a large artificial network of connections that uses deep learning (Koehn, 2020). Once a text is fed the system, an encoder converts each sentence into a fixed-length vector, which is a sequence of numbers that represent its meaning; from that, a decoder generates a well-formed translation in the target language (Cho et al., 2014). During the encoding phase, the system assigns an embedding (i.e., a mathematical code) to each isolated word in source language. The isolated neural embeddings are then combined to produce contextualized embeddings at the sentence level. The system then performs the inverse procedure during the decoding phrase, having the sentence-level embeddings unraveled to predict every single word in the target sentence (Pérez-Ortiz et al., 2022). Neural systems are also trained using neural network-based end-to-end learning protocols together with focus mechanisms (Koehn, 2020). And so on.

A trickier question is whether neural machine translation is the basis for the translation capacity of generative AI. Some writers with a background in translation studies assure us it is; others – for example, Jiang et al. (2023) and Hendy et al. (2023) – insist it is not. Although neural machine translation systems and generative AI models are both based on transformer architecture (Vaswani et al., 2017), they vary in a few aspects. Unlike the encoder-decoder architecture of neural machine translation (see above), generative AI (or at least GPT) adopts decoder-only models that both process an input (i.e., the start text) and generate the output. As mentioned in Chapter 1 above, generative AI does not work on curated parallel data but on large databases, reportedly with a dominant bias toward English. The difference can sometimes be seen in the products. If we use machine translation from Catalan to English, the output occasionally has traces of a passage through Spanish, particularly in names – which shows that parallel data have been used. In generative AI, we have so far found no such traces. Another example would be the different ways the systems translate the verb *to become* (see the activity

"Use generative AI to solve translation problems" in Chapter 5): generative AI answers your questions; neural machine translation tells you about what translators have done.

More up-to-date explanations of large language models should not be too hard to find. Good luck!

How should we work with technologies?

Happily, some of the students' questions are more on the level of how to drive a car, rather than how the automatic transmission works. Most of those questions can be addressed through class activities, by getting the students to explore driving skills – there are not a lot of things they can crash into, after all, and there is an abundance of help available in online videos, user forums, and instruction manuals. There are nevertheless a few general questions that can be tackled with conceptual pirouettes.

Will automation kill creativity?

In a seminar we gave in 2023 for teachers of translation in Venice, Italy, the participants' initial questions overwhelmingly concerned the negative aspects of translation technologies, especially for creativity (which was the most frequent value referred to in the questions, ahead of "context," "nuance," and "emotions," all of which were presumed to be in danger). If students ask about these kinds of negative consequences of using any technology, the replying teacher should not fall into the trap of pure negativity. Invite them to draw up an initial list of advantages and disadvantages, since their preconceptions should be operating in *both* ledgers. It makes no sense to focus on the negative aspects alone. That said, here are some of the considerations that should arise.

All language automation is fallible, give or take technical domains where terminology is very stable and some syntactic patterns are obligatory (as in controlled authoring). This means that whenever someone picks up an automatized translation suggestion and accepts it as *the* definitive translation, they are running the risk of ignoring alternatives. That is the main negative aspect: users are likely to accept what "the machine" says and reproduce it mindlessly. How can one avoid that? As we have suggested, you do this by interacting with the system, exploring alternative translations, and using language skills to improve the suggestions.

Consider for a moment the idea that the core translation skills are the ability to generate alternative renditions and the ability to select one of them, quickly and with ethical confidence (Pym, 2003). The more alternatives, the more creative the selection process. And the one thing that all translation technologies do is generate alternatives. Translators still have to do the selecting themselves, but there is no reason why technology should be opposed to creativity.

Beware of misleading examples, though. A pamphlet that largely comprises arguments against machine translation claims that the technology produces an "anchoring bias," which means that translators will tend to reproduce the first proposal that is made by machine translation (Association pour la promotion de la traduction littéraire, 2023, p. 7). The one example, taken from Hemingway's *A Very Short Story*, is the sentence "Luz sat on the bed" (from an experiment in Kolb, 2010). This could mean "Luz sat down" or "Luz was sitting," and many languages require that a choice be made between the two. So how should the translator decide? The students in the experiment rendered the phrase *differently* when unaided, but the students who were post-editing machine translation all gave the *same* translation. That proves, apparently, that machine translation kills creativity. Does it really? In this case, there is nothing to be gained or lost by either of the two ways of rendering the verb: nothing in Hemingway's story depends on whether Luz was sitting or sat down, so there is nothing at stake. In those circumstances, it seems quite rational for a translator to follow the path of least effort and copy the machine translation proposal. There is no need to seek variation for the mere sake of variation.

The logic of this example should tell us something basic about how to teach translation technologies: if your purpose is to foster creativity, do not give activities where everyone can rationally copy from the same machine translation system. If you do, the lack of creativity is in the task prescribed, not in the translations completed.

Will machines translate better than humans?

This is a version of the perennial question about automation replacing humans. It is impossible to answer seriously. But students ask it, so it should be addressed one way or another.

There can be no doubt that, if you map the progress of language automation, its quality improves faster than has the quality of human translation. In theory, there should come a time when automation surpasses human translation, as posited by the theory of the singularity addressed in Chapter 1 above.

A better way to answer the question is to raise doubts about the extent to which the two terms in the question can be separated. Are "machines" and "humans" really two different worlds (cf. Pym, 2011; Mihalache, 2021; O'Brien, 2023)? There are at least two arguments to consider here.

First, almost everything in the databases that are used by language automation has been the result of human translating at one time or another. Automation is fundamentally recycling human work, so it cannot simply be opposed to human work.

Second, human language skills have been augmented by technology ever since the invention of writing, the book, the printing press, the dictionary, the written grammar, and so on. Those technologies extend our language capacities, fundamentally by supplementing our memory (Pym, 2011). Indeed, the Catalan paleontologist Eudald Carbonell (in Carbonell & Sala, 2003), working on the remains of the first Europeans, claims that the use of technology is what distinguishes humans from the higher apes. The more technology we master, the more human we become. (From this perspective, talk about the "post-human" does not mean very much.)

If you pursue those two lines of argument, your students might start to look at technology in a different way. They still have every right to be concerned about the future, of course, but some might enjoy thinking about the many new ways in which human capacities will be augmented.

What are the ethical problems of translation technologies?

Here we find a set of questions that, to be honest, students do not ask enough. If you have grown up with technologies and social media, you tend to accept that everything can be copied, everything is free, and there is no limit to usage. That might be why many of our first-year students are genuinely perplexed by academic rules against plagiarism, and why those same rules are struggling to adapt to the age of generative AI. The ethical problems are now truly problematic – if ever there were an area for debate in the classical for-versus-against style (one team has to be in favor of a proposition, the other against it), this is it. But the questions can also be dealt with one by one.

Is automation really theft of intellectual property?

The question of intellectual property can be approached as an extension of the debate about what belongs to humans and what could be the preserve of machines. Doubts about intellectual property have long concerned translation technologies (cf. Koponen et al., 2022). They were with us in the 1990s, when translators were first asked to deliver their translation memories along with their translations, so who owned the translation memory? That basic issue has become more extreme with the advent of generative AI, where the technology draws on knowledge of all kinds and presents it mostly without recognizing authorship (see the associated question of confidentiality below).

In many of the discussions of intellectual property, the translator is cast in the role of victim, exploited by companies that steal the translator's work by feeding it into databases. Students should be made aware that this happens. When we first do projects in class with the more sophisticated translation memory suites, we sign the students up as Linguists, have them complete a translation task, and then ask them to download their translation, translation memory, and glossary. With the main current suites, they often find that the fruits of their labor cannot be downloaded for future recycling – their work has already been whisked away into the hands of the Project Manager, nominally in the interests of security. Later we sign all students up as Project Managers, so they can at least see what is going on.

In that immediate removal of translation data, our work is fed into databases where it can be used by future translators employed on the same or similar projects. If that seems scandalous, it is also worth recalling that many otherwise normal translation activities are also working from similar databases. Translators draw on the work of other translators whenever they use a public or shared translation memory, whenever they use machine translation, whenever they consult an online reference like Linguee, and in fact whenever they use a bilingual dictionary (where the entries were produced by translators at some point in the workflow). If you have therefore benefited from the work of previous translators, is the translation you produce now wholly yours to sell? The legal frameworks become murky and differ from country to country (cf. Megale, 2004). However, one important difference remains between the general case and what happens in the translation memory suites. When we all draw on each other's work, each of us at least retains the texts and the databases and we are free to re-use them (we have some degree of sovereignty over them). On the other hand, when the technology whisks away our work, all sovereignty is lost: the linguistic capital belongs exclusively to our employer.

Students should be able to come up with reasonable arguments for and against such practices, if only because they have grown up with online usage of all kinds of data. They should know what is going on, even if they have not thought about it in terms of ethics. The arguments can be presented in dialectical spirals. For example, one might argue that copyright is needed to encourage people to be creative – so they can receive profits from their intellectual efforts – but copyright is said to protect only the people and countries that are rich enough to enforce it; and then the presence of free public content can enhance the sales of private content, so there are virtues in breaking copyright, and so on.

Here are two more general debates, from an increasingly unfashionable intellectual tradition that can still put some foxes in the henhouse.

First, ask if anyone owns a language (a natural language like French or Chinese). Then ask how a language stays alive and changes. Answer, we hope: by collective usage, with innovation happening all the time and some new creations becoming shared as part of the language. So does the language steal intellectual property from its users? Not really. As Stalin put it in a famous intervention into Soviet linguistics, "language has been created precisely in order to serve society as whole, [...] serving members of society equally, irrespective of their class status" (1950/2008, p. 5). So why should this same logic not apply when machine translation systems pool our individual work and generative AI draws its solutions from the Internet?

Second debate: There can be no doubt that automation takes the language work of many people and stores it in a database, which then becomes a resource for future production. In Marxist terms, that resource is capital, the accumulated surplus value of anonymized language workers, dead labor. In this, it is functioning in the same way as any of the collective infrastructure and research projects that improve daily life. The real question is not the source of that capital or its capacity to produce value – capital can be private or public, and profit is never guaranteed. The problem is *who* reaps future benefits from it. When translators are asked about working with translation memories and machine translation, many of them are fine with the technologies as such (cf. Vieira, 2020), but they are not happy with the business practices that see the major profits going to large companies rather than to working translators.

"Property" could be a misleading word in these debates. It can make more sense simply to follow the money. *Cui bono?*

Should we work with proprietary translation systems?

Close to the concept of "property," "proprietary" software is developed and marketed for profit, which means that it is paid for by users or their intermediaries (perhaps it is pre-installed on a computer or the user's institution pays for it) or it otherwise seeks profit by extracting data from the user or by showing publicity. The user is mostly not able to adapt the system to their own specific needs and is often not aware that, in using the system, they are providing data for free. Proprietary software can be opposed to software that is free ("libre") and open-source (called FOSS, FLOSS, or sometimes "libreware") that genuinely requires no payment and that the user can often modify, especially with respect to retaining sovereignty over their data. The best-known example is perhaps Linux as an operating system and LibreOffice, but in the translation field we have examples like Tatoeba, Apertium, MinT, LibreTranslate, Translate You, and so on – students will be able to locate further examples, probably more recent and probably better.

For the more activist positions, proprietary software serves the interests of capitalism, exploiting translators and stealing the products of their labor. Free and open software enables translators to resist this exploitation, boycotting the profit-seeking capitalist software and, in a not uncommon extension, boycotting companies that use those translation systems.

Any discussion of this issue should bring in several voices. As difficult as it may be to defend big-business capitalism, you could ask students if they want to work for profit, and then whether profit is inherently bad (big companies not paying taxes could be a side discussion). You might also suggest that the major advances in translation technologies would not have been possible without risk-taking investments – without the accumulation of surplus value, in other words, capital, either private or state.

At the end of the day, everyone should feel free to translate with the system they feel comfortable with. At the same time, though, all those with an interest in translation technologies – especially the technicians and the users – should feel completely free to talk with each other. Technicians within even the most evil of enterprises are surprisingly keen on solving problems in the interests of good causes – the post-hippie ideology of progress through technology is not completely dead. The lack of dialogue across those divides remains one of the main problems of our age, and boycott-based discourses that simplistically oppose a purist activist "we" to a nefarious capitalist "they" do little to seek mutually beneficial cooperation.

Why are online technologies free?

Good question! The quick answer is that nothing is ever really free. When you use an online GPS system to find your way in traffic, you think you are getting real-time information for free, but of course you are sending the provider real-time information on where you go and how fast you are getting there, giving information not just on traffic jams and the like but also on the movements in your life: where you work, where you shop, who you like to see, in short, who you are. That kind of information is gold for targeted marketing practices. The relation could be cooperative: you give some information, you receive other information, and each party attributes more value to what it receives than to what it gives – if and when they are aware of what is going on. In terms of legal principle, no gift is ever entirely free.

This is happening all over the place in translation technologies. Students can be asked to search the fine print whenever one signs up as a user of software. Most translation memory systems promise they will not divulge an uploaded text or its translation to any "third party," which implies that they themselves (the "second party") assume the right to use the text and the translation for their own purposes. Most interactive machine translation systems and AI text generators explain that the user's choices will be used to improve the quality of future translations, which is not entirely wrong. In the development of these technologies, one of the developer's main assets is a relatively clean and reliable database, verified by human feedback as much as possible. They are effectively building up their stock-in-trade, their core capital, for free.

Is it wrong to translate for free?

Online technologies now enable us to integrate something of the "free gift" economy into our teaching, and not just in the sense of using online systems.

As noted in Chapter 5, students of subtitling, for example, can be invited to join one of the many online fan-sub communities around the world, where they can gain on-the-job training and guidance for free at the same time as they translate cultural products that are of genuine interest to them (to the extent that they can choose which group to join and what audiovisual material they work on). Similarly, until 2022 Facebook had an interface for crowdsourced translations, where Facebook users could offer their own translations of texts from the site and then vote on other translations. This was reportedly the world's most successful crowdsourcing of translation activities – it also provided some great in-class discussions.

Should students be doing translations for free? The technologies certainly make the activity possible, and individual students almost always find there is an acceptable trade-off between the labor they put in and the experience they gain. (When the trade-off no longer works for them, they can stop working for free.) Once they have gained experience, the fansubbers can sometimes move into the professional sphere (Çavuşoğlu, 2020), assuming that the professional sphere still remains intact. Zwischenberger (2022), drawing on Wertheimer (1999), nevertheless argues that these work-for-free relations can still be exploitative. Even when the trade-off is beneficial for the individual, even when the translator is fully aware of their personal costs and benefits, the exchanges may have negative consequences for a third party: if the community of professional translators loses work overall, the student's future employment prospects will worsen as a result. (Arguments against that argument, which could also concern unpaid work placements, are presented in Pym, 2021.)

An important consideration here becomes the status of languages with limited electronic resources. Sometimes we translate for free simply to build up the capacity of a threatened language to benefit from automation.

Should you tell everyone which technologies you use?

When French literary translators feel threatened by "AI," as noted above, they assume that technology presents a heightened risk of error. The correct ethical response is therefore to have all translations carry a warning about what kind of workflow they come from. The catch-cry is "transparency" (Association pour la promotion de la traduction littéraire, 2023), perhaps like food labels that indicate the ingredients and country of origin. That sounds quite reasonable. Who could ever be against transparency?

In times of technological transition, when there is uncertainty and fear, can too much transparency have negative effects? If you tell your client that you have suddenly started to post-edit machine translation, you may run the risk of losing that client – at least until they really understand what post-editing is and they look at the results rather than follow scaremongering about the process.

A classroom discussion can take the issue further. Should we also be transparent about the dictionaries we use? What about the friends and family whose L1 intuitions we ask about? And surely the same principle should apply to all language production, not just translations? Or is transparency only for the technologies we don't trust?

Can confidential texts be translated online?

This question technically follows on from the issue of intellectual property, but the arguments are a little different. A widespread concern among the translation community is that any text uploaded to an online machine-translation system can be accessed and used by the controllers of that system, and probably by others as well. For that reason, several generations of teachers, including us, have been telling students never to upload any text that is of a confidential nature. If a professional translator does this, we say, their client's high-value industrial secrets will be known to the world and the translator is likely to be out of a job. And yet translating can be made easier by using online technologies. How do we skirt around the problem?

Lyu et al. (2023) suggest that translators anonymize start texts and then de-anonymize the translations. Would that work? It is hard to see how that would make the actual information significantly less visible. The basic problem seems only to be resolved by using technologies that are downloaded to the translator's physical computer, are in-house in the sense of belonging to the translation company or its client, or are subscription services (cf. Canfora & Ottmann, 2020).

Although translation studies has been concerned with issues of confidentiality for some time (Bennett, 2021), there may be an element of folklore to claims of high-stakes exposure. The risk of breaching confidentiality has been with us at least from the early 1990s, when the translation memories that were controlled by client companies were turning uploaded private texts into databases. As we have seen, those bilingual databases then became valuable language assets, with no recognition of authorship or prior ownership, and no separate payment for the data. The same situation applies to AI technologies that build their texts by drawing on everyone else's texts, allowing criteria of confidentiality to go the same way as concerns about intellectual property. That said, the language industries seem to have accepted this, at least tacitly. Ethical principles specifically related to translation technology were virtually absent prior to the code of the Translators Association of China in 2019 (Ren, 2019). The ISO standard for post-editing (ISO, 2017) makes no mention of confidentiality (as noted in Moorkens, 2022). And then, if the issue had really been of widespread importance since the 1990s, one would expect to find court cases involving violation of intellectual property through translation technologies. Strangely, we have found no such cases. There are various instances where translators are accused of plagiarizing other translators, and some intriguing cases concerning the divorce of the CEO of TransPerfect, the largest translation company in the world at the time. But we have found nothing about technology leaking secrets. It may be that the cases were settled out of court. Perhaps clever students can find some.

In the meantime, we will continue to teach students about the risks of uploading confidential documents. And the easy answer to the problem for companies is to set up their own in-house machine-translation systems, for translators to download systems to their hard disks (as can be done with OPUS-CAT, for instance), and for users to pay for a generative AI service that at least promises some degree of confidentiality.

Will translation automation destroy the climate?

Questions concerning climate effects are not actually among those that our students have asked, but it is one that they should have asked, with increasing urgency. It is also one of the issues that should be dealt with as a part of the ethics of translation technology (Cronin, 2017; Moorkens & Rocchi, 2021).

As with most of the above questions, you can send students out in search of evidence. One finds, for example, that the training of one machine-translation engine leaves the same carbon footprint as five cars over the lifetime of the cars (Strubell et al., 2019). That need not be scandalous in itself. The hard part is to conceptualize the social benefits that could justify that ecological cost.

The public debates over generative AI have tended to muddy this issue, along with many others, and a fair share of urban legends have evolved. One hears, for example, that Google's electricity bill is about the same as Ireland's, which would indeed be quite surprising, not to say shocking. When one goes looking for the truth of the rumor, you find the calculation mentioned as the worst-case scenario if and when all of Google's standard search operations became LLM interactions (De Vries, 2023, p. 2192). As it stands, Google's AI electricity bill in 2021 was about 8.3% of Ireland's (ibid.), which is still indicative of a serious environmental problem.

The kind of progress we are experiencing now cannot be unlimited.

*   *

*

In considering these questions, we have repeatedly mentioned the need for spoken debate between students. In some education situations, those debates might then become issues for essay writing (admittedly a disappearing species in the zoo of testing procedures). In all situations, though, the discussions should be accompanied by practical, hands-on activities as much as possible.

Note

1 An alternative source of questions could be the 'Getting established' forum on the online translation marketplace ProZ.com. Plaza-Lara (2023) analyzes the queries expressed there and strangely finds no concerns about technology. The absence could be due to her use of higher-level categories from PACTE (2018) that do not mention technology.

8

WAYS FORWARD

Here we step back and broadly summarize what we have said about the way language technologies are likely to affect the language industries, particularly with respect to the skillsets that should become the most sought after. We consider the main possible threats, and then a series of desiderata for a future in which technologies will help translators, language learners, and the diversity of languages.

What has really changed in the use of languages?

Through to the 1970s, the most advanced technology used by top-flight translators was probably a Dictaphone to record their spoken rendition. Typists would later come in to transcribe the recording, using a pedal to stop and start the tape. In language teaching, the most advanced technologies in the same years were probably a textbook for structuralist drills and then the pre-electronic tools of the audiovisual method, where images and recorded dialogues helped students follow and mimic language use in concrete situations. Those technologies were clearly *augmenting* language skills. The strange thing is that no one, as far as we can tell, argued that the Dictaphones and spoken cartoons were replacing anyone or had a negative effect on the quality of the translating or learning process.[1] So why should the same positive view not hold today? Why are contemporary reactions to technology far more divisive and increasingly taken to extremes in mainstream public discourse?

Part of the reason, we suggest, is the historical democratization of the technologies. We now live in a world where virtually everyone can have fun learning a language online, and virtually everyone has access to automated

DOI: 10.4324/9781032648033-8

translations as they do that learning. In countries where access to computers is still a privilege, learning content on mobile phones is far more accessible and widespread. The technologies have helped spread language learning and translation well beyond the narrow social cliques of the foreign-language experts and top-flight translators and interpreters of the 1960s and 1970s. This is a part of general trends. In 1960, some 44% of the world population was literate (in the sense of being able to read and write); by 2020, that percentage had more or less doubled to 87% (World in Data, 2023). In the 1970s, 10.1% of the world's population had enrolled in higher education within five years of completing secondary education; in 2020, that percentage had multiplied by four to reach 40.3% (World in Data, 2023). With that greater democratization, we find not infrequent claims that the general standards of language learning and translation have declined: there was once an age where properly qualified people worked hard and were able to produce language products of a quality that is now scarce – or so the narrative goes. There is some anecdotal evidence of this. For instance, restaurant menus translated in the 1970s and 1980s have been found to have far fewer errors than those translated in the 1990s (Fallada Pouget, 2000); English novels translated into Chinese in the 1950s and 1960s were more consistent and had fewer errors than their retranslations in the 1990s (Tian, 2023). In both cases, the decline in quality might be attributed to a widening of the social base: in the earlier decades, only a few people mastered foreign languages, so the translators tended to be professionals; in the more recent decades, language acquisition may be to variable degrees of semi-mastery, many translations are done by non-professionals, and electronic communication has the added disadvantage of making plagiarism and textual piracy easier to achieve, including the scamming of professional profiles (Pym et al., 2016). Yes, it can be claimed that quality has slid downhill in some quarters.

An associated argument against technologies is that, as automation reduces the need for human effort, our human capacities decline accordingly. "Disuse atrophy" means that if you do not use a muscle, it becomes weaker. By analogy, if learners do not *work* to acquire a foreign language, they will not become strong in it; and if translators are simply asked to *approve* automated translations, then their translation skills will similarly waste away – or so the argument goes. The values of the past will no longer be attainable because we will have forgotten the skills.

And then there is the rather more worrying associated argument that a massive increase in quick translations will stop people from learning additional languages, so we will forget how to learn languages, and there will be a decline in the social pool of interlingual mediators.

As we have had occasion to remark, such views tend to be espoused by professionals who used previous technologies to reach the top of their profession. Brian Mossop, for example, after a full career as a government translator in Canada, reflects on the impact of translation technologies (which he reduces to "Memory") and claims that the concept of quality has been redefined (implicitly downwards). This fails to satisfy his professional habitus: "I became a translator in order to translate (compose suitable wordings in the target language), not to fix someone else's recycled wordings" (Mossop, 2019, p. 315). Work done with automated translation solutions, implies Mossop, is simply not translation in the proper sense of the word.

Once you reach the top of a profession using a certain ladder, you are necessarily threatened when alternative ladders are set in place: the technologies of the younger generation will always seem inferior; the uncultured hoards use them to invade privileged space. In a similar way, priestly scribes once sought to impede writing from spreading to the general populace.

How might one argue against that reactionary, pessimistic position? It could be enough to point to the virtues of user-based democratic participation, to the huge quantities of texts that are rendered every day by non-professionals, to the tight deadlines that can now be met, and to the evolution of the translation concept itself, which no longer implies homage to *the* translation completed by *the* faceless professional in perfectly readable standard language, but increasingly allows for a series of publicly visible alternative translations, from which each user can select in accordance with myriad situational purposes.

As much as one might claim that the quality of translations and language learning was higher in a past heroic age, the Dictaphones and recorded cartoons have been well and truly superseded by more advanced technologies. The newer technologies allow for a lot *more* translating to be done, and the resulting variation in quality is not due to the technology itself but to the very irregular social distribution of the skills needed for its use.

Since much therefore depends on *how* technologies are used, here we offer a short list of desiderata, of admittedly unequal importance and possible impact.

How might translation technologies develop in positive ways?

We have necessarily been working on the *current* state of the various translation technologies. Our teaching should nevertheless be for societies of the future, for technologies that are likely to head in one direction or another. Here we sketch out a few of the ways in which automation might advance, particularly the improvements that would address not just the aspects that translators are currently unhappy with (as in the gripes summarized in Mossop, 2019), but also a few issues that concern the development of multilingual society.

Greater accessibility

If one accepts that translation technologies bring more good than bad, then it makes sense to have them as generalized as possible. Price and complexity should not be obstacles; the technologies should be as freely available as possible, in as many languages as possible, and with as much data sovereignty as possible for the user. How one moves toward those goals does not matter much. It could be through an activist user base, altruistic language workers, educational institutions, state intervention, or private companies that make their basic language tools widely available, as is currently the case for generative AI. Ideally, all such stakeholders should be able to talk with each other freely, in search of cooperation.

Greater interactivity

We hope and believe that all translation interfaces will incorporate alternative translation suggestions in such a way that the user selects from them, and the rest of the translation is adjusted automatically. At the time of writing, this happens in DeepL and to a lesser extent in Lilt, but it seems not to have been generalized. This mode of translating, which effectively becomes a type of ongoing post-editing, is reported to be faster and more conducive to a better translator experience than traditional post-editing (Knowles et al., 2019). For language learning, users of most machine-translation systems can freely modify the start text and immediately see the effects in the translation, thus bringing out rather than hiding the differences between languages. That kind of interactivity has the potential to provide quick contextualized information about comparative grammar and terminology. And once we have drop-down menus giving alternatives for each item in the *start text* (rather than just for the target text), the potential will be even greater.

Increased use of speech

Automated solutions increasingly allow for speech-to-text and text-to-speech tools that have been gaining in quality. At the same time, transcription technologies such as Sonix offer a built-in machine-translation tool that gives very reasonable results. These technologies invite us to return to the days when translators spoke their renditions, except that the spoken act can now draw on a plurality of written translation suggestions.

Why is this desirable? Our written technologies have long been criticized for promoting literalist translation solutions, stifling creativity, and producing unexciting language based on middle-of-the-road probabilities. When you speak rather than write, many of those negative effects tend to be overcome. And your wrists, back, and neck will be much healthier.

In the language class, this more generally means using the written technologies as support for role-play activities and spoken renditions.

And in all classes, the ability to talk about technologies and to enhance human relations is predominantly a set of spoken skills. In our classroom activities, we should have students speaking as much as possible.

Instant glossaries

Generative AI allows contextualized target-language notes to pop up when a mysterious term is clicked (this currently happens in Matecat), in effect offering a quick focused dictionary search. There may come a day when computers have built-in eye trackers that enable the notes to pop up when the user stares longer than usual at an item (as envisaged by Arnt Lykke Jakobsen in private conversations). Awaiting that day, we look forward to the incorporation of instant glossaries in language-learning materials and translation software.

Greater control over segmentation

One of the long-standing technical problems of translation memory software has been the breaking of continuous text into segments, usually into sentences. This has the positive effect of ensuring that nothing is skipped, and the negative effect of making the translator focus on the segment, often to the detriment of coherence and textual flow. When a translation of any complexity is exported out of the translation memory suite and revised as continuous text, many of those problems become immediately obvious and must be repaired. This is a possible reason why translation memories have never had much impact on the language class, although language corpora have, perhaps with similar effects.

One of the solutions introduced into the more advanced suites is to have the continuous text visible in another part of the interface. That is sometimes useful, since the translator can see what is coming next. For instance, the in-context function of Phrase allows users to access a real-time preview of the whole original and translated texts. This preview is in a pull-up window below the primary editing area ("editor"). When the user clicks on a segment in the editor, the corresponding text is colored within the preview to provide additional contextual information; similarly, clicking on a text in the preview window prompts the editor grid to indicate the segment for editing. An even more useful step forward, however, would be to allow the translator to interact directly with that continuous text. As machine translation proposals steadily become more useful than any fuzzy matches, this should be where we are heading anyway: the segments could disappear. And then the degree of terminological control allowed by translation memories will be achieved by simply giving those preferences priority over the translation-memory suggestions within the continuous text.

That sounds so logical that it must exist somewhere already.

Caveats to the user

We note that when ChatGPT and Gemini are asked to give advice on any legal matter, their responses include advice to consult a professional lawyer. For financial matters, they tell you to talk with a financial professional. For medical matters, they recommend seeing a doctor. This is an implicit recognition that the help offered by automated procedures is not replacing the advice of human professionals – for low-stakes problems, the automated solutions can help; for high-stakes problems, you need a human. We hope that the same kind of recognition will be extended to translations: the AI solutions should close with a recommendation to consult a professional translator. (We have requested this from OpenAI and Google, so far without response.)

Forget about counting words

This is just a detail. As automation takes care of the many boring and repetitive translation problems of translating a text, the number of words in the text becomes increasingly irrelevant. The translator should therefore be paid not by the number of words but by the hour, by the project, or by being contracted for a long-term maintenance program (all the updates to a website over two years, for example). Do you pay a lawyer on the basis of how many words are in a contract? Do doctors get paid for the length of their diagnoses? Is a teacher paid on the basis of how many words they address to students?

This detail concerns the technologies to the extent that the more sophisticated translation memories incorporate project-management tools that still sometimes (not always) refer to payment by number of words.

Ways forward for translation work

Recall Mossop's complaint (2019, p. 315n): "I became a translator in order to translate (compose suitable wordings in the target language)." That is a noble statement, spoken in defense of a noble profession. There will no doubt remain a demand for experts in the art of high-quality translation, but the technologies we have been looking at have encroached on that territory and are very likely to take much more ground in the future.

We have outlined three possible ways of future-proofing translation skills with respect to professional employment: using the technologies creatively (especially as support for various degrees of transcreation), doing what the technologies are *not* good at (gaining personal trust in client or user relations, with or without some degree of content development), and working with the technologies (post-editing, but not only). Of those three, the post-editing option is increasingly portrayed as the poorest, the one most given to exploitation. Yet it need not be. In times of technological uncertainty, clients need the authoritative voice of a human who can assure them that a translation is valid, just as a notary gives validity to a legal document. It may take a good while for translators to gain that status. In the meantime, our main point is that there is no radical need to choose between the three options: most training situations should allow for all those avenues to be explored, and the basic communication skills should be highly transversal, across that range and beyond.

There have been many attempts to reconceptualize that space, right the way from the wide view of "translatorial action" (Holz-Mänttäri, 1984) as doing whatever it takes to achieve the client's cross-lingual aim, through to the "language engineer" (Briva-Iglesias & O'Brien, 2022) who knows how to use appropriate technologies as part of that action. One might also add some sanguine advice from the International Translators Federation: "professionals should act as language services advisors or language consultants, advising their customers on the best approach to a particular assignment and explaining the benefits or drawbacks of certain translation methods" (FIT, 2017, p. 2). That is, professionals must know what can be done with the technologies.

Our wider call, however, has been for translation technologies to be used intelligently and creatively by all, in the first place by anyone who has learned an additional language. That does not mean taking anything away from professional translators; it simply aims to improve something that is already happening. A call to address a wide range of non-professional translators need not entail any "unprofessional" standards either: the wider world is translating, and in many cases doing so astutely and creatively.

Is there an alternative? When Mumford studied the first industrial revolution, he was fascinated that one of the things the industrial workers bought with their salaries was a watch: "to own a watch was for long a definite symbol of success" (Mumford, 1946, p. 16). In the new industrial environment, where work was regulated by mechanical time rather than by the sun, workers willingly embraced the prime technology of what might be seen as their own enslavement – that is one possible reading. Is the personal computer the watch of our time? Is our embrace of translation technologies a rush forward to our own enslavement? We have argued that the encounter has more to do with empowerment: if the worker does not have a watch or does not know how to use it, then time is entirely controlled by the factory owner, who can adjust it to their advantage. The way forward will not be reached by refusing new technologies and returning to a cottage industry.

That does not mean, we have argued, that *more* technology is the only way forward. It also makes sense to train people to do what translation technologies cannot yet do, notably in content development. But even there, you cannot leave the technology entirely behind. One of the effects of improved translation technologies should be a narrowing of the high-stakes cases in which professional translation is required. Translation companies can thus be expected to move toward transcreation. For instance, one Melbourne company now offers "multilingual generation and translation." They offer to do market surveys, then write the publicity copy, then translate it in a way that is adapted to each target group, adjusting the images and layout as well as the language. And how might they get ideas for the new content? That is one of the things that generative AI is proving to be quite good at (Li, Pang, et al., 2023). We are thus seeing the development of workplaces that bring together translators, technology, and advanced language users (technical writers who know about creativity and cultures). Those are jobs for graduates of both translation and language education. That is another reason why we need teachers and teaching practices that work on both sides of that false divide.

Will a more democratized use of technology overcome the main historical effect of automation: the widening income gap between those who benefit and those who do not? Perhaps surprisingly, there is some evidence of a gradual narrowing of the global income gap (Chancel & Picketty, 2021). This is due to the rise of Asian economies but also, in part, to increased access to knowledge: "the poor catch up to the rich to the extent that they achieve the same level of technological know-how, skill, and education, not by becoming the property of the wealthy" (Picketty, 2017, p. 91). General literacy in translation technologies can help in this process, not only as knowledge in itself but more obviously in opening access to all the knowledge that is digitized.

Translation vs. multilingualism?

One final future prospect needs to be addressed. At several points we have mentioned the risk that a generalized use of translation technologies could curtail social motivations to learn languages, thus threatening multilingualism. That is, translation technologies could work to the detriment both of societies that require a lingua franca (Australia, for example, where the policy is for everyone to learn English) and of societies that seek to maintain multilingualism (the European Union, for instance, where the official languages of member states are supposed to remain strong, which means that many linguistic mediators are required – as envisaged in the *Common European Framework of Reference*). The opposition between translation and multilingualism is a frequent enough assumption. Here, for instance, is a United Kingdom Communities Secretary doing his best to thwart a black future:

> Stopping the automatic use of translation and interpretation services into foreign languages will provide further incentive for all migrant communities to learn English, which is the basis for an individual's ability to progress in British society. It will promote cohesion and better community relations.
>
> *(Pickles, 2013)*

What could be wrong with that logic? Over the years, we have collected arguments and information on this issue.

One argument comes from literary translation. If an author works in a less-disseminated language but is well translated into major languages or lingua francas, then the fact of translation encourages them to keep working in the smaller language (this argument has been made by Susan Bernofsky in several talks). And if that translation process is aided by technology, then the result should be more translations and thus more indirect promotion of linguistic diversity.

A different kind of insight comes from immigration studies. In a series of interviews with asylum seekers in Europe (reported in Fiedler & Wohlfarth, 2018; Pokorn & Čibej, 2018a, 2018b; Pym, 2018), we found that (1) everyone with intentions of long-term mobility was learning the host languages, (2) no one would stop learning the host language if professional interpreters were provided on all occasions, and (3) machine translation was often used in preference to human mediation because it gave the user control (official interpreters are not always trusted), it offered confidentiality (no one is overhearing you) (cf. Cox & Maryns, 2021), and it provided a way to learn key resources in the host language.

It could always be that those interviewees were telling the researchers what they thought they wanted to hear. Then again, reflect for a moment on what it means to seek a place in a vibrant multilingual society, to develop long-term emotional involvement across language differences. No one in their right mind would *prefer* translation technologies as anything more than a quick solution to an immediate problem. In any question of long-term belonging, language learning remains the key, and the technologies can provide some pathways to its development.

Possibly because of that underlying logic, we have found *no* patterned evidence of the apparently logical link espoused by the United Kingdom Communities Secretary. The use of translation can positively enhance language learning, in our societies and in our classrooms. The challenge is to use it well.

These are all reasons not to be afraid of translation technologies. Instead, we have to explore and experiment with them in our classrooms.

Note

1 On the other hand, there were clear reactions against the use of headphones and microphones for simultaneous conference interpreting. The older generation of consecutive interpreters pejoratively referred to the younger generation as *les téléphonistes* (telephone operators) (Baigorri-Jalón, 2004, pp. 55, 70–71).

REFERENCES

Agar, M. H. (1994). *Language Shock: Understanding the Culture of Conversation.* William Morrow.

ALPAC (1966). *Languages and Machines: Computers in Translation and Linguistics.* A report by the Automatic Language Processing Advisory Committee, Division of Behavioral Sciences. National Academy of Sciences, National Research Council.

Al Qahtani, M. M. (2023). Utilizing Computer-Aided Translation Tools in Saudi Translation Agencies. *Arab World English Journal for Translation and Literary Studies, 7*(3), 87–98. http://doi.org/10.24093/awejtls/vol7no3.6

Álvarez-Álvarez, S., & Arnáiz-Uzquiza, V. (2017). Translation and Interpreting Graduates under Construction: Do Spanish Translation and Interpreting Studies Curricula Answer the Challenges of Employability? *The Interpreter and Translator Trainer, 11*(2–3), 139–159.

Andrade, H. L. (2019). A Critical Review of Research on Student Self-assessment. *Frontiers in Education, 4,* 1–13.

ANECA (2004). *Libro blanco. Título de Grado en Traducción e Interpretación.* Agencia Nacional de Evaluación de la Calidad y Acreditación.

Association pour la promotion de la traduction littéraire (2023). *AI and Literary Translation: Translators Call for Transparency.* Translated by S. Whiteside. https://www.atlas-citl.org/tribune-ia

Aston, G. (2011). Applied Corpus Linguistics and the Learning Experience. In V. Vander, S. Zyngier, & G. Barnbrook (Eds.), *Perspectives on Corpus Linguistics* (pp. 1–16). John Benjamins.

Austermühl, F. (2013). Future (and Not-so-future) Trends in the Teaching of Translation Technology. *Tradumàtica, 11,* 326–337.

Autor, D. H. (2015). Why Are There Still So Many Jobs? The History and Future of Workplace Automation. *The Journal of Economic Perspectives, 29*(3), 3–30.

Ayvazyan, N., Hao Y., & Pym, A. (2024). Things to do in the translation class when technologies change: The case of generative AI. In Y. Peng, H. Huang, & D. Li (Eds.), *New Advances in Translation and Interpreting Technology: Theories, Applications and Training* (pp. 219–238). Springer.

Bai, L., & Hu, G. (2017). In the Face of Fallible AWE Feedback: How do Students Respond? *Educational Psychology, 37*(1), 67–81.

Baigorri-Jalón, J. (2004). *Interpreters at the United Nations: A History*. Translated from Spanish by A. Barr. Ediciones Universidad de Salamanca.

Baigorri-Jalón, J. (2014/2000). *From Paris to Nuremberg: The Birth of Conference Interpreting*. Translated from Spanish by H. Mikkelson & B. S. Olsen. John Benjamins. https://doi.org/10.1075/btl.111

Barrot, J. S. (2018). Using the Sociocognitive-Transformative Approach in Writing Classrooms: Effects on L2 Learners' Writing Performance. *Reading & Writing Quarterly, 34*(2), 187–201.

Barrot, J. S. (2023a). Using Automated Written Corrective Feedback in the Writing Classroom: Effects on L2 Writing Accuracy. *Computer Assisted Language Learning, 36*(4), 584–607.

Barrot, J. S. (2023b). Using ChatGPT for Second Language Writing: Pitfalls and Potentials. *Assessing Writing, 57*, 1–6.

Bašić, Ž., Banovac, A., Kružić, I., & Jerković, I. (2023). Better by You, Better than Me? ChatGPT-3 as Writing Assistance in Students' Essays. arXiv:2302.04536

Beaulieu, E., Boutet, M., Bowker, L., Burelli, T., Carnegie, J., Lillo, A., MacDonald, D., Montpetit, C., & Ousko, S. (2020). *Using Game-Based Learning Online: A Cookbook of Recipes*. eCampus Ontario Open Library.

Bender, E., Gebru, T., McMillan-Major, A., & Shmitchell, S. (2021). On the Dangers of Stochastic Parrots: Can Language Models Be Too Big? *FAccT '21: Proceedings of the 2021 ACM Conference on Fairness, Accountability, and Transparency*. https://dl.acm.org/doi/10.1145/3442188.3445922

Bennett, P. M. (2021). Ethics in translation practice. A comparison of professional codes of conduct. *Verba Hispanica, 29*(1), 31–52. https://doi.org/10.4312/vh.29.1.31-52

Berber-Irabien, D. (2010). *Information and Communication Technologies in Conference Interpreting* [Doctoral thesis]. Universitat Rovira i Virgili. http://hdl.handle.net/10803/8775

Berlitz, M. (1888/1916). *The Berlitz Method for Teaching Modern Languages*. English Part. Revised American Edition. Berlitz.

Bessen, J. E. (2015). *Learning by Doing: The Real Connection between Innovation, Wages, and Wealth*. Yale University Press.

Bessen, J. E. (2016). *How Computer Automation Affects Occupations: Technology, Jobs, and Skills*. Law and Economics Research Paper No. 15-49. Boston University School of Law. http://doi.org/10.2139/ssrn.2690435

Biggs, J. (2003). Aligning Teaching and Assessing to Course Objectives. *Teaching and Learning in Higher Education: New Trends and Innovations, 2*(4), 13–17.

Bitchener, J., & Knoch, U. (2010). The Contribution of Written Corrective Feedback to Language Development: A Ten-month Investigation. *Applied Linguistics, 31*, 193–214.

Black, S. (2021). The Potential Benefits of Subtitles for Enhancing Language Acquisition and Literacy in Children: An Integrative Review of Experimental Research. *Translation, Cognition & Behavior, 4*(1), 74–97. https://doi.org/10.1075/tcb.00051.bla

Bocanegra-Valle, A. (2016). Needs Analysis for Curriculum Design. In K. Hayland (Ed.), *The Routledge Handbook of English for Academic Purposes* (pp. 560–576). Routledge.

Bol, L., Campbell, K. D. Y., Perez, T., & Yen, C. J. (2016). The Effects of Self-Regulated Learning Training on Community College Students' Metacognition and Achievement in Developmental Math Courses. *Community College Journal of Research and Practice, 40*, 480–495.

Bond, E. (2018). The Stunning Variety of Job Titles in the Language Industry. *Slator.* https:// slator.com/features/the-stunning-variety-of-job-titles-in-the-language-industry

Borgonovi, F., Hervé, J., & Seitz, H. (2023). Not Lost in Translation: The Implications of Machine Translation Technologies for Language Professionals and for Broader Society. *OECD Social, Employment and Migration Working Papers No. 291.* OECD Publishing. https://doi.org/10.1787/e1d1d170-en

Bourdieu, P. (1982). *Ce que parler veut dire.* Fayard.

Bowker, L. (2015). Computer-Aided Translation: Translator Training. In S. W. Chan (Ed.), *Routledge Encyclopedia of Translation Technology* (pp. 88–104). Routledge.

Bowker, L., & Buitrago Ciro, J. (2019). *Machine Translation and Global Research: Towards Improved Machine Translation Literacy in the Scholarly Community.* Emerald Publishing.

Briva-Iglesias, V., & O'Brien, S. (2022). The Language Engineer: A Transversal, Emerging Role for the Automation Age. *Quaderns de Filologia: Estudis Lingüístics, 27*, 17–48. https://doi.org/10.7203/QF.27.24622

Briva-Iglesias, V., O'Brien, S., & Cowan, B. R. (2023). The Impact of Traditional and Interactive Post-editing on Machine Translation User Experience, Quality, and Productivity. *Translation, Cognition & Behavior, 6*(1), 60–86.

Brown, G., & Harris, L. R. (2014). The Future of Self-Assessment in Classroom Practice: Reframing Self-assessment as a Core Competency. *Frontline Learning Research, 2*(1), 22–30.

Bureau of Labor Statistics, US Department of Labor (2020). *Occupational Outlook Handbook, Interpreters and Translators.* Updated April 12, 2020. https://www.bls.gov/ooh/media-and-communication/interpreters-and-translators.htm

Bureau of Labor Statistics, US Department of Labor (2023). *Occupational Outlook Handbook, Interpreters and Translators.* Updated September 5, 2023. https://www.bls.gov/ooh/media-and-communication/interpreters-and-translators.htm

Canfora, C., & Ottmann, A. (2020). Risks in Neural Machine Translation. *Translation Spaces, 9*(1), 58–77.

Carbonell, E., & Sala, R. (2003). *Aún no somos humanos. Propuestas de humanización para el tercer milenio.* Península.

Carl, M., & Schaeffer, M. J. (2017). Why Translation Is Difficult: A Corpus-Based Study of Non-Literality in Post-editing and From-Scratch Translation. *Hermes. Journal of Language and Communication in Business, 56*, 43–57.

Carré, A., Kenny, D., Rossi, C., Sánchez Gijón, P., & Torres-Hostench, O. (2022). Machine Translation in Language Learning. In D. Kenny (Ed.), *Machine Translation for Everyone. Empowering Users in the Age of Artificial Intelligence* (pp. 187–207). Language Science Press.

Carreres, Á., & Noriega-Sánchez, M. (2021). The Translation Turn: A Communicative Approach to Translation in the Language Classroom. In T. Beaven & F. Rosell-Aguilar (Eds.), *Innovative Language Pedagogy Report* (pp. 83–89). Research-publishing.net. https://doi.org/10.14705/rpnet.2021.50.1240

Castilho, S., Mallon, C., Meister, R., & Yue, S. (2023). Do Online Machine Translation Systems Care for Context? What about a GPT Model? *24th Annual*

Conference of the European Association for Machine Translation (EAMT 2023), European Association for Machine Translation.

Çavuşoğlu, E. (2020). The Best of Both Worlds: From Volunteer Subtitling to Professional Subtitling. *transLogos, 3*(2), 83–102. https://doi.org/10.29228/transLogos.28

Chan, W. S., Kruger, J.-L., & Doherty, S. (2019). Comparing the Impact of Automatically Generated and Corrected Subtitles on Cognitive Load and Learning in a First- and Second-Language Educational Context. *Linguistica Antverpiensia, 18*, 237–272. https://lans-tts.uantwerpen.be/index.php/LANS-TTS/article/view/506/

Chancel, L., & Piketty, T. (2021). Global Income Inequality, 1820–2020: The Persistence and Mutation of Extreme Inequality. *Journal of the European Economic Association, 19*(6), 3025–3062.

Chang, C. C., Liang, C., & Chen, Y. H. (2013). Is Learner Self-Assessment Reliable and Valid in a Web-based Portfolio Environment for High School Students? *Computers & Education, 60*(1), 325–334.

Chen, S., & Kruger, J. L. (2022). The Effectiveness of Computer-Assisted Interpreting. A Preliminary Study Based on English-Chinese Consecutive Interpreting. *Translation and Interpreting Studies.* https://doi.org/10.1075/tis.21036.che

Chernov, S. (2016). At the Dawn of Simultaneous Interpreting in the USSR. Filling Some Gaps in History. In K. Takeda & J. Baigorri-Jalón (Eds.), *New Insights in the History of Interpreting* (pp. 135–166). https://doi.org/10.1075/btl.122.06che

China Academy of Translation, & Translators Association of China. (2023). *2023 China Language Service Industry Development Report.* Beijing

Cho, K., van Merrienboer, B., Bahdanau, D., & Bengio, Y. (2014). On the Properties of Neural Machine Translation: Encoder-Decoder Approaches. *ArXiv Preprint.* https://arxiv.org/abs/1409.1259

Chomsky, N. (2022, Nov. 15). Debunking the Great AI Lie. Interview. https://youtu.be/PBdZi_JtV4c?si=d2FJQ7qRI0xa5gzb

Chomsky, N., Roberts, I., & Watumull, J. (2023, March 10). AI Unravelled: The False Promise of ChatGPT. *The New York Times.*

Chung, E. S., & Ahn, S. (2022). The Effect of Using Machine Translation on Linguistic Features in L2 Writing across Proficiency Levels and Text Genres. *Computer Assisted Language Learning, 35*(9), 2239–2264. https://doi.org/10.1080/09588221.2020.1871029

Chung, H. Y. (2020). Automatic Evaluation of Human Translation: BLEU vs. METEOR. *Lebende Sprachen, 65*(1), 181–205.

Church, K., & Hovy, E. (1993). Good Applications for Crummy Machine Translation. *Machine Translation, 8*(4), 239–258.

Clifford, J., Merschel, L., & Munné, J. (2013). Surveying the Landscape: What is the Role of Machine Translation in Language Learning? *@tic. Revista d'Innovació Educativa, 10*, 108–121.

Cnnic. (2021). *The 49th Statistical Report on China's Internet Development.* China Internet Network Information Center.

Commeyras, M. (1995). What Can We Learn from Students' Questions? Theory into Practice, 34(2), 564–570.

Cook, G. (2010). *Translation in Language Teaching.* Oxford University Press.

Cooper, A. (2004). *The Inmates Are Running the Asylum: Why High Tech Products Drive Us Crazy and How to Restore the Sanity.* Sams Publishing.

Corpas Pastor, G., & Defrancq, B. (Eds.). (2023). *Interpreting Technologies – Current and Future Trends.* John Benjamins.

Correa, M. (2011). Academic Dishonesty in the Second Language Classroom: Instructors' Perspectives. *Modern Journal of Language Teaching Methods, 1,* 65–79.

Correa, M. (2014). Leaving the 'Peer' Out of Peer-editing: Online Translators as a Pedagogical Tool in the Spanish as a Second Language Classroom. *Latin American Journal of Content and Language Integrated Learning, 7*(1), 1–20.

Council of Europe (2001). *Common European Framework of Reference for Languages: Learning, Teaching.* Cambridge University Press.

Council of Europe (2018). *Common European Framework of Reference for Languages: Learning, Teaching, Assessment.* Companion Volume with New Descriptors. https://www.coe.int/en/

Cox, A., & Maryns, K. (2021). Multilingual Consultations in Urgent Medical Care. *The Translator, 27*(1), 75–93. https://doi.org/10.1080/13556509.2020.1857501

Creswell, J. W., & Creswell, J. D. (2017). *Research Design: Qualitative, Quantitative, and Mixed Methods Approaches.* Sage.

Cronin, M. (2017). *Eco-translation: Translation and Ecology in the Age of the Anthropocene.* Routledge.

Cui, Q. (2017). *A Survey Report on China's MTI Education and Employment.* University of International Business and Economics Press.

Cui, Q. (2019). MTI Programs: Employment Investigation. In F. Yue, Y. Tao, H. Wang, Q. Cui, & B. Xu (Eds.), *Restructuring Translation Education: Implications from China for the Rest of the World* (pp. 55–68). Springer.

Davies, G., & Higgins, J. (1982). *Computers, Language and Language Learning.* CILT.

Delisle, J. (1980). *L'analyse du discours comme méthode de traduction.* Presses Universitaires d'Ottawa.

Deming, D., & Kahn, L. B. (2018). Skill Requirements across Firms and Labor Markets: Evidence from Job Postings for Professionals. *Journal of Labor Economics, 36*(S1), S337–S369.

De Vries, A. (2023). The Growing Energy Footprint of Artificial Intelligence. *Joule, 7,* 2191–2194. https://doi.org/10.1016/j.joule.2023.09.004

Durban, C. (2011). *Translation. Getting It Right.* American Translators Association.

ELIS Research (2023). European Language Industry Survey 2023. Trends, Expectations and Concerns of the European Language Industry. https://elis-survey.org

Eloundou, T., Manning, S., Mishkin, P., and Rock, D. (2023, March 20). GPTs are GPTs: An Early Look at the Labor Market Impact Potential of Large Language Models. https://arxiv.org/abs/2303.10130

EMT (2017). *Competence Framework 2017.* European Commission.

EMT (2022). *Competence Framework 2022.* European Commission.

EMT Expert Group (2009). *Competences for Professional Translators, Experts in Multilingual and Multimedia Communication.* European Commission.

Enkin, E., & Mejías-Bikandi, E. (2016). Using Online Translators in the Second Language Classroom: Ideas for Advanced-level Spanish. *Latin American Journal of Content and Language Integrated Learning, 9*(1), 138–158.

Enríquez Raído, V., & Austermühl, F. (2003). Translation Technology and Software Localization. In L. Pérez González (Ed.), *Speaking in Tongues: Language Across Contexts and Users* (pp. 225–250). Universidad de Valencia.

Epstein, R. M., Siegel, D. J., & Silberman, J. (2008). Self-Monitoring in Clinical Practice: A Challenge for Medical Educators. *Journal of Continuing Education in the Health Professions, 28*(1), 5–13.

European Commission (2023). *European Master's in Translation (EMT) Explained.* https://commission.europa.eu/resources-partners/european-masters-translation-emt/european-masters-translation-emt-explained

Fallada Pouget, C. (2000). Are Menu Translations Getting Worse? Restaurant Menus in English in the Tarragona Area. *Target, 12*(2), 323–332.

Fantinuoli, C. (2023). Towards AI-Enhanced Computer-Assisted Interpreting. In G. Corpas Pastor & B. Defrancq (Eds.), *Interpreting Technologies – Current and Future Trends* (pp. 46–71). John Benjamins.

Farzi, R. (2016). *Taming Translation Technology for L2 Writing: Documenting the Use of Free Online Translation Tools by ESL Students in a Writing Course* [Unpublished doctoral dissertation]. University of Ottawa.

Ferris, D., & Roberts, B. (2001). Error Feedback in L2 Writing Classes: How Explicit does It Need to Be? *Journal of Second Language Writing, 10*, 161–184.

Fiedler, S., & Wohlfarth, A. (2018). Language Choices and Practices of Migrants in Germany: An Interview Study. *Language Problems and Language Planning, 42*(3), 267–287.

FIT (Fédération Internationale des Traducteurs) (2017). *FIT Position Paper on the Future for Professional Translators.* https://www.fit-ift.org/publications/papers/

Fredholm, K. (2014). Effects of Online Translation on Morphosyntactic and Lexical-pragmatic Accuracy in Essay Writing in Spanish as a Foreign Language. In S. Jager, L. Bradley, E. J. Meima, & S. Thouësny (Eds.), *CALL Design: Principles and Practice. Proceedings of the 2014 EUROCALL Conference* (pp. 96–101). Research-publishing.net.

Fredholm, K. (2015). Online Translation Use in Spanish as a Foreign Language Essay Writing: Effects on Fluency, Complexity and Accuracy. *Revista Nebrija de Lingüística Aplicada a la Enseñanza de las Lenguas, 18*, 1–18.

Fredholm, K. (2019). Effects of Google Translate on Lexical Diversity: Vocabulary Development among Learners of Spanish as a Foreign Language. *Revista Nebrija de Lingüística Aplicada a la Enseñanza de las Lenguas, 13*(26), 98–117.

Freigang, K. H. (1998). Machine-aided Translation. In M. Baker (Ed.), *Routledge Encyclopedia of Translation Studies* (pp. 134–136). Routledge.

Frey, C. B., & Osborne, M. A. (2017). The Future of Employment: How Susceptible are Jobs to Computerisation? *Technological Forecasting and Social Change, 114*, 254–280.

Galán-Mañas, A. (2019). Employment Rate and Market Sector Occupation of Graduates in Translation and Interpreting at the Universitat Autònoma de Barcelona. *Revista Sinalizar, 4.* https://doi.org/10.5216/rs.v4.57515

García, I. (2009). Beyond Translation Memory: Computers and the Professional Translator. *The Journal of Specialised Translation, 12*(2), 199–214.

García, I. (2010). Is Machine Translation Ready Yet? *Target, 22*(1), 7–21.

García, I. (2011). Translating by Post-editing: Is It the Way Forward? *Machine Translation, 25*(3), 217–237.

García, I., & Peña, M. I. (2011). Machine Translation-Assisted Language Learning: Writing for Beginners. *Computer Assisted Language Learning, 24*(5), 471–487. https://doi.org/10.1080/09588221.2011.582687

Gaspari, F., Almaghout, H., & Doherty, S. (2015). A Survey of Machine Translation Competences: Insights for Translation Technology Educators and Practitioners. *Perspectives, 23*(3), 333–358. https://doi.org/10.1080/0907676X.2014.979842

González-Davies, M. (2004). *Multiple Voices in the Translation Classroom: Activities, Tasks and Projects.* John Benjamins.

Gouadec, D. (2003). Notes on Translator Training. In A. Pym, C. Fallada, J. R. Biau Gil, & J. Orenstein (Eds.), *Innovation and E-Learning in Translator Training. Reports on Online Symposia* (pp. 11–19). Intercultural Studies Group.

Gouadec, D. (2007). *Translation as a Profession.* John Benjamins.

Guerberof-Arenas, A., & Toral, A. (2022). Creativity in Translation: Machine Translation as A Constraint for Literary Texts. *Translation Spaces, 11*(2), 184–212.

Han, C., & Lu, X. (2023). Can Automated Machine Translation Evaluation Metrics be Used to Assess Students' Interpretation in the Language Learning Classroom? *Computer Assisted Language Learning, 36*(5–6), 1064–1087.

Hao, Y. (2023). Students' Perceptions and Expectations of Translation Technology in the Training Setting: What Can Emotional Narratives Tell Us? *Translation & Interpreting, 15*(2), 157–175. https://doi.org/10.12807/ti.115202.2023.a10

Hao, Y, & Pym, A. (2021). Translation Skills Required by Master Graduates for Employment: Which Are Needed, Which Are Not? *Across Languages and Cultures, 22*(2), 158–175.

Hao, Y., & Pym, A. (2022). Teaching How to Teach Translation: Tribulations of a Tandem-Learning Model. *Perspectives. Studies in Translation Theory and Practice, 30*(2), 275–291. https://doi.org/10.1080/0907676X.2021.1913197

Hao, Y., & Pym, A. (2023a). Where Do Translation Students Go? A Study of the Employment and Mobility of Master Graduates. *The Interpreter and Translator Trainer, 17*(2), 211–229. https://doi.org/10.1080/1750399X.2022.2084595

Hao Y., & Pym, A. (2023b). Choosing Effective Teaching Methods for Translation Technology Classrooms: Teachers' Perspectives. *Forum, 21*(2), 190–202 https://doi.org/10.1075/forum.22017.hao

Hao, Y., Pym, A., & Wang, Y. (2023). Chinese Students in Australia: Motivations and Mobility in the Face of COVID-19. *Melbourne Asia Review, 14.* https://doi.org/10.37839/mar2652-550x14.1

Hao Y., Hu, K., & Pym, A. (2024). Who's afraid of literary post-editing? Performances and reflections of student translators. In In Y. Peng, H. Huang, & D. Li (Eds.) *New Advances in Translation and Interpreting Technology: Theories, Applications and Training* (pp. 263–282). Springer. 10.1007/978-981-97-2958-6_13

Harpaz, Y., & Lefstein, A. (2000). Communities of Thinking. *Educational Leadership, 58*(3), 54–58.

Harris, H. (2010). Machine Translations Revisited: Issues and Treatment Protocol. *The Language Teacher, 34*(3), 25–29.

Hartshorn, K. J., Evans, N. W., Merrill, P. F., Strong-Krause, D., & Anderson, N. J. (2010). Effects of Dynamic Corrective Feedback on ESL Writing Accuracy. *TESOL Quarterly, 44,* 84–109.

Hassan, H., Aue, A., Chen, C., Chowdhary, V., Clark, J., Federmann, C., Huang, X., Junczys-Dowmunt, M., Lewis, W., Li, M., Liu, S., Liu, T.-Y., Luo, R., Menezes, A., Qin, T., Seide, F., Tan, X., Tian, F., Wu, L., ... Zhou, M. (2018). Achieving Human Parity on Automatic Chinese to English News Translation. http://arxiv.org/abs/1803.05567

Hatim, B. (1997). *English-Arabic/Arabic-English Translation. A Practical Guide.* Saqi.

Hatim, B., & Munday, J. (2004). *Translation. An Advanced Resource Book.* Routledge.

Hendy, A., Abdelrehim, M., Sharaf, A., Raunak, V., Gabr, M., Matsushita, H., Young, J. K., Afify, M., & Awadalla, H. H. (2023). How Good are GPT Models at Machine Translation? A Comprehensive Evaluation. https://arxiv.org/abs/2302.09210

Hoang, G. T. L. (2022). Feedback Precision and Learners' Responses: A Study into ETS 'Criterion' Automated Corrective Feedback in EFL Writing Classrooms. *JALT CALL Journal, 18*(3), 444–467.

Holz-Mänttäri, J. (1984). *Translatorisches Handeln: Theorie und Methode.* Suomalainen Tiedeakatemia.

Horbačauskienė, J., Kasperavičienė, R., & Petronienė, S. (2017). Translation Studies: Translator Training vs Employers' Expectations. *Journal of Language and Cultural Education, 5*(1), 145–159. https://doi.org/10.1515/jolace-2017-0009

Inboxtranslation (2023). *Freelance Translator Survey 2023.* https://inboxtranslation. com/resources/research/freelance-translator-survey-2023

ISO (2017). ISO 18857:2017. *Translation Services – Post-editing of Machine Translation Output: Requirements.* https://www.iso.org/standard/62970.html

Jespersen, O. (1901/1904). *How to Teach a Foreign Language.* Translated by S. Yhlen-Olsen Bertelsen. George Allen and Unwin.

Jiang, Z., Lv, Q., & Zhang, Z. (2023). Distinguishing Translations by Human, NMT, and ChatGPT: A Linguistic and Statistical Approach. https://arxiv.org/abs/2312.10750

Jiao, W., Wang, W., Huang, J. T., Wang, X., & Tu, Z. (2023). Is ChatGPT a Good Translator? A Preliminary Study. arXiv preprint arXiv:2301.08745.

Jolley, J., & Maimone, L. (2015). Free Online Machine Translation: Use and Perceptions by Spanish Students and Instructors. In A. J. Moeller (Ed.), *Learn Languages, Explore Cultures, Transform Lives* (pp. 181–200). Central States Conference on the Teaching of Foreign Languages.

Jolley, J. R., & Maimone, L. (2022). Thirty Years of Machine Translation in Language Teaching and Learning: A Review of the Literature. *L2 Journal, 14*(1), 26–44. https://doi.org/10.5070/L214151760

Jordan, R. R. (1997). *English for Academic Purposes: A Guide and Resource Book for Teachers.* Cambridge University Press.

Josselson, R. (2013). *Interviewing for Qualitative Inquiry: A Relational Approach.* Guilford Press.

Katan, D. (2009). Occupation or Profession. A Survey of the Translator's World. *Translation and Interpreting Studies, 4*(2), 187–209.

Kelly, D. (2005/2014). *A Handbook for Translator Trainers.* Routledge.

Kelly, L. G. (1969). *25 Centuries of Language Teaching; An Inquiry into the Science, Art, and Development of Language Teaching Methodology, 500 B.C.-1969.* Newbury House.

Kenny, D. (2018). Sustaining Disruption. On the Transition from Statistical to Neural Machine Translation. *Tradumàtica, 16,* 59–70.

Kenny, D. (2020). Technology in Translator Training. In M. O'Hagan (Ed.), *The Routledge Handbook of Translation Technology* (pp. 498–515). Routledge.

Kenny, D. (Ed.) (2022). *Machine Translation for Everyone. Empowering Users in the Age of Artificial Intelligence.* Language Science Press.

Kenny, D., & Way, A. (2001). Teaching Machine Translation and Translation Technology: A Contrastive Study. In M. Carl & A. Way (Eds.), *Proceedings of Workshop on Example-based Machine Translation.* Machine Translation Summit VII. https://aclanthology.org/2001.mtsummit-teach.6

Kim, H. R., & Bowles, M. (2019). How Deeply do Second Language Learners Process Written Corrective Feedback? Insights Gained from Think-Alouds. *Tesol Quarterly, 53*(4), 913–938.

Kiraly, D. (2000). *A Social Constructivist Approach to Translator Education.* St. Jerome.

Kiraly, D. (2014). From Assumptions about Knowing and Learning to Praxis in Translator Education. *inTRAlinea Special Issue: Challenges in Translation Pedagogy.* Unpaginated. https://www.intralinea.org/specials/article/2100

Knowles, C. (2016). *Investigating Instructor Perceptions of Online Machine Translation and Second Language Acquisition within Most Commonly Taught Language Courses* [Doctoral dissertation, The University of Memphis]. ProQuest Dissertations Publishing.

Knowles, R., Sánchez-Torron, M., & Koehn, P. (2019). A User Study of Neural Interactive Translation Prediction. *Machine Translation, 33,* 135–154. https://doi.org/10.1007/s10590-019-09235-8

Koehn, P. (2020). *Neural Machine Translation.* Cambridge University Press.

Kol, S., Schcolnik, M., & Spector-Cohen, E. (2018). Google Translate in Academic Writing Courses? *The EuroCALL Review, 26*(2), 50–57.

Kolb, W. (2010). 'Who Are They?'. Decision-Making in Literary Translation. In C. Way et al. (Eds.), *Tracks and Treks in Translation Studies* (pp. 207–221). John Benjamins.

Koponen, M. (2015). How to teach machine translation post-editing? Experiences from a post-editing course. In S. O'Brien & M. Simard (Eds.) *Proceedings of the 4th Workshop on Post-editing Technology and Practice,* pp. 2–15. AMTA. https://aclanthology.org/2015.mtsummit-wptp.1

Koponen, M., Nyqvist, S., & Taivalkoski-Shilov, K. (2022). Translating with Technology. How Digitalisation Affects Authorship and Copyright of Literary Texts. In J. L. Hadley, K. Taivalkoski-Shilov, C. S. C. Teixeira, & A. Toral (Eds.), *Using Technologies for Creative-Text Translation* (pp. 182–198). Routledge.

Koskinen, K., & Ruokonen, M. (2017). Love Letters or Hate Mail? Translators' Technology Acceptance in the Light of their Emotional Narratives. In D. Kenny (Ed.), *Human Issues in Translation Technology* (pp. 26–42). Routledge.

Krüger, R., & Hackenbuchner, J. (2022). Outline of a Didactic Framework for Combined Data Literacy and Machine Translation Literacy Teaching. *Current Trends in Translation Teaching and Learning E,* 375–432.

Krusche, S., & Seitz, A. (2018, February). Artemis: An Automatic Assessment Management System for Interactive Learning. *Proceedings of the 49th ACM technical symposium on computer science education* (pp. 284–289). http://arxiv.org/abs/2308.07938v1

Kumaravadivelu, B. (1994). The Postmethod Condition: (E)merging Strategies for Second/Foreign Language Teaching. *TESOL Quarterly, 28*(1), 27–48.

Kurzweil, R. (2005) *The Singularity Is Near.* Viking Books.

Kuznik, A., & Olalla-Soler, C. (2018). Results of PACTE Group's Experimental Research on Translation Competence Acquisition. The Acquisition of the Instrumental Sub-Competence. *Across Languages and Cultures, 19*(1), 19–51. https://doi.org/10.1556/084.2018.19.1.2

Lafeber, A. (2012a). *Translation at Inter-governmental Organizations the Set of Skills and Knowledge Required and the Implications for Recruitment Testing* [Doctoral thesis. Universitat Rovira i Virgili]. http://hdl.handle.net/10803/83500

Lafeber, A. (2012b). Translation Skills and Knowledge – Preliminary Findings of a Survey of Translators and Revisers Working at Inter-governmental Organizations. *Meta, 57*(1), 108–131. https://doi.org/10.7202/1012744ar

Lagoudaki, E. (2006). Translation Memories Survey 2006: Users' Perceptions Around TM Use. In *Proceedings of the ASLIB International Conference Translating & the Computer 28*, 1–29. https://aclanthology.org/2006.tc-1.2.pdf

Läubli, S., Sennrich, R., & Volk, M. (2018). Has Machine Translation Achieved Human Parity? A Case for Document-level Evaluation. https://arxiv.org/pdf/1808.07048.pdf

Laviosa, S. (2014). *Translation and Language Education: Pedagogic Approaches Explored*. Routledge.

Laviosa, S. (2019). Translanguaging and Translation Pedagogies. In H. V. Dam, M. N. Brøgger, & K. K. Zethsen (Eds.), *Moving Boundaries in Translation Studies* (pp. 181–199). Routledge.

Lee, S. M. (2020). The Impact of Using Machine Translation on EFL Students' Writing. *Computer Assisted Language Learning, 33*(3), 157–175.

Lee, S. M. (2023). The Effectiveness of Machine Translation in Foreign Language Education: A Systematic Review and Meta-analysis. *Computer Assisted Language Learning, 36*(1–2), 103–125. https://doi.org/10.1080/09588221.2021.1901745

Lewis, D. (1997). Machine Translation in a Modern Languages Curriculum, *Computer-Assisted Language Learning, 10*(3), 255–271.

Li, L., Dang, Q., & Zhao, K. (2023). Embracing Transdisciplinarity to Prepare for the Future: Revisiting the Gap between the Labour Market and Translator Education. *The Interpreter and Translator Trainer, 17*(3), 454–478. https://doi.org/10.1080/1750399X.2023.2237324

Li, Y., Pang, J., & Tan, B. (2023, June 8). Comparative Study of Artificial Intelligence and Human Creativity: A Dual Perspective of Experts and Consumers [In Chinese]. *Journal of Business Economics, 43*(10), 1–13.

Lin, M. P. C., & Chang, D. (2020). Enhancing Post-secondary Writers' Writing Skills with a Chatbot. *Journal of Educational Technology & Society, 23*(1), 78–92.

Litwin, M. (2023). The Jakobson Controversy: Toward an Understanding of the Glottocentric Drift in Translation Studies. *Translation Studies*. https://doi.org/10.1080/14781700.2023.2210584

Long, D., & Magerko, B. (2020). What Is AI Literacy? Competencies and Design Considerations. In R. Bernhaupt, et al. (Eds.), *CHI '20: Proceedings of the 2020 CHI Conference on Human Factors in Computing Systems* (pp. 1–16). Association for Computing Machinery. https://doi.org/10.1145/3313831.3376727

Loock, R., Lechaugette, S., & Holt, B. (2022). Dealing with the 'Elephant in the Classroom': Developing Language Students' Machine Translation Literacy. *Australian Journal of Applied Linguistics, 5*(3), 118–134. https://doi.org/10.29140/ajal.v5n3.53si2

Lotz, S., & Van Rensburg, A. (2016). Omission and Other Sins: Tracking the Quality of Online Machine Translation Output over Four Years. *Stellenbosch Papers in Linguistics, 46*, 77–97.

Lu, X., & Han, C. (2023). Automatic Assessment of Spoken-Language Interpreting Based on Machine-translation Evaluation Metrics: A Multi-Scenario Exploratory Study. *Interpreting, 25*(1), 109–143.

Lyu, C., Xu, J., & Wang, L. (2023). New Trends in Machine Translation using Large Language Models: Case Examples with ChatGPT. https://arxiv.org/pdf/2305.01181.pdf

Mainardes, E., Alves, H., & Raposo, M. (2012). A Model for Stakeholder Classification and Stakeholder Relationships. *Management Decision, 50*(10), 1861–1879.

Marczak, M., & Bondarenko, O. (2022). Translator Education in Poland and Ukraine: Does the Academia vs Industry Gap Persist? *The Interpreter and Translator Trainer, 16*(1), 115–134. https://doi.org/10.1080/1750399X.2021.1891516

McCambridge, J., Witton, J., & Elbourne, D. R. (2014). Systematic Review of the Hawthorne Effect: New Concepts are Needed to Study Research Participation Effects. *Journal of Clinical Epidemiology, 67*(3), 267–277.

McCracken, G. (1988). *The Long Interview.* Sage.

Megale, F. (2004). *Diritto d'autore del traduttore.* Editoriale Scientifica.

Meier, G. S. (2017). The Multilingual Turn as a Critical Movement in Education: Assumptions, Challenges and a Need for Reflection. *Applied Linguistics Review, 8*(1), 131–161. https://doi.org/10.1515/applirev-2016-2010

Meijer, H., Hoekstra, R., Brouwer, J., & Strijbos, J. W. (2020). Unfolding Collaborative Learning Assessment Literacy: A Reflection on Current Assessment Methods in Higher Education. *Assessment & Evaluation in Higher Education, 45*(8), 1222–1240.

Mellinger, C. D. (2017). Translators and Machine Translation: Knowledge and Skills Gaps in Translator Pedagogy. *The Interpreter and Translator Trainer, 11*(4), 280–293.

Mihalache, I. (2021). Human and Non-human Crossover: Translators Partnering with Digital Tools. In R. Desjardins, C. Larsonneur, & P. Lacour (Eds.), *When Translation Goes Digital: Case Studies and Critical Reflections* (pp. 19–43). Palgrave Macmillan.

Miller, K., Gates, D., Underwood, N., & Magdalen, J. (2001). *Evaluation of Machine Translation Output for an Unknown Source Language.* https://www.issco.unige.ch/en/staff/nancy/miller-2.pdf

Moorkens, J. (2022). Ethics and Machine Translation. In D. Kenny (Ed.), *Machine Translation for Everyone. Empowering Users in the Age of Artificial Intelligence* (pp. 121–140). Language Science Press.

Moorkens, J., & Rocchi, M. (2021). Ethics in the Translation Industry. In K. Koskinen & N. K. Pokorn (Eds.), *The Routledge Handbook of Translation and Ethics* (pp. 320–337). Routledge.

Morse, J. M. (2016). *Mixed Method Design: Principles and Procedures.* Routledge.

Mossop, B. (2003). What Should be Taught at Translation School? In A. Pym, C. Fallada, J. R. Biau-Gil, & J. Orenstein (Eds.), *Innovation and E-learning in Translator Training* (pp. 20–22). Intercultural Studies Group.

Mossop, B. (2019). Subjective Responses to Translation Memory Policy in the Workplace. *TTR, 32*(1), 309–339. https://doi.org/10.7202/1068023ar

Mumford, L. (1946). *Technics and Civilization.* Secker and Warburg.

Munby, J. (1978). *Communicative Syllabus Design.* Cambridge University Press.

Munday, P. (2016). The Case for Using DUOLINGO as Part of the Language Classroom Experience. *Revista iberoamericana de educación a distancia, 19*(1), 83–101.

Mundt, K., & Groves, M. (2016). A Double-Edged Sword: The Merits and the Policy Implications of Google Translate in Higher Education. *European Journal of Higher Education, 6*(4), 387–401.

NAATI. (2019). *Certified Translator.* National Accreditation Authority for Translators and Interpreters.

Narayan, K., & George, K. M. (2003). Personal and Folk Narrative as Cultural Representation: Stories about Getting Stories. In J. A. Holstein & J. F. Gubrium (Eds.), *Inside Interviewing: New Lenses, New Concerns* (pp. 449–465). Sage.

Niño, A. (2008). Evaluating the Use of Machine Translation Post-editing in the Foreign Language Class. *Computer Assisted Language Learning, 21*(1), 29–49.

Niño, A. (2009). Machine Translation in Foreign Language Learning: Language Learners' and Tutors' Perceptions of its Advantages and Disadvantages. *ReCALL, 21*(2), 241–258.

Nord, C. (1996). 'Wer nimmt denn mal den ersten Satz?': Überlegungen zu neuen Arbeitsformen im Übersetzungsunterricht ['Who'll Take the First Sentence?': Reflections on New Strategies in Translation Didactics]. In A. Lauer, H. Gerzymisch-Arbogast, J. Haller, & E. Steiner (Eds.), *Übersetzungswissenschaft im Umbruch* [Translation Studies in Transition] (pp. 313–327). Gunter Narr.

Norton, L. (2019). *Action Research in Teaching and Learning*. Routledge.

Nunan, D. (1988). *Syllabus Design*. Oxford University Press.

O'Brien, S. (2002). Teaching Post-editing: A Proposal for Course Content. In *6th EAMT Workshop Teaching Machine Translation* (pp. 99–106). European Association for Machine Translation.

O'Brien, S. (2017). Machine Translation and Cognition. In J. W. Schwieter & A. Ferreira (Eds.), *The Handbook of Translation and Cognition* (pp. 311–331). Wiley.

O'Brien, S. (2023). Human-Centered Augmented Translation: Against Antagonistic Dualisms. *Perspectives*, 1–16. https://doi.org/10.1080/0907676X.2023.2247423

O'Brien, S. & Rossetti, A. (2021). Neural Machine Translation and Evolution of the Localisation Sector. Implications for Training. *Journal of Internationalization and Localization, 7*(1/2), 95–121.

Occupational Information Network (O*Net) (2023). Details Report for 27-3091.00 - Interpreters and Translators (updated 2023). O*NET 27.2 27-3091.00 - Interpreters and Translators (onetonline.org).

O'Hagan, M. (2007). Video Games as a New Domain for Translation Research: From Translating Text to Translating Experience. *Revista Tradumàtica: Tradumàtica: Traducció i Tecnologies de la Informació i la Comunicació, 5*, 1–7.

O'Neill, E. M. (2019). Training Students to Use Online Translators and Dictionaries: The Impact on Second Language Writing Scores. *International Journal of Research Studies in Language Learning, 8*(2), 47–65.

Organ, A. (2023). Attitudes to the Use of Google Translate for L2 Production: Analysis of Chatroom Discussions among UK Secondary School Students. *The Language Learning Journal, 51*(3), 328–343. https://doi.org/10.1080/09571736.2021.2023896

OTTIAQ (2020). Machine Translation. For and Against. https://ottiaq.org/en/general-public/advantages-of-working-with-a-certified-professional/

PACTE (2018). Competence Levels in Translation: Working Towards a European Framework. *The Interpreter and Translator Trainer, 12*(2), 111–131. https://doi.org/10.1080/1750399X.2018.1466093

PACTE (2022). Procés d'Adquisició de la Competència Traductora i Avaluació – PACTE. https://ddd.uab.cat/record/273075

PACTE Group (2000). Acquiring Translation Competence: Hypotheses and Methodological Problems in a Research Project. In A. Beeby, D. Ensinger, & M. Presas (Eds.), *Investigating Translation* (pp. 99–106). John Benjamins.

PACTE Group (2003). Building a Translation Competence Model. In F. Alves (Ed.), *Triangulating Translation: Perspectives in Process-oriented Research* (pp. 43–66). John Benjamins.

PACTE Group (2017). Conclusions: Defining features of Translation Competence. In A. Hurtado Albir (Ed.), *Researching Translation Competence by PACTE Group* (pp. 281–302). John Benjamins.

Panadero, E., Jonsson, A., & Strijbos, J. W. (2016). Scaffolding Self-regulated Learning through Self-assessment and Peer Assessment: Guidelines for Classroom Implementation. In D. Laveault & L. Allal (Eds.), *Assessment for Learning: Meeting the Challenge of Implementation* (pp. 311–326). Springer.

Patton, M. Q. (2014). *Qualitative Research & Evaluation Methods: Integrating Theory and Practice*. Sage Publications.

Pedersen, D. (2014). Exploring the Concept of Transcreation – Transcreation as 'More Than Translation'? *Cultus, 7*, 57–71.

Pérez-Ortiz, J. A., Forcada, M. L., & Sánchez-Martínez., F. (2022). How Neural Machine Translation Works. In D. Kenny (Ed.), *Machine Translation for Everyone: Empowering Users in the Age of Artificial Intelligence* (pp. 141–164). Language Science Press. https://doi.org/10.5281/zenodo.6760020

Petrilli, S. (2014). The Critique of Glottocentrism: European Signatures. *Chinese Semiotic Studies, 10*(1), 25–41. https://doi.org/10.1515/css-2014-0006

Piccoli, V. (2022). Plurilingualism, Multimodality and Machine Translation in Medical Consultations: A Case Study. *Translation and Interpreting Studies, 17*(1), 42–65. https://doi.org/10.1075/tis.21012.pic

Picketty, T. (2017). *Capital in the Twenty-First Century*. Harvard University Press.

Pickles, E. (2013). *Translation into Foreign Languages. Written Ministerial Statement by Communities Secretary Eric Pickles on the Use of Translation Services by Local Authorities*. https://www.gov.uk/government/speeches/translation-into-foreign-languages

Pickles, K., Cvejic, E., Nickel, B., Copp, T., Bonner, C., Leask, J., Ayre, J., Batcup, C., Cornell, S., Dakin, T., Dodd, R. H., Isautier, J. M. J., & McCaffery, K. (2021). COVID-19 Misinformation Trends in Australia: Prospective Longitudinal National Survey. *Journal of Medical Internet Research, 23*(1), e23805. https://doi.org/10.2196/23805

Plaza-Lara, C. (2023). Future Translators' Concerns Regarding Professional Competences: A Corpus Study. *Íkala, 28*(3), 1–16.

Poibeau, T. (2017). *Machine Translation*. MIT Press.

Pokorn, N., & Čibej, J. (2018a). Interpreting and Linguistic Inclusion – Friends or Foes? Results from a Field Study. *The Translator, 24*(2), 111–127.

Pokorn, N., & Čibej, J. (2018b). 'It's So Vital to Learn Slovene'. Mediation Choices by Asylum Seekers in Slovenia. *Language Problems and Language Planning, 42*(3), 288–307.

Prabhu, N. S. (1990). There Is No Best Method – Why? *TESOL Quarterly, 24*(2), 161–176.

Prates, M., Avelar, P., & Lamb, L. C. (2020). Assessing Gender Bias in Machine Translation. A Case Study with Google Translate. *Neural Computing and Applications, 32*(1), 6363–6381. https://doi.org/10.1007/s00521-019-04144-6

Presas, M. (2000). Bilingual Competence and Translation Competence. In C. Schäffner & B. Adab (Eds.), *Developing Translation Competence* (pp. 19–31). John Benjamins. https://doi.org/10.1075/btl.38.04pre

Prieto Ramos, F., & Guzmán, D. (2023). Translating Legal Terms at International Organisations: Do Institutional Term Banks Meet Translators' Needs? In F. Prieto Ramos & D. Guzmán (Eds.), *New Advances in Legal Translation and Interpreting* (pp. 243–264). Springer Nature Singapore.

Pym, A. (1992). Translation Error Analysis and the Interface with Language Teaching. In C. Dollerup & A. Loddegaard (Eds.), *The Teaching of Translation* (pp. 279–288). John Benjamins.

Pym, A. (1998). Translation History and the Manufacture of Paper. In R. Ellis, R. Tixier, & B. Weitemeier (Eds.), *The Medieval Translator / Traduire au Moyen Âge* 6 (pp. 57–71). Brepols. https://doi.org/10.1484/M.TMT-EB.4.00015

Pym, A. (2003). Redefining Translation Competence in an Electronic Age. In Defence of a Minimalist Approach. *Meta*, 48(4), 481–497.

Pym, A. (2009). Using process studies in translator training. Self-discovery through lousy experiments. In S. Göpferich, F. Alves & I. M. Mees (Eds.), *Methodology, Technology and Innovation in Translation Process Research* (pp. 135–156). Samfundslitteratur.

Pym, A. (2011). What Technology does to Translating. *Translation & Interpreting*, 3(1), 1–9.

Pym, A. (2013). Translation Skill Sets in a Machine-Translation Age. *Meta*, 58(3), 487–503. https://doi.org/10.7202/1025047ar

Pym, A. (2015). The Medieval Postmodern in Translation Studies. In A. Fuertes & E. Torres-Simón (Eds.), *And Translation Changed the World (and the World Changed Translation)* (pp. 105–123). Cambridge Scholars Publishing.

Pym, A. (2016). *Translation Solutions for Many Languages – Histories of a Flawed Dream*. Bloomsbury.

Pym, A. (2018). Why Mediation Strategies are Important. *Language Problems and Language Planning*, 42(3), 255–266. https://doi.org/10.1075/lplp.00022.pym

Pym, A. (2019). Teaching Translation in a Multilingual Practice Class. In D. B. Sawyer, F. Austermühl, & V. Enríquez Raído (Eds.), *The Evolving Curriculum in Interpreter and Translator Education. Stakeholder Perspectives and Voices* (pp. 319–340). John Benjamins.

Pym, A. (2020). Quality. In M. O'Hagan (Ed.), *The Routledge Handbook of Translation and Technology* (pp. 437–452). Routledge.

Pym, A. (2021). Cooperation, Risk, Trust: A Restatement of Translator Ethics. *Stridon: Studies in Translation and Interpreting*, 1(2), 5–24. https://doi.org/10.4312/stridon.1.2.5-24

Pym, A. (2023). A Naïve Inquiry into Translation between Aboriginal Languages in Pre-Invasion Australia. In I. Feinauer, A. Marais, & M. Swart (Eds.), *Translation Flows: Exploring Networks of People, Processes and Products* (pp. 3–22). John Benjamins. https://doi.org/10.1075/btl.163.01pym

Pym, A., & Ayvazyan, N. (2018). Linguistics, Translation and Interpreting in Foreign-Language Teaching Contexts. In K. Malmkjær (Ed.), *The Routledge Handbook of Translation and Linguistics* (pp. 393–407). Routledge. https://doi.org/10.4324/9781315692845

Pym, A., Fallada, C., Biau-Gil, R., & Orenstein, J. (Eds.). (2003). *Innovation and E-learning in Translator Training*. Intercultural Studies Group.

Pym, A., & Hu, B. (2022). Trust and Cooperation through Social Media. COVID-19 Translations for Chinese Communities in Melbourne. In T. K. Lee & D. Wang

(Eds.), *Translation and Social Media Communication in the Age of the Pandemic* (pp. 44–61). Routledge. https://doi.org/10.4324/9781003183907-4

Pym, A., & Hu, K. (forthcoming). Trade-offs in Translation Effects. Illustrations and Methodological Concerns. *Target*.

Pym, A., Malmkjær, K., & Gutiérrez, M. (2013). *Translation and Language Learning*. European Commission.

Pym, A., Orrego-Carmona, D., & Torres-Simón, E. (2016). Status and Technology in the Professionalization of Translators. Market Disorder and the Return of Hierarchy. *The Journal of Specialised Translation, 25,* 33–53.

Pym, A., & Torres-Simón, E. (2016). Designing a Course in Translation Studies to Respond to Students' Questions. *The Interpreter and Translator Trainer, 10*(2), 183–203. https://doi.org/10.1080/1750399X.2016.1198179

Pym, A., & Torres-Simón, E. (2021). Is Automation Changing the Translation Profession? *International Journal of the Sociology of Language, 270,* 39–57. https://doi.org/10.1515/ijsl-2020-0015

Quine, W. V. O. (1969). Linguistics and Philosophy. In S. Hook (Ed.), *Language and Philosophy. A Symposium* (pp. 95–98). New York University Press.

Rakus-Andersson, E. (2004). The Polish Brains Behind the Breaking of the Enigma Code Before and During the Second World War. In C. Teuscher (Ed.), *Alan Turing: Life and Legacy of a Great Thinker* (pp. 419–439). Springer.

Ranalli, J. (2018). Automated Written Corrective Feedback: How Well can Students Make Use of It? *Computer Assisted Language Learning, 31*(7), 653–674.

Ren, W. (2019). Ethical Challenges Posed by and Ethical Principles Proposed for Machine Translation [机器翻译伦理的挑战与导向]. *Shanghai Journal of Translators, 5,* 46–52.

Revzin, I. I., & Rozentsveyg, V. I. (1964). Основы Общего И Машинного Перевода [Fundamentals of General and Machine Translation]. Moscow.

Richmond, I. M. (1994). Doing It Backwards: Using Translation Software to Teach Target-language Grammaticality. *Computer Assisted Language Learning, 7*(1), 65–78.

Rodríguez de Céspedes, B. (2018). Mind the Gap: Language Service Providers' Views on the Technological Training of Professional Translators. In E. Pinazo (Ed.), *Nuevas tecnologías, procesos cognitivos y estrategias para la optimización de las competencias del traductor e intérprete* (pp. 143–161). Frank and Timme.

Rodríguez de Céspedes, B. (2019). Translator Education at a Crossroads: The Impact of Automation. *Lebende Sprachen, 64*(1), 103–121.

Rothwell, A., & Svoboda, T. (2018). Tracking Translator Training in Tools and Technologies: Findings of the EMT Survey 2017. *The Journal of Specialised Translation, 32,* 26–60.

Rudolph, J., Tan, S., & Tan, S. (2023). ChatGPT: Bullshit Spewer or the End of Traditional Assessments in Higher Education? *Journal of Applied Learning & Teaching, 6*(1), 342–263. https://doi.org/10.37074/jalt.2023.6.1.9

Ruokonen, M., & Koskinen, K. (2017). Dancing with Technology: Translators' Narratives on the Dance of Human and Machinic Agency in Translation Work. *The Translator, 23*(3), 310–323. https://doi.org/10.1080/13556509.2017.1301846

Sahari, Y., Al-Kadi, A. M. T., & Ali, J. K. M. (2023). A Cross Sectional Study of ChatGPT in Translation: Magnitude of Use, Attitudes, and Uncertainties. *Journal of Psycholinguistic Research*. https://doi.org/10.1007/s10936-023-10031-y

Saito, M., & Sato, M. (2023). *Tsūji, Interpreters in and Around Early Modern Japan.* Palgrave Macmillan.

Saldanha, G., & O'Brien, S. (2014). *Research Methodologies in Translation Studies.* Routledge.

Saricaoglu, A., & Bilki, Z. (2021). Voluntary Use of Automated Writing Evaluation by Content Course Students. *ReCALL, 33*(3), 265–277.

Schmitt, P., Gernstmeyer, L., & Müller, S. (2016). *Übersetzer und Dolmetscher – Eine internationale Umfrage zur Berufspraxis.* DBÜ Fachverlag.

Sengupta, M., Pym, A., Hao, Y., Hajek, J., Karidakis, M., Woodward-Kron, R., Amorati, R. (2024). On the Transcreation, Format and Actionability of Health-care Translations. *Translation & Interpreting, 16*(1), 121–141.

Serres, M. (1974). *Hermès III. La Traduction.* Minuit.

Sevilla, J., Heim, L., Ho, A., Besiroglu, T., Hobbhahn, M., & Villalobos, P. (2022). Compute Trends across Three Eras of Machine Learning. https://arxiv.org/abs/2202.05924

SFT (Société Française des Traducteurs) (2022). *Rapport de l'enquête 2022 sur les pratiques professionnelles en traduction.* https://www.sft.fr/fr/chiffres-cles

Shei, C. C. (2002). Teaching MT through Pre-editing: Three Case Studies. In *Proceedings of the 6th EAMT Workshop on Teaching Machine Translation* (pp. 89–98). European Association for Machine Translation.

Shoemaker, S. J., Wolf, M. S., & Brach, C. (2014). Development of the Patient Education Materials Assessment Tool (PEMAT): A New Measure of Understandability and Actionability for Print and Audiovisual Patient Information. *Patient Education and Counseling, 96*(3), 395–403. https://doi.org/10.1016/j.pec.2014.05.027

Simmons, V. N., Quinn, G., Litvin, E. B., Rojas, A., Jimenez, J., Castro, E., ... & Brandon, T. H. (2011). Transcreation of Validated Smoking Relapse-Prevention Booklets for Use with Hispanic Populations. *Journal of Health Care for the Poor and Underserved, 22*(3), 886–893.

Slavin, R. E. (2020). How Evidence-based Reform will Transform Research and Practice in Education. *Educational Psychologist, 55*(1), 21–31.

Somers, H. (1997). A Practical Approach to Using Machine Translation Software: 'Post-editing' the Source Text. *The Translator, 3*(2), 193–212.

Song, Y., Sznajder, K., Bai, Q., Xu, Y., Dong, Y., & Yang, X. (2023). English as a Foreign Language Writing Anxiety and Its Relationship with Self-esteem and Mobile Phone Addiction among Chinese Medical Students – A Structural Equation Model Analysis. *Plos one, 18*(4), e0284335.

Stalin, J. V. (1950/2008). Concerning Marxism and Linguistics. *Pravda,* June 20, 1950. Translated in *Marxism and Problems of Linguistics* (pp. 3–32). Wildside Press.

Stern, H. H. (1983). *Fundamental Concepts of Language Teaching.* Oxford University Press.

Strubell, E., Ganesh, A., & McCallum, A. (2019). Energy and Policy Considerations for Deep Learning in NLP. Paper presented to the 57th Annual Meeting of the Association for Computational Linguistics, Florence, Italy. July 2019. https://arxiv.org/abs/1906.02243

Su, Y., Lin, Y., & Lai, C. (2023). Collaborating with ChatGPT in Argumentative Writing Classrooms. *Assessing Writing, 57,* 1–11.

Tabari, M. A., Sato, M., & Wang, Y. (2023). Engagement with Written Corrective Feedback: Examination of Feedback Types and Think-aloud Protocol as

Pedagogical Interventions. *Language Teaching Research*, 1–34. https://doi.org/10.1177/13621688231202574

Taibi, M. (2017). Quality Assurance in Community Translation. In M. Taibi (Ed.), *Translating for the Community* (pp. 7–23). Multilingual Matters.

Takeda, K., & Yamada, M. (2019). 'TI Literacy' for General Undergraduate Education. In D. B. Sawyer et al. (Eds.), *The Evolving Curriculum in Interpreter and Translator Education: Stakeholder Perspectives and Voices* (pp. 53–74). John Benjamins.

Tejeiro, R. A., Gomez-Vallecillo, J. L., Romero, A. F., Pelegrina, M., Wallace, A., & Emberley, E. (2012). Summative Self-Assessment in Higher Education: Implications of its Counting towards the Final Mark. *Electronic Journal of Research in Educational Psychology, 10*(2), 789–812.

Thomas, P. A., Kern, D. E., Hughes, M. T., Tackett, S. A., & Chen, B. Y. (Eds.). (2022). *Curriculum Development for Medical Education: A Six-Step Approach.* John Hopkins University Press.

Thue Vold, E. (2018). Using Machine-Translated Texts to Generate L3 Learners' Metalinguistic Talk. In Å. Haukås, C. Bjørke & M. Dypedahl (Eds.), *Metacognition in Language Learning and Teaching* (pp. 67–97). Routledge. https://doi.org/10.4324/9781351049146

Tian, C. (2023). *A Sociocultural Analysis of Chinese Retranslations of English Novels.* Lambert Academic.

Tian, S., Jia, L., & Zhang, Z. (2023). Investigating Students' Attitudes towards Translation Technology: The Status Quo and Structural Relations with Translation Mindsets and Future Work Self. *Frontiers in Psychology, 14*, 1–16. https://doi.org/10.3389/fpsyg.2023.1122612

Tinedo Rodríguez, A. J., & Frumuselu, A. D. (2023). SDH as a Pedagogical Tool: L2, Interculturality and EDI. *Translation and Translanguaging in Multilingual Contexts, 9*(3), 316–336. https://doi.org/10.1075/ttmc.00116.tin

Topping, K. (1998). Peer Assessment between Students in Colleges and Universities. *Review of Educational Research, 68*(3), 249–276.

Torres-Hostench, O. (2012). Occupational Integration Training in Translation. *Meta, 57*(3), 787–811.

Torres-Simón, E., & Pym, A. (2016). The Professional Backgrounds of Translation Scholars. Report on a Survey. *Target, 28*(1), 110–131. https://doi.org/10.1075/target.28.1.05tor

Torres-Simón, E., & Pym, A. (2019). European Masters in Translation. A Comparative Study. In D. Sawyer, F. Austermühl, & V. Enríquez Raído (Eds.), *Translator Education: The Evolving Curriculum* (pp. 319–340). John Benjamins.

Toudic, D. (2012). *Employer Consultation Synthesis Report, OPTIMALE Academic Network Project on Translator Education and Training.* Rennes.

Toudic, D. (2017a). *Graduate Employment Survey.* Report to the EMT Network Meeting in Brussels.

Toudic, D. (2017b). *Maintaining Standards in a Changing Market: The New EMT Competence Framework.* PowerPoint presented EMT meeting in Prague.

Translators Association of China (2022). *2022 China Language Service Industry Development Report.* Beijing.

Tsai, S. C. (2019). Using Google Translate in EFL Drafts: A Preliminary Investigation. *Computer Assisted Language Learning, 32*(5–6), 510–526. https://doi.org/10.1080/09588221.2018.1527361

Tsvetkova, M., Yasseri, T., Meyer, E. T., Pickering, J. B., Engen, V., Walland, P., & Bravos, G. (2017). Understanding Human-machine Networks: A Cross-Disciplinary Survey. *ACM Computing Surveys (CSUR), 50*(1), 1–35.

van Dis, E. A., Bollen, J., Zuidema, W., van Rooij, R., & Bockting, C. L. (2023). ChatGPT: Five Priorities for Research. *Nature, 614*, 224–226.

Vaswani, A., Shazeer, N., Parmar, N., Uszkoreit, J., Jones, L., Gomez, A. N., Kaiser, L., & Polosukhin, I. (2017). Attention Is All You Need. *Advances in Neural Information Processing Systems*. https://arxiv.org/abs/1706.03762

Venkatesh, V., & Bala, H. (2008). Technology Acceptance Model 3 and a Research Agenda on Interventions. *Decision Sciences, 39*(2), 273–315.

Vieira, L. N. (2020). Automation Anxiety and Translators. *Translation Studies, 13*(1), 1–21. https://doi.org/10.1080/14781700.2018.1543613

Vieira, L. N., O'Sullivan, C., Zhang, X., & O'Hagan, M. (2023). Machine Translation in Society: Insights from UK Users. *Language Resources & Evaluation, 57*, 893–914. https://doi.org/10.1007/s10579-022-09589-1

Vygotsky, L. S. (1978). Interaction between Learning and Development. Translated by M. Lopez-Morillas. In M. Cole, V. John-Steiner, S. Scribner, & E. Souberman (Eds.), *Mind in Society: The Development of Higher Psychological Processes* (pp. 79–91). Harvard University Press.

Wang, H., Li, D., & Lei, V. (2018). 翻译专业硕士(MTI)翻译技术教学研究:问题与对策 [Translation Technology Teaching in MTI Programs in China: Problems and Suggestions]. *Technology Enhanced Foreign Language Education (TEFLE), 181*, 76–94.

Webb, L. E. (2000). *Advantages and Disadvantages of Translation Memory* [MA thesis]. Monterey Institute for International Studies.

Wertheimer, A. (1999). *Exploitation*. Princeton University Press.

West, R. (1994). Needs Analysis in Language Teaching. *Language Teaching, 27*(1), 1–19.

Wood, E. (2018). Twenty Years of Building for Everyone. *Company Announcements*. https://www.blog.google/inside-google/company-announcements/twenty-years-building-everyone

World in Data (2023, Oct. 26). Our World in Data. https://ourworldindata.org/

Wu, Y., & Jiang, Z. (2021). Educating a Multilingual Workforce in Chinese universities: Employability of Master of Translation and Interpreting Graduates. *Círculo de Lingüística Aplicada a la Comunicación, 86*, 1–15. https://doi.org/10.5209/clac.75491

Wu, Y., Schuster, M., Chen, Z., Le, Q. V., & Norouzi, M. (2016). Google's Neural Machine Translation System: Bridging the Gap between Human and Machine Translation. https://arxiv.org/pdf/1609.08144.pdf

Yamada, M. (2023). Optimizing Machine Translation through Prompt Engineering: An Investigation into ChatGPT's Customizability. https://arxiv.org/abs/2308.01391

Yilmaz, E. D., Naumovska, I., & Aggarwal, V. A. (2023). AI-Driven Labor Substitution: Evidence from Google Translate and ChatGPT. *INSEAD Working Paper No. 2023/24/EFE*. http://doi.org/10.2139/ssrn.4400516

Zhang, H. (2019). *Formación en posedición de traducción automática para estudiantes de lenguas extranjeras* [Doctoral thesis]. Universitat Autònoma de Barcelona. http://hdl.handle.net/10803/669645

Zhang, T. (2021). The Effect of Highly Focused versus Mid-focused Written Corrective Feedback on EFL Learners' Explicit and Implicit Knowledge Development. *System, 99*, 1–16.

Zhang, X., & Vieira, L. N. (2021). CAT Teaching Practices: An International Survey. *The Journal of Specialised Translation, 36*, 99–124.

Zhou, J., Cao, Y., Wang, X., Li, P., & Xu, W. (2016). Deep Recurrent Models with Fast-forward Connections for Neural Machine Translation. *Transactions of the Association for Computational Linguistics, 4*, 371–383.

Zurich University of Applied Sciences (2020). AbsolventInnenbefragung ein Jahr nach der Diplomfeier. MA Angewandte Linguistik: Vertiefungen Fachübersetzen und Konferenzdolmetschen. Unpublished Document.

Zwischenberger, C. (2022). Online Collaborative Translation: Its Ethical, Social, and Conceptual Conditions and Consequences. *Perspectives, 30*(1), 1–18. https://doi.org/10.1080/0907676X.2021.1872662

INDEX